STRATEGIES FOR CREATIVE PROBLEM SOLVING

Taken from:
Strategies for Creative Problem Solving, Second Edition
by H. Scott Fogler and Steven E. LeBlanc

PEARSON

Custom
Publishing

PEARSON

Prentice
Hall

Cover image: courtesy of PhotoDisc/Getty Images

Taken from:

Strategies for Creative Problem Solving, Second Edition
by H. Scott Fogler and Steven E. LeBlanc
Copyright © 2008 by Pearson Education, Inc.
Published by Prentice Hall
Upper Saddle River, New Jersey 07458

This special edition published in cooperation with Pearson Custom Publishing.

Printed in the United States of America

10 9 8 7

ISBN 0-536-08783-0

2007361207

KL

Please visit our web site at *www.pearsoncustom.com*

PEARSON CUSTOM PUBLISHING
501 Boylston Street, Suite 900, Boston, MA 02116
A Pearson Education Company

CONTENTS

PREFACE

The purpose of this book is to help problem solvers improve their "street smarts." We know that every individual possesses creative skills of one type or another, and that these skills can be sharpened if they are exercised regularly. This book provides a framework to hone and polish these creative problem-solving skills.

Strategies for Creative Problem Solving is intended for students, new engineers, practitioners, or anyone else who wants to increase his or her problem-solving skills. After studying this book, you will be able to encounter an ill-defined problem, identify the real problem, generate and implement solutions, and then evaluate what you have accomplished. You will develop the skills needed to achieve these goals by examining the components of a problem-solving algorithm and studying a series of graduated exercises intended to familiarize, reinforce, challenge, and stretch your creativity in the problem-solving process.

To cut through the maze of obstacles blocking the pathway to the solution to the problem, we need skills analogous to a pair of scissors with two special blades.

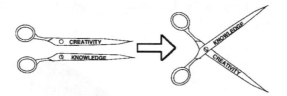

One of the shears is made of the **knowledge** necessary to understand the problem and to develop technically feasible solutions. Of course, no cutting can be done—and no problems of invention can be solved—with just one shear. The other shear contains creativity that can generate new and **creative** ideas. Likewise, creativity alone will not necessarily generate solutions that are technically feasible—and no cutting can be done with just this single shear, either. Instead, the combination of creativity with a strong technical foundation allows us to cut through the problem to obtain original solutions.

With the aid of a major grant from the National Science Foundation, we researched the wide variety of problem-solving techniques used in industry. Teams of students and faculty visited a number of companies (see the list of acknowledgments later in this preface) to study their problem-solving strategies. We also carried out an extensive survey of new employees, experienced engineers, and managers in industry to collect information on the problem-solving process. As a result of our research, which we share in this text, we know you can become a better problem solver.

A number of the engineers and managers provided examples of industrial problems that were incorrectly defined. These examples of ill-defined problems vividly illustrate the need to define the *real* problem as opposed to the *perceived* problem. We believe that if a problem-solving heuristic had been applied to some of these problems in the first place, then the real problem would have been uncovered more rapidly.

A problem-solving heuristic is a systematic approach to problem solving that helps guide us through the solution process and generate alternative solution pathways. The heuristic in this book is quite robust and is applicable to many types of problems. The problem-solving techniques presented in this book provide an organized, logical approach to generating more creative solutions.

This book is designed to guide you step by step through the problem-solving process. Chapter 1 illustrates the need to apply an organized method of solving problems and gives an overview of the heuristic (i.e., a systematic approach) introduced in this text. Chapter 2 discusses the need to approach the problem with a positive attitude and emphasizes the importance of teamwork. Chapter 3 describes how to gather more information to learn more about the problem.

The next chapters move step by step through the five building blocks of the problem-solving heuristic (shown below) to increase your problem-solving "street smarts." We start by laying down the first building block, *Define the Problem*, and then lay one building block upon another as we move through the problem-solving process. The last block to be laid down is *Evaluate the Solution,* where we analyze all we have accomplished.

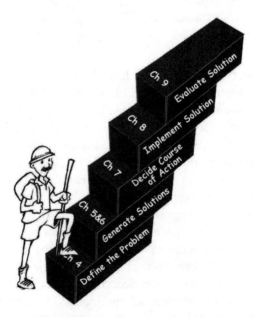

The Five Building Blocks of the Problem-Solving Heuristic

Chapter 10 extends the material in Chapter 4 on defining the problem to discuss techniques for troubleshooting both everyday problems and highly technical problems. We close with Chapter 11, which includes two case studies that incorporate the principles of the first 10 chapters. The first case study focuses on a project carried out by Engineers Without Borders (EWB) and was provided by Dr. Marina Melitic. The second case study is from a term project in a senior-level problem-solving course at the University of Michigan, entitled "Problem Solving, Troubleshooting, and Making the Transition to the Workplace," in which a draft of the second edition of this book was used as the text.

Chapter Objectives

The chapter-by-chapter objectives for this new edition of the text are shown below. They provide a logical pathway to help improve and exercise your problem-solving skills.

- **Chapter 1: Problem-Solving Strategies: Why Bother?** Chapter 1 documents several examples where people defined and proceeded to solve the *perceived problem* instead of defining and solving the *real problem*. This chapter also introduces a problem-solving heuristic that can help define the real problem.
- **Chapter 2: The Characteristics, Attitudes, and Environment Necessary for Effective Problem Solving.** Chapter 2 takes an introspective look at the characteristics, habits, and actions that effective problem solvers use and helps readers develop the skills necessary to be an effective and productive members of a team that is working together to solve problems.
- **Chapter 3: Gathering Information on the Problem.** Chapter 3 describes different methods to gather information so as to define and solve the real problem. These techniques include collecting and analyzing information, talking with people who are familiar with the problem, viewing the problem firsthand, and confirming all findings.
- **Chapter 4: Problem Definition.** Chapter 4 provides four techniques you can use to help ensure that you have defined the real problem instead of the perceived problem: critical thinking, the Duncker diagram, the statement–restatement technique, and Kepner–Tregoe (K.T.) problem analysis.
- **Chapter 5: Breaking Down the Barriers to Generating Ideas.** Chapter 5 provides techniques that will help you break down barriers and preconceived notions that get in the way when you are trying to generate solutions to the problem. It also suggests ways to try to enhance your risk taking, because most truly innovative solutions require some risk.

- **Chapter 6: Generating Solutions.** Chapter 6 provides a number of techniques to help you generate solutions to the correctly defined problem, including brainstorming, vertical and lateral thinking, futuring, analogy, and TRIZ.
- **Chapter 7: Deciding the Course of Action.** Chapter 7 provides algorithms that will help you decide which problem you should work on first, which solution you should choose, how to identify potential problems, and how you can prevent problems from occurring in the future.
- **Chapter 8: Implementing the Solution.** Chapter 8 describes the steps necessary to implement the decisions you made using the techniques described in Chapter 7.
- **Chapter 9: Evaluation.** Chapter 9 shows you how to evaluate the solution you have implemented, making sure it completely solves the problem, is ethical, and is safe for both people and the environment.
- **Chapter 10: Troubleshooting.** Chapter 10 provides an algorithm and a worksheet that you can use for troubleshooting problems of malfunctioning industrial equipment and systems. This algorithm also finds application to nontechnical problems.
- **Chapter 11: Putting It All Together.** Chapter 11 shows how all of the problem-solving techniques presented in Chapters 1 through 10 can be applied to two real-life case studies.

What's New in the Second Edition

- **Reorganization.** Related topics are more appropriately grouped together in a more coherent manner.
- **Teamwork.** The text provides guidelines to help team members work together more effectively and to resolve any conflicts they experience.
- **Critical Thinking.** Socratic Questioning and critical thinking are suggested as strategies to define the real problem.
- **New Examples.** A number of new examples are used in problem definition techniques, brainstorming, and implementation.
- **TRIZ.** This approach to problem solving helps resolve contradictions.
- **Troubleshooting.** Algorithms for troubleshooting to find the root cause of industrial equipment and process problems are presented.
- **Real-Life Case Studies.** Chapter 11 includes two new case studies that illustrate the techniques presented in the first 10 chapters. One is based on a project carried out by Engineers Without Borders in India, and the other focuses on a class term project involving employees at a local restaurant.

ACKNOWLEDGMENTS

We wish to thank the following companies for participating in this project to provide real examples and share their problem-solving methodology:

Amoco
Chevron Specialty Chemicals
Dow Chemical
Dow Corning
DuPont
Eli Lilly
General Mills
KMS Fusion
Kraft General Foods
Mobil
Monsanto
Procter & Gamble
Shell
3M
Upjohn

We would also like to thank Professors Peggy Ruff, Gabrielle Bonner, Lina Karam, and Susan Montgomery, along with Jeff Siirola and Michael Senra, for their detailed and invaluable comments on the draft manuscript. In addition, students in the fall 2006 class of Chemical Engineering 496, "Problem Solving, Troubleshooting, and Making the Transition to the Workplace," provided detailed comments on every chapter. These students are Adesina Aladetohun, Bobby Beasley, Ken Brown, Ana Butka, Halley Crast, Charlene Dobbs, Scott Dombrowski, Carly Ehrenberger, Stephanie Fraley, Jim Freeman, Jamila Grant, James Herbin, Tim Harms, Tyrika Johnson, Jaclyn Kaufman, Monica Lichty, Curt Longcore, Jason Rhode McGauley, Jessica Moreno, Jane (Jin Wei) Ni, Paul Niezguski, Jessica Nunn, Yuliya Polyachenko, Kyle Scarlett, Sara Schulze, Carlo Spagnuolo, Mara Tobin, Sarah Tschirhart, and Israel Vicars. Michael Senra did an excellent job as the graduate student instructor (GSI) working with these students to make the class and term projects a success.

We are particularly grateful to Professor Donald Woods for his pioneering work in bringing a structure of problem solving and troubleshooting to the engineering professions as well as initiating and stimulating the authors' interest in teaching problem solving.

The production staff at Prentice Hall was outstanding as usual. We also would like to recognize our publisher, Bernard Goodwin; our production editor, Julie Nahil; and our copyeditor, Jill Hobbs, for their excellent work.

Last but not least, we recognize Laura Bracken, who caught many, many inconsistencies in the numbering and organization in the initial drafts, and who typed and retyped what must have seemed like a never-ending succession of revisions as we converged on the final version.

One person who deserves special recognition for her work in making this book possible is Janet Fogler, our de facto editor. Janet spent endless hours going through every page of the manuscript, rewriting sentences, making sure things followed logically, giving us suggestions on how to make things clearer, and helping in many other ways. She took our original manuscript and raised it to a higher level and, indeed, is an integral part of this work.

H. Scott Fogler, Ann Arbor, Michigan
Steven E. LeBlanc, Toledo, Ohio
June 2007

1   PROBLEM-SOLVING STRATEGIES: WHY BOTHER?

Everyone is called upon to solve problems every day—from such mundane decisions as what to wear or where to go for lunch, to the much more difficult problems that are encountered in school or on the job. Most real-world problems have many possible solutions. The more complex the problem, the larger the number of alternative solutions. The goal is to choose the best solution. All of us will be better able to achieve this goal if we exercise our problem-solving skills frequently to make them sharper. By understanding and practicing the techniques discussed in this book, you will develop problem-solving "street smarts" and become a much more efficient problem solver.

WHAT'S THE REAL PROBLEM?

With the aid of a grant from the National Science Foundation, the authors of this book carried out an extensive study of problem solving in industry. Teams of students and faculty from the University of Michigan visited many U.S. companies to learn how they approached problem solving, to collect their problem-solving techniques, and to learn about the difficulties that occurred in solving real-world problems. When we summarized the results, we found that the greatest challenge was making sure that the **real problem** was defined instead of the **perceived problem.** The difference between a perceived problem and a real problem is illustrated in the following humorous example.

The Case of the Hungry Grizzly Bear[1]
or
An Exercise in Defining the "Real Problem"

A student and his professor are backpacking in Alaska when a grizzly bear starts to chase them from a distance. Both start running, but it's clear that eventually the bear will catch up with them. The student takes off his backpack, gets his running shoes out, and starts putting them on. His professor says, "You can't outrun the bear, even in running shoes!" The student replies, "I don't need to outrun the bear; I only need to outrun you!"

1

Of course, the student quickly realized that that the perceived problem was to outrun the bear while the real problem was to not get caught by the bear. This example illustrates a very important issue: **problem definition.**

Problem definition is a common but difficult task because true problems are often disguised in a variety of ways. It takes a skillful individual to analyze a situation and extract the real problem from a sea of information. Ill-defined or poorly posed problems can lead novice—and not-so-novice—problem solvers down the wrong path to a series of impossible or spurious solutions. Defining the real problem is critical to finding a workable solution.

Sometimes we can be "tricked" into treating the symptoms instead of solving the root problem. Treating symptoms (e.g., putting a bucket under a leaking roof) can give us the satisfaction of a quick fix, but finding and solving the real problem (i.e., the cause of the leak) are important to minimize lost time, money, and effort. Implementing real solutions to real problems requires discipline, and sometimes stubbornness, to avoid being pressured into accepting a less desirable quick-fix solution because of time constraints.

The next four pages present a series of real-life examples from case histories showing how easy it is to fall into the trap of defining and solving the wrong problem. In these examples and the discussions that follow, the perceived problem refers to a problem that is thought to be correctly defined but that actually is not. These examples provide evidence of how millions of dollars and thousands of hours can be wasted as a consequence of poor problem definition and solution.

Impatient Guests

Shortly after the upper floors of a high-rise hotel had been renovated to increase the hotel's room capacity, guests complained that the elevators were too slow. The building manager assembled his assistants. His instructions to solve the perceived problem: "Find a way to speed up the elevators."

After calling the elevator company and an independent expert on elevators, it was determined that nothing could be done to speed up the elevators. The manager then issued new directions: "Find a location and design a shaft to install another elevator." An architectural firm was hired to carry out this request.

Ultimately, neither the shaft nor the new elevator was installed because shortly after the firm was hired, the real problem was uncovered. The real problem statement was "Find a way to minimize the complaints by taking the guests' minds off their wait rather than installing more elevators." The guests stopped complaining when mirrors were installed on each floor in front of the elevators.[2] Few people can resist taking the time to check or admire their appearance in the mirror.

Better Printing Inks

In 1990, the Bureau of Engraving and Printing (BEP) initiated a program to redesign and improve the quality of paper money being printed in the United States. When the design was completed and the new printing machines were installed, a few trial printings were carried out. Unfortunately, it was found that the ink on the new bills smeared when touched. The following instructions were given to solve the perceived problem: "Develop a program to find better printing inks."

A number of workshops and panels were convened to work on this problem. After a year and a half of hard work by both government officials and college faculty on the perceived problem, research programs at several universities were chosen to try to develop better printing inks.

Just as these programs were to be initiated, BEP withdrew the funds, stating that the real problem was not with the inks but rather with the printing machines. The new machines were not putting sufficient pressure on the new type of paper to force the ink down into the paper far enough to avoid smearing. Consequently, the funds earmarked for research on inks were diverted to the purchase of new printing machines.

By originally defining the wrong problem, BEP wasted thousands of hours of effort by government officials and college faculty. The real problem statement should have been "Find out why the ink is smearing."

Coca-Cola's New Soft Drink

Pepsi-Cola developed an advertising campaign, "Take the Pepsi Challenge," that increased the company's market share at the expense of its bitter rival, Coca-Cola. As part of this campaign, Pepsi set up stations at various locations in which it conducted blind tastings of both Pepsi and Coke. As the individuals took the taste test, whose results mostly favored Pepsi, they were videotaped. These sessions were then shown on Pepsi's television commercials.

Coca-Cola's management responded to the decrease in market share that followed Pepsi's campaign by issuing the following instruction: "Develop a soft drink that tastes more like Pepsi." Coke developed the product, dubbed "New Coke," and put it on the market to replace the existing version of Coke. Customers tried New Coke, but did not like it. The product was withdrawn from the market after 77 days and replaced by the original Coca-Cola recipe, which was called "Classic Coke." The real problem statement should have been "Develop a marketing campaign to regain Coke's market share."[3]

Leaking Flow Meter

Flow meters, such as the ones used at gasoline pumps to measure the number of gallons of gas delivered to your gas tank, are commonplace in industry. A flow meter was installed in a chemical plant to measure the flow rate of a corrosive fluid. A few months after its installation, the corrosive fluid ate through the flow meter and began to leak onto the plant floor. The following instruction was given to solve the perceived problem: "Find material from which to make a flow meter that will not corrode and cause leakage of the dangerous fluid."

An extensive, time-consuming search was carried out to find such a material and a company that would construct a cost-effective flow meter. None was found. The real problem statement should have been "Prevent the flow meter from leaking." The solution was to institute a program in which workers simply replaced the existing flow meter on a regular basis before corrosion caused a failure.[4]

Where Is the Oil?

Water flooding is a technique commonly used in oil recovery in which water is injected into a well, displacing the oil and pushing it out of another nearby well. In many cases, expensive chemicals are injected along with the water to facilitate pushing out the oil.

A major oil company was having problems with a Canadian light-oil reservoir where the recovery was turning out to be much lower than expected. The following instruction was given to solve the perceived problem: "Find ways to improve the oil recovery rate."

Several studies costing hundreds of thousands of dollars were carried out over a 20-year period aimed at determining how to get more oil from the reservoir through improved water-flooding techniques. Unfortunately, this situation was not really a case of low oil recovery efficiency but rather one of miscalculation—the estimate of the amount of recoverable oil was wrong. In other words, there just wasn't much oil down there to recover![5] The real problem statement was "Learn why the well is not producing as expected," rather than "Find ways to improve the oil recovery rate."

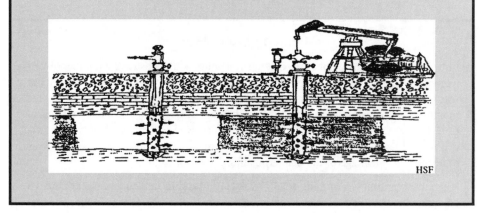

CORRECT PROBLEM DEFINITION/WRONG SOLUTION

In this section, we discuss some examples where the real problem has been correctly defined, but the solutions to the problem were woefully inadequate, incorrect, or unnecessary. The individuals who made the decisions in the situations described in these examples were all competent, hard-working professionals. Unfortunately, they overlooked some essential details that might have prevented the accidents and mistakes. Using 20/20 hindsight, consider whether the following situations could have been avoided if an organized problem-solving approach had been applied.

Dam the Torpedoes or Torpedo the Dam?

The Australian government wanted to increase agricultural production by finding ways to grow crops on wastelands. It was decided to cultivate land in the New South Wales region of southeastern Australia, which is very arid. Some wild plants could be seen growing in the soil from time to time, but there was insufficient moisture to grow crops. It was believed that the land could be irrigated and that agricultural food crops could be grown. The Murray River, which flows naturally from the mountains to the sea, passes through the region. The solution chosen by the Australian government was this: "Design and build a dam to divert the river water inland to irrigate the land."

A multimillion-dollar dam was built, and the water was diverted. Unfortunately, when the irrigation was achieved, absolutely no new vegetation grew, and even the vegetation that had previously grown on some of the land died. It was determined that this infertility of the soil occurred because the diverted water dissolved abnormally high concentrations of salts present in the soil, which then entered the plant roots. Little of the vegetation could tolerate the salts at such high concentrations; as a result, even the existing vegetation died. A potential problem analysis (Chapter 7) might have prevented this costly experiment.[6] Currently, efforts are under way to deal with this salinity problem, with proposed solutions ranging from desalination to the construction of salt ponds.

What's the Disease?

On a lighter note, we end with the following true example of right problem/wrong solution. At an American Medical Association (AMA) convention on respiratory diseases a number of years ago, an upper-body X-ray was displayed at the booth of one of the pharmaceutical vendors.

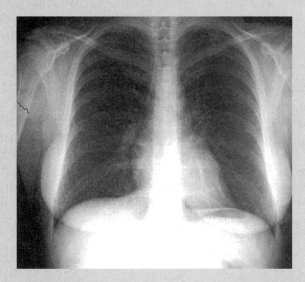

The following instructions were given to the physicians: "Diagnose the ailment from the X-ray, and place your answer in the contest box near the display" (a correct problem statement). The winner of a valuable prize would be drawn from those who had made the correct diagnosis. Because of the focus on the upper torso, virtually every known lung disease treatment was suggested by one physician or another. There was no need to hold a drawing from the correct diagnoses submitted because only one person discovered the true solution: "Set a broken right arm."[7]

Nearly all project design failures, such as those described in the preceding examples, result from faulty judgments rather than faulty calculations. While there is nothing we can do that will guarantee that you will never make mistakes or faulty judgments, we believe that if you use the methods and techniques discussed in this book, you will be less likely to do so.

A HEURISTIC FOR SUCCESSFUL PROBLEM SOLVING

In the preceding sections, you saw several examples of ill-defined and incorrectly solved problems. The people who defined these perceived problems were bright and conscientious people. So how could they have made these mistakes? And how can we avoid the same pitfalls that ensnared the people in these examples? The goal of this book is to structure the process of defining and solving real problems in a way that will be useful to you in everyday life, both on and off the job. We shall achieve this goal by providing a structure to the problem-solving process called a **heuristic.** A problem-solving heuristic is a systematic approach that helps guide us through the solution process and generate alternative solution pathways. While a heuristic cannot prevent people from making errors, it provides a uniform, systematic approach to deal with any problem.

A heuristic is analogous to a road map. It can tell you where you are, where you want to go, and how to get there. Heuristics, like road maps, can also help you determine alternative routes to a destination. A complex problem, such as route selection, can be ill defined, may have many solutions, or might not have any feasible solution as posed. While there is no unique or preferred way to solve these types of problems, we believe the use of a heuristic is an effective technique.

Building Blocks of the Heuristic

The five-step problem-solving heuristic that we will use is illustrated below and finds its origins in the McMaster Five-Point Strategy.[8] The figure shows the order in which these building blocks are laid down, starting with defining the problem and then laying each of the other building blocks on top of one another as we solve the problem and then evaluate the solution.

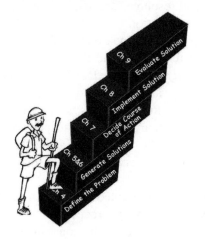

The Five Building Blocks of the Problem-Solving Heuristic

Problem definition is the important first step in our problem-solving heuristic. In practice, this phase can resurface at any point of the problem-solving process as we encounter dead ends or as the criteria or conditions change. First we gather information, and then we use several specific techniques to help **define** the problem to arrive at the correct problem definition. Once you have defined the real problem, it is then important to ask the following questions: Has this problem been solved before? Is it worth solving? Which resources (e.g., time, money, personnel) are available to obtain a solution?

After defining the real problem, you can proceed to **generate** solutions to solve the problem—the next step in the heuristic. One of the most popular techniques used in industry to generate ideas is brainstorming. This technique is useful in expanding thinking about what *is* possible and what *is not* possible. In addition to brainstorming, other methods to facilitate idea generation include futuring, analogies, and blockbusting.

The next building block, **decide,** is discussed in the context of the Kepner–Tregoe strategy.[9] Situation appraisal helps you to decide which project to tackle first. Problem analysis helps you to find the root cause of the problem. Decision analysis is where you generate a number of solution alternatives, and then decide which alternative to choose. In potential problem analysis, you plan to ensure the success of the solution by identifying everything that might potentially go wrong, the causes of each potential problem, the preventive actions that could be taken, and the steps of last resort.

Having made the decision and planned for its success through potential problem analysis, you are now ready to **implement** the solution. The first step is to plan the activities you need to perform to solve the problem. A number of techniques to allocate time and resources are available to help you carry the solution through to its successful completion.

In the **evaluation** phase, you look back and make sure all of the criteria in the problem statement were fulfilled and that none of the constraints were violated. Has the problem *really* been solved, and is the solution you chose the best solution? Is the solution innovative, new, and novel, or is it merely an application of existing principles (which, in some cases, may be all that's necessary)? Is the solution ethical, safe, and environmentally responsible? Although evaluation appears at the end of the heuristic, you should also evaluate the problem solution at various points along the way, especially when major decisions are made or branch points occur.

The heuristic we have just presented will serve as a handy road map for your journey through the problem-solving process. Of course, even when they are armed with a good road map, travelers may sometimes arrive at the wrong destination or take an excessive amount of time to reach the correct destination. In a similar way, problem solvers may come to the wrong solution or take too much time to obtain a solution. Travelers also have to approach the trip with a positive attitude and draw upon the knowledge of expert travelers who have navigated the road before them. Finally, they need to make sure there is agreement on the route among themselves—conflicts between the travelers can make the trip unpleasant, sometimes with a disastrous outcome. Similarly, problem-solving groups can be much more efficient when they work well together in teams. In Chapter 2, we discuss the attributes and characteristics of experienced problem solvers, the need to approach each problem in a positive manner, and some ideas on how to solve problems successfully in teams. After this chapter, we begin discussing the first block of our problem-solving heuristic.

SUMMARY

Why bother with using a problem-solving strategy? This chapter presented a number of factual case histories that illustrate what happens when the real problem isn't defined or when there is no organized approach to problem solving. In the chapters that follow, we present a heuristic and a number of techniques that can greatly enhance your chances of defining and solving the real problem instead of the perceived problem and identifying potential roadblocks during the problem-solving process.

REFERENCES

1. Prof. John Falconer, University of Colorado, Boulder, CO 80302.
2. Adapted from *Chemtech,* 22, 1, p. 24, 1992.
3. Zyman, S., and A. A. Brott, *Renovate Before You Innovate,* Portfolio, a member of the Penguin Group, 2005.
4. Dr. R. G. McNally, Dow Chemical Company, Midland, MI 48667.
5. Dr. Mark Hoefner, Mobil Research and Development Corporation, Dallas, TX 75387.
6. http://www.environment.sa.gov.au/reporting/inland/murray.html
7. Prof. Brymer Williams, University of Michigan, Ann Arbor, MI 48109.
8. Woods, D. R., "The McMaster Five-Point Strategy," notes and personal communication, 1982.
9. Kepner, C. H., and B. B. Tregoe, *The New Rational Manager,* Princeton Research Press, Princeton, NJ, 1981.

EXERCISES

1.1. What were the three most important things you learned in this chapter?

1.2. Think of a recurring problem or situation in your life that you would like to resolve or manage better. Try viewing it as an ill-defined problem, and try to redefine this issue. Do new possibilities come to mind?

1.3. Is there a common thread running through the ill-defined problems on pages 3 to 6? If so, what is it?

1.4. Start to keep a journal or record as we progress through this text on problem solving. Write down things of interest as well as questions that you think will help your problem-solving capabilities. Write down what doesn't work for you as well as what does. List the types of problems you would like to become more skilled in solving.

1.5. Collect two or more ill-defined problems similar to the case histories described in this chapter.

1.6. Write a paragraph discussing problems you might have with the different building blocks as you use the heuristic discussed in this chapter.

FURTHER READING

Copulsky, William. "Stories from the Front," *Chemtech,* 22, p. 154, 1992. More anecdotal cases of histories of ill-defined situations and solutions.

2 THE CHARACTERISTICS, ATTITUDES, AND ENVIRONMENT NECESSARY FOR EFFECTIVE PROBLEM SOLVING

In this chapter we present ways to improve your problem-solving skills both individually and as a team member. We first discuss ways to improve your individual skills—namely, by practicing the habits of effective problem solvers, adopting a positive attitude, and embracing advice from industry on how to be successful in a creative environment. Next we encourage you to take notes, have a vision of the "big picture," and look for paradigm shifts. We close the chapter with a discussion of problem solving in teams and an exploration of ways that team members can work together effectively to solve problems.

GETTING IN THE RIGHT FRAME OF MIND

Characteristics of Effective Problem Solvers

Extensive research has been carried out in an effort to determine the differences between effective problem solvers and ineffective problem solvers.[1,2] The most important factors that appear to distinguish effective from ineffective problem solvers are the attitudes with which they approach the problem, their aggressiveness in the problem-solving process, their concern for accuracy, and the solution procedures they use. For example, effective problem solvers believe that problems can be solved through the use of heuristics and careful persistent analysis. By contrast, ineffective problem solvers think, "You either know it or you don't." Effective problem solvers become very active in the problem-solving process: They draw figures, make sketches, and ask questions of themselves and others. Ineffective problem solvers don't seem to understand the level of personal effort needed to solve the problem. Effective problem solvers take great care to understand all the facts and relationships accurately; ineffective problem solvers make judgments without checking for accuracy.

If you think you can— you will.

If you think you can't— you won't.

The following table identifies even more differences between effective and ineffective problem solvers. By approaching a situation using the characteristic attitudes and actions of an effective problem solver, you will be well on your way to finding the real problem and generating an outstanding solution.

Characteristics of Effective and Ineffective Problem Solvers[1,2]

Effective	Ineffective
Attitude	
Believe the problem can be solved.	Give up easily.
Are proactive in solving the problem.	Lie back and hope a solution will occur.
Actions	
Ask themselves and others questions.	Are passive in their approach to finding a solution.
Reread the problem several times. Redescribe the problem. Don't jump to conclusions. Create a mental picture. Draw sketches; write equations.	Do not reread the problem. Cannot redescribe the problem. Jump to conclusions. Are not actively involved in the solution. Do not draw sketches or write equations.

Effective	Ineffective
Solution Procedures	
Keep track of their progress.	Don't know where to start.
Break the problem into subproblems. Start at a point they first understand. Use a few key fundamental concepts as building blocks. Use heuristics. Persevere when stuck. Use quantitative formulas and descriptions.	Don't break the problem apart. Fail to identify key concepts. Guess. Use no special format. Quit. Do not use quantitative formulas and descriptions.
Accuracy	
Check and recheck.	Do not check.
Validate assumptions.	Don't bother to validate assumptions.

Characteristics that students have found particularly useful in solving single-answer, closed-ended problems given as homework include (1) redescribing/rephrasing the problem statement and (2) starting at a point they can first understand even though it may not be what, at first glance, appears the most logical point. The following example shows how these characteristics can be applied to solving closed-ended problems.

Closed-Ended Problem Algorithm

Problem Statement:

How many jelly beans will fit in a cylindrical jar 10 inches high and 8 inches in diameter?

ATTITUDE

This is a fun problem that may prove useful in the future for winning a guessing contest.

ACTIONS

Redescribe the problem:

What is the volume of the jar, what is the volume of a jelly bean, and what is the packing factor (i.e., what is the volume fraction of the jelly beans in the filled jar—remembering there will be some empty space between the beans)?

Assumptions:

Assume the jelly beans are spheres.

Sketch the system:

10 inches

8 inches

SOLUTION PROCEDURE

Identify:

Knowns

Jar height (H = 10 inches) and diameter (D = 8 inches)

Jelly bean diameter (d = 0.5 inch)

Unknowns

Solid fraction (the fraction of the jar volume occupied by beans, not including the void space between the beans)

Fundamentals:

Volume of the cylinder $= \pi(D^2/4)H = 3.1416 \times ((8^2)/4) \times 10 = 502.6$ in^3

Volume of one jelly bean $= \pi(D^3/6) = 3.1416 \times (0.5^3/6) = 0.0654$ in^3

Look up the solid fraction of spheres packed together. It is ~0.65.

Volume of Beans = (Jar Volume) $\times$ (Solid Fraction) = $502.6 \times 0.65 = 326.7$ in^3

Number of Beans = (Volume of Beans)/(Volume of One Bean)

$\qquad = (326.7$ in$^3) / (0.0654$ in^3 per bean)

$\qquad = 4995$ beans in the jar

ACCURACY

Check and recheck:

Explore the effects of cylindrical beans rather than spherical beans.

Check the jelly bean dimensions.

If beans are cylindrical ($D = 0.5$ in, $H = 0.5$ in), redo the calculations.

Volume of one jelly bean $= \pi(D^2/4) \times H = 3.1416 \times (0.5^2/4) \times 0.5 = 0.0982$ in^3

Look up the solid fraction of cylinders packed together in jar. It is ~0.67.

Volume of Beans = (Jar Volume) $\times$ (Solid Fraction) = $502.6 \times 0.67 = 336.7$ in^3

Number of Beans = (Volume of Beans) / (Volume of One Bean)

$\qquad = (336.7$ in$^3) / (0.0982$ in^3 per bean)

$\qquad = 3429$ beans in the jar

The true number of jelly beans in the jar is probably between these two figures, because the beans are not truly spheres or cylinders. Nevertheless, this technique gives us a range that likely includes the true answer.

Attitudes for Effective Problem Solving

Effective problem solvers develop mindsets and habits that aid them in dealing with difficult problems. They approach the problem with a positive attitude. Stephen Covey's research on highly effective people revealed that these people adopt a similar set of habits.[3] We encourage you to practice the seven habits shown in the table below.

The Seven Habits of Highly Effective People

Habit 1: Be Proactive.	Take the initiative and make things happen. Aggressively seek new ideas and innovations. Don't let a negative environment affect your behavior and decisions. Work on things that you can do something about. If you make a mistake, acknowledge it, learn from it, and move on.
Habit 2: Begin with the End in Mind.	Know where you are going, and make sure all the steps you take are in the right direction. First determine the right things to accomplish and then identify how to best accomplish them. Write a personal mission statement describing where you want to go, what you want to do, and how you will accomplish these things.
Habit 3: Put First Things First.	List your top priorities each day for the upcoming week and schedule time to work on them. Continually review and prioritize your goals. Say "no" to unimportant tasks. Focus on the important tasks, the ones that will have the greatest impact if they are carefully thought out and planned.
Habit 4: Think Win/Win.	Win/win is the frame of mind that seeks mutual benefits for all people involved in solutions and agreements. Identify the key issues and results that would constitute a fully acceptable solution to all. Make everyone who is involved in the decision feel good about the decision and committed to a plan of action.

Habit 5: Seek First to Understand, Then to Be Understood.	Learn as much as you can about the situation. "Listen, listen, listen." Try to see the problem from the other person's perspective. Be willing to be adaptable in seeking to be understood. Present things logically, not emotionally. Be credible, empathetic, and logical.
Habit 6: Synergize. $$2 + 2 = 5$$	Make the whole greater than the sum of its parts. Value the differences in the people you work with. Foster open and honest communication. Help everyone bring out the best in everyone else.
Habit 7: Practice Renewal.	Renew the four dimensions of your nature: Physical: exercise, nutrition, stress management Mental: reading, thinking, visualizing, planning, writing Spiritual: value clarification and commitment, study and meditation Social/emotional: service, empathy, self-esteem, synergy The upward spiral: Learn, Commit, Do; Learn, Commit, Do; Learn, . . .

This table is meant to give only a thumbnail sketch of the Seven Habits. You are referred to Covey's best-selling book for a more complete discussion, which includes numerous examples that illustrate these habits in action.

We continue our discussion of what constitutes a winning attitude by presenting advice for new graduates that was collected from company vice presidents, managers, recent company hires, and seminar speakers at the University of Michigan. This advice was distilled and formulated into the list of Seven Actions Necessary for a Successful Career.

The Seven Actions Necessary for a Successful Career

Action 1: Enjoy.
Find a job where you enjoy what you do and it doesn't really feel like work. Feel good about what you do or else do something different. Find time for health care. Work hard, but have fun. Life is short, so leave time for yourself.

Action 2: Learn.
Continue to learn, and renew and expand your skills set. Build a network of peers and mentors. Never stop asking questions. Listen, question, and learn. Recognize what you know and what you don't know, and don't pretend to know what you don't. Take advantage of other people's knowledge. Don't reinvent the wheel. Learn how to take feedback, both positive and negative, and listen, listen, listen. Learn how to communicate and "market" yourself and your results.

Action 3: Communicate.
Develop strong communication skills—oral, written, and listening. The best work is of little value if you can't communicate it clearly and succinctly. Develop "active listening" skills. When you have something valuable to say, say it. Develop a network of colleagues who can provide excellent advice and guidance. As your experience grows, share your knowledge with others. Peers are great sounding boards.

Action 4: Work Hard.
The harder you work, the better you'll do. The most effective results come from the synergy created in effective team efforts, rather than as individual efforts. Focus on results. Learn about the business, the culture, and the politics of the organization to which you belong. Figure out what it takes to succeed. Learn to manage up and down. If the criteria for success in your organization are incompatible with your beliefs and your style, maybe that organization is not the right place for you.

Action 5: Evolve.
Be prepared for changes in your career, and remember that every change is accompanied by new opportunities. Challenge yourself. Find useful problems to work on. Be willing to tackle different problems.

Action 6: Plan.
Be proactive in everything you do, but especially in your career plans. You own your career, and no one cares as much about you as yourself. Figure out what you want to do in your career and life. Talk to people who are doing what you want to do 10 years from now to learn what experiences you will need to get there. Pick a job (or a series of jobs) that meet your objectives. Will they help you be where you want to be in 20 years from your career, financial, and personal points of view?

Action 7: Share.
Find a way to give something back to society.

Adopting and practicing the Seven Habits and Seven Actions will lead to better problem solving—but also to your individual growth as a professional.

HAVING A VISION

To make a difference, you must have a vision. A **vision** is the ability to see the way things ought to be or will be in the future. Implementing a vision requires a master plan. Each one of us must look to find the voids in our organization, our community, and our lives and try to fill these holes. We can formulate a coherent, powerful vision by listening, reading, talking, and focusing our thoughts on bettering the current conditions. A vision with a master plan makes day-to-day decisions easier by targeting our actions to achieve our desired outcomes. Our ethical and moral values help us establish our vision, which should be consistent with our personal belief system.

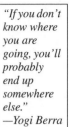

"If you don't know where you are going, you'll probably end up somewhere else."
—Yogi Berra

To develop a vision, you must occasionally set aside a block of time (anywhere from a few minutes to several hours), become introspective, and step back and look at the "big picture." Determine which direction your life (or your organization) should be taking, identify what needs to be accomplished, and devise a plan to meet your goals.

Joel Barker, in his book *The Business of Paradigms*, speaks of the concepts of paradigm shifts, paradigm paralysis, and paradigm pioneers.[4] A **paradigm** is a model or pattern based on a set of rules that defines boundaries and specifies how to be successful at and within these boundaries. Success is measured in terms of the problems you solve using these rules.

Paradigm shifts can occur instantaneously, or they can evolve over a period of time. These transitions move us from seeing the world in one way to seeing it in an entirely different way. When a paradigm shifts, a new model based on a new set of rules replaces the old model. The new rules establish new boundaries and allow for solutions to problems that were previously deemed unsolvable. All practitioners of the old paradigm are returned to "the starting line" and are again on equal footing because the old rules no longer apply.

For example, the guidelines (rules) followed by the most successful manufacturer of slide rules became useless as a result of the paradigm shift in computation brought about by the invention of pocket calculators. Other more recent paradigm shifts include the ability to purchase products or services online. Traditional travel agencies have been forced to adapt and offer expanded services to compete with online services such as Travelocity and Orbitz. Other paradigm shifts have pitted DVDs against VHS tapes; online music sales against in-store sales; flash drives against floppy disks; digital photography against film photography; dial-up modems against cable and DSL; MapQuest and Google maps and GPS units against AAA Trip-Tiks and gas-station maps; word processors against typewriters; online banking for standard recurring bills against paper checks each month; Google and online resources against encyclopedias; spell-checkers against dictionaries; and on-demand movies provided via the Internet against in-store rentals.

Barker describes **paradigm paralysis** as a situation in which someone (or some organization) becomes frozen—that is, hopelessly locked into the idea that what was successful in the past will continue to be successful in the future. **Paradigm pioneers** are people who have the courage to escape from paradigm paralysis by breaking the existing rules when success is not guaranteed. They realize that there are no easy roads when traveling in uncharted territory, so they cut new pathways, making the route safe and easy for others to follow. The characteristics of a paradigm pioneer are (1) the intuition to recognize a big idea, (2) the courage to move forward in the face of great risk, and (3) the perseverance to bring the idea to fruition.

You need to be a paradigm pioneer—not only as you generate alternative solutions to a problem, but also as you look for ways to improve things even when no apparent problems exist. Paradigm pioneers are continually searching for opportunities to initiate a paradigm shift to improve their process, product, organization, and so on. Barker uses the example of the Swiss watch industry to make this point about paradigms.[4]

A Paradigm Shift

In 1968, Switzerland, which had a long and highly respected history of making fine watches, accounted for approximately 80% of the world market in watch sales. Today, Swiss manufacturers hold less than 10% of this market. Their downfall: the emergence of the quartz digital watch.

You might be surprised to discover, however, that the Swiss invented the quartz digital watch. So why didn't these manufacturers capitalize on this invention? A paradigm shift in wristwatch technology had occurred. The Swiss failed to adopt the new technology because they were caught in a paradigm paralysis—the idea that what was successful in the past will continue to be successful in the future. After all, "the digital watch didn't have a mainspring, and it didn't tick; who would buy such a watch?" As a consequence of their paradigm paralysis, the inventors did not protect the digital watch with a patent, allowing Seiko of Japan and Texas Instruments (TI) to capitalize on the idea and market it. As a result of their miscalculation, the employment in the Swiss watch industry dropped from about 65,000 to about 15,000 over a period of a little more than three years.

Of course, even if the Swiss *had* decided to manufacture the digital watch after realizing its success, they would have been simply on equal footing with Seiko and TI because of the paradigm shift. That is, all of the Swiss companies' vast experience in making watches with gears and mainsprings would have given them absolutely no advantage in manufacturing digital watches.

By now, the importance of paradigms, paradigm shifts, and having a vision should be obvious. New York Yankees catcher Yogi Berra best described the need to have a vision when he said, "If you don't know where you are going, any road will take you there." Once you have your vision of the future, it is important that you move forward with your vision.

> Vision without action is merely a dream.
> Action without vision merely passes the time.
> Vision with action can change the world.
> —Joel Barker

It is important not only to create a vision but also to periodically reevaluate your vision, modify it as necessary, and rework your implementation plan to accomplish it. Barker further discusses the importance of vision using a number of examples in his excellent video *The Power of Vision.*[4]

WORKING TOGETHER IN TEAMS

As problems become more complex and interdisciplinary in nature, their solutions tend to require the assembly of groups of people with different areas of expertise. These kinds of problem-solving activities will require your interaction with other people, either one-on-one or in group meetings.

The 1990s saw a dramatic increase in the use of teams in industry to formulate and solve problems. This shift away from individual problem solving and toward group-based processes came in response to the advent of global competition, which created a need to respond rapidly to changes in the market and changes in technology. As a result, universities were encouraged to give students more experience in working in teams. In the material that follows, we have only enough time to give a thumbnail sketch of effective team problem solving. For a more in-depth study, you are referred to resources such as *The 17 Indisputable Laws of Teamwork.*[5]

As a member of a team, you will learn and practice collective decision making and collaboration. You will gain an appreciation of conflict and differences of opinion, learn to balance the time demands of the team with your other commitments, and, most of all, learn to appreciate the importance of mutual support.

Tuckman identified four stages of team development: forming, storming, norming, and performing.[6] Just as a child crawls before walking and then running, teams go through maturation stages before they become an effectively functioning unit. If members are aware of these stages of team development, the team will be less likely to flounder and become frustrated during the initial, more chaotic phases.

- **Forming stage:** Team members introduce themselves and get to know one another. In this stage, they should agree on group goals and establish ground rules. Team members have an initial discussion of the project they have been assigned. There is great excitement and expectations are high.
- **Storming stage:** As work on the project continues, a general state of chaos typically develops. Team interactions are characterized by a lot of talking, little listening, no common vision, and very little progress. The team should realize that this stage is a common phase teams go through and should not be discouraged. Disagreements will certainly occur. However, the team needs to develop strategies for encouraging constructive controversy and respecting differences of opinion. The team must work hard to establish an atmosphere that supports robust dialogue and disagreement.
- **Norming stage:** The team gels and develops a common vision. This stage is characterized by good communication between team members as tasks are identified and mapped into a timetable.
- **Performing stage:** In this final stage, the team makes progress in achieving the objectives and goals. Creative brainstorming is fostered, and ideas rather than personal agendas are debated. The team takes collective pride in their work and produces their final product.

Meetings are essential tools for team problem solving. They should be carefully planned and skillfully run to realize their maximum benefit. Because everyone's time is valuable, it is imperative that these meetings be both effective and efficient.

The importance of meetings and positive group interactions cannot be overemphasized. For the problem-solving process to function smoothly, group members must learn to work smoothly together. All members of the team may not "like" all other members of the team, but they still must work together for the common good.

If you are working in a team environment, always be courteous, no matter how much you disagree with a team member. Because mistakes will inevitably arise in the problem-solving process, focus on correcting these mistakes and preventing them from recurring, and then "move on." This focus on the issues forestalls defensive behavior and consequent loss of productivity. Provide positive reinforcement and encouragement to your team members. In many instances, the success of the project will depend on how well people communicate and interact with one another.

Another key ingredient of successful teams is the ability to work together creatively. John Sculley (former chairman of Apple Computer, one of the more creative companies of the past decade) has discussed the philosophy of maintaining a creative environment for product development.[7] Some of the ideas that he suggests for team leaders or managers to foster a creative environment are shown here.

Establishing a Creative Team Environment[7]

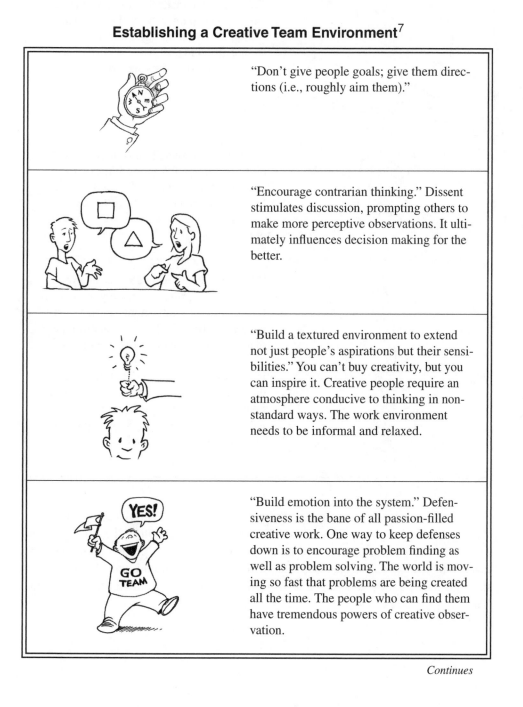

"Don't give people goals; give them directions (i.e., roughly aim them)."

"Encourage contrarian thinking." Dissent stimulates discussion, prompting others to make more perceptive observations. It ultimately influences decision making for the better.

"Build a textured environment to extend not just people's aspirations but their sensibilities." You can't buy creativity, but you can inspire it. Creative people require an atmosphere conducive to thinking in nonstandard ways. The work environment needs to be informal and relaxed.

"Build emotion into the system." Defensiveness is the bane of all passion-filled creative work. One way to keep defenses down is to encourage problem finding as well as problem solving. The world is moving so fast that problems are being created all the time. The people who can find them have tremendous powers of creative observation.

Continues

Establishing a Creative Team Environment[7] (Continued)

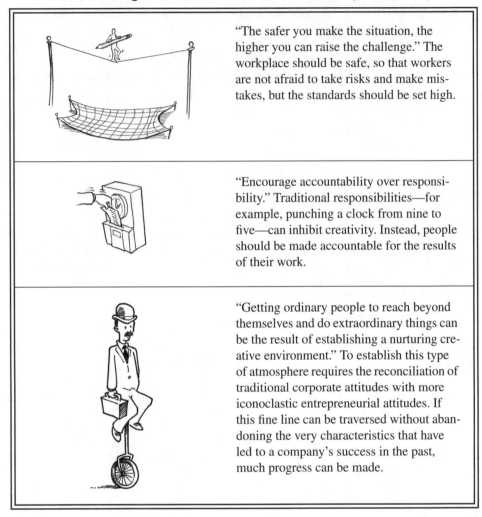

"The safer you make the situation, the higher you can raise the challenge." The workplace should be safe, so that workers are not afraid to take risks and make mistakes, but the standards should be set high.

"Encourage accountability over responsibility." Traditional responsibilities—for example, punching a clock from nine to five—can inhibit creativity. Instead, people should be made accountable for the results of their work.

"Getting ordinary people to reach beyond themselves and do extraordinary things can be the result of establishing a nurturing creative environment." To establish this type of atmosphere requires the reconciliation of traditional corporate attitudes with more iconoclastic entrepreneurial attitudes. If this fine line can be traversed without abandoning the very characteristics that have led to a company's success in the past, much progress can be made.

As you become more involved in group problem solving, you will discover that personal traits inevitably surface among individuals within the group. Some traits will be positive; others will be a barrier to the group problem-solving process. When these challenges arise, the following table should help the group get through these issues and continue working toward a solution to the problem at hand.

Suggestions on How to Handle the Top Ten List of Group Problems[8]

Problem	Strategies to Minimize the Problem
Floundering	Make sure the mission is clear and everyone understands what is needed to move forward.
Overbearing experts	Have an agreement among team members that all members have the right to explore and question all areas. Be courteous to everyone no matter how they are behaving.
Dominating participants	List "balance of participation" as a goal, and evaluate this issue regularly. Practice "gatekeeping" to limit a dominant participant.
Reluctant participants	Encourage everyone to participate. Ask opinions of quiet members and encourage them by validation. Require individual assignments and reports.
Unquestioned acceptance of opinion	Play the devil's advocate; ask for supporting data and reasoning. Accept and encourage conflicting ideas. Be careful with criticism; criticize only ideas—not individuals.

Continues

Suggestions on How to Handle the Top Ten List of Group Problems[8]

Problem	Strategies to Minimize the Problem
Rush to accomplishment	Confront those doing the rushing and remind them not to compromise the best solution. Even though achieving total agreement among all team members may not be possible, make sure a general consensus is reached. Everyone may not be able to get everything they want from each team decision, but there should not be serious internal opposition to team actions.
Attribution of motives to others	Ask for data to support statements. Verify that the attribution is correct—for example, "John is just saying this because he is angry with the Sales Department."
Discounting or ignoring a group member's statement	Listening effectively is a must for all. Provide training in effective listening. Support the discounted person. Talk off-line with anyone who continually discounts the opinions and contributions of other team members.
Wanderlust: digression and tangents	Follow an agenda that includes time estimates. Keep the topics in full view of the team, and direct the conversation back to the topic.

Problem	Strategies to Minimize the Problem
Feuding team members	Focus on ideas—not personalities. Get adversaries to discuss the issues off-line or get them to agree to a standard of behavior during meetings.

For a more complete discussion of ways to further minimize these top ten problems, you are referred to Scholtes's work.[8]

CONFLICT RESOLUTION

Controversy can be a positive contributor to the creative process; however, keeping controversy properly focused so that it does not degenerate into interpersonal conflict is a challenge for teams. Personality conflicts consume energy that would be much better spent on achieving team goals. The following material was adapted from the University of Colorado's Web site on *Introductory Engineering Design: A Project-Based Approach* (http://itll.colorado.edu/GEEN1400/index.cfm?fuseaction=Textbook).[9]

Johnson and Johnson suggest the following negotiating steps to resolve a problem that arises from conflict between team members.[10]

Step 1: Describe Your Interests and What You Want

Tactfully describe your perception of the problem and what you want as a desired outcome. Define the conflict as small and specific, not general and global.

- Define your views in as short and as specific a manner as possible.
- Acknowledge the legitimate goals of the other person as part of the challenge to be addressed.
- Focus on a long-term cooperative relationship with statements such as "I think it's in the best interests of the team for us to talk about our argument."
- Be a good listener; face the other person and be quiet while that individual takes his or her turn.
- Show that you understand by paraphrasing what the other person said.

Step 2: Describe Your Feelings

Feelings must be openly expressed for the issue to be resolved. Acknowledging that every person's feelings are valid is essential for furthering the negotiation.

Step 3: Exchange Underlying Reasons for Your Opinions and Positions Relative to the Problem at Hand

It is now appropriate to better understand the underlying reasons both parties have for taking their positions.

- Present your reasons and listen to the reasons given by the other person. State the underlying reason(s) for what you want and work to understand the other party's reasons. Only through this empathetic understanding can you search for creative, win/win solutions.
- Empower the other person by being flexible and providing a choice of options.

Step 4: Understand the Other Person's Perspective

Clarifying the intentions of your teammate may help you realize that his or her intentions are not the same as your fears. Be sure that you understand both perspectives, and openly discuss opposing perceptions.

   Some Tips for Effective Listening
   - Make eye contact.
   - Avoid negative body language (e.g., constantly looking at your watch).
   - Practice "active listening" by using encouraging verbal cues to elicit further information (e.g., "Can you expand on that?" or "Tell me more.").
   - Frequently confirm your understanding by restating what you think you have heard others say.
   - Use Covey's Habit No. 5 of Highly Effective People: "Seek first to understand, then to be understood."

Step 5: Generate Options for Mutual Gain

Use each other's perspective to promote the generation of new, creative solutions. Brainstorm to generate at least three workable alternative agreements before selecting the one solution that you will jointly employ. Use the techniques discussed in Chapters 5 and 6 to help generate options.

Step 6: Reach a Wise Agreement

- Does everyone have an equal chance of benefiting?
- Does the agreement meet the legitimate needs of everyone in the team (or at least those people who are directly affected by the conflict)?
- Are the gains and losses of all parties roughly in balance?

TEAM DECISIONS

When working together as a team, there are several ways to arrive at a decision. In Chapter 7, we discuss the use of the Kepner–Tregoe (K.T.) decision analysis strategy to choose between a number of alternative solutions by filling out a K.T. decision analysis table. After each team member individually completes the K.T. table, the team members should compare and discuss the results. If it turns out that no single alternative is the clear choice of all members of the team, then further discussion should ensue until a consensus is reached. With a consensus, an alternative can be chosen that all members support and that no one actively opposes, even though not everyone is totally satisfied. The most important thing in reaching a consensus is to have an open, interactive discussion in which everyone participates.

Two techniques can be used to help narrow the number of alternatives: multivoting and nominal group techniques.[10] **Multivoting** is useful when there are a large number of alternatives from which to choose. With this technique, each team member is given a number of votes that is one-third the total number of choices (i.e., 10 votes for 30 alternatives). A vote is taken, and the top 15 vote-getters advance to the next round of voting. The next round of voting begins with each team member now having five 5 to distribute among the remaining 15 items. This process continues until a choice emerges. If no clear choice is evident, then further discussion should ensue and a final vote should be taken.

The **nominal group technique (NGT)** is particularly useful when the team members are new to one another, when the issue is highly controversial, or when the team is stuck. With this technique, each team member receives four to eight blank cards (e.g., 3" × 5" index cards) or pieces of paper. Scholtes suggests distributing four cards if there are 20 or fewer items, six cards for 20 to 35 items, and eight cards for 35 to 50 choices. For example, if there are 30 items, six cards are given to each member. Each team member first writes one choice on each of the six cards and then assigns a point total to each card, starting with the member's first choice, which receives a 6 (8 if there are eight cards); the second choice receives a 5, the third choice a 4, and so on. Members may vote only once for an alternative. The points are then tallied and the alternative with the highest score is chosen.

SUMMARY

This chapter began by emphasizing the importance of approaching the problem with a positive, "can do" attitude, striving to develop the traits of expert problem solvers, and practicing the Seven Habits of Highly Effective People. We continued with a discussion of the need to have a vision and to look for paradigm shifts and exploit them. Finally, we presented a micro-summary of ideas for working effectively in teams to solve problems.

- **Practice**
  - Recognize and cultivate the characteristics of expert problem solvers.
  - Practice the Seven Habits of Highly Effective People.
  - Practice the Seven Actions for a Successful Career.

- **Paradigms**
  - Welcome change and paradigm shifts as opportunities to make inroads and advancements.
  - A **paradigm** is a model or pattern based on a set of rules that defines boundaries and specifies how to be successful within these boundaries.
  - **Paradigm shifts** occur when a new model based on a new set of rules replaces the old rules, we establish new boundaries, and we allow more problems to be solved.
  - **Paradigm paralysis** occurs when someone or some organization is stuck on the idea that what was successful in the past will be successful in the future.
  - **Paradigm pioneers** are individuals who have the courage to move forward and to break existing rules when success is not guaranteed.

- **Vision**
  - Look for and fill the voids in your organization. Try to provide a vision to fill those holes and move the organization forward.
  - Develop an atmosphere that encourages and fosters creativity in your co-workers.
  - Listen to your customers and work with them as a unit to develop creative solutions.

- **Teamwork**
  - Understand that the four stages of teamwork are forming, storming, norming, and performing.
  - Seek ways to establish a creative team environment.
  - Follow the suggestions on ways to handle the top ten group problems.
  - Pursue conflict resolution to ensure that your team will work effectively and efficiently.

REFERENCES

1. Whimbey, A., and J. Lochhead, *Problem Solving and Comprehension: A Short Course in Analytical Reasoning*, Franklin Institute Press, Philadelphia, 1980.
2. Wankat, P. C., and F. S. Oreovicz, *Teaching Engineering*, McGraw-Hill, New York, 1992.
3. Covey, Stephen R., *The Seven Habits of Highly Effective People*. © 1989. Reprinted with permission of Simon & Schuster, New York, 1989.
4. Barker, J. A., *Discovering the Future: The Business of Paradigms*, ILI Press, St. Paul, MN, 1985; *The New Business of Paradigms, 21st Century Editions,* distributed by Star Thrower (800-242-3220); *Paradigm Pioneers and the Power of Vision, 21st Century Editions,* distributed by Star Thrower (800-242-3220).
5. Maxwell, John C., *The 17 Indisputable Laws of Teamwork*, Thomas Nelson, Nashville, TN, 2001.
6. Tuckman, Bruce W., "Developmental Sequence in Small Groups," *Psychological Bulletin*, 63, pp. 384–399, 1965. The article was reprinted in *Group Facilitation: A Research and Applications Journal,* 3, Spring 2001, http://dennislearningcenter.osu.edu/references/GROUP%20DEV%20ARTICLE.doc; accessed January 14, 2005. Also see Hanwit, Jessie, *Four Stages of Teambuilding,* http://www.ttacev.org/articles/team.html.
7. Sculley, John, and John A. Byrne, *Odyssey: Pepsi to Apple . . . A Journey of Advertising Ideas and the Future.* © 1987 by John Sculley. Reprinted by permission of HarperCollins Publishers, Inc.
8. Scholtes, Peter R. *The Team Handbook.* Oriel, Inc. (formerly Joiner Associates, Inc.), Madison, WI, 1988.
9. Bedard, A., D. Carlson, L. Carlson, J. Hertzberg, B. Louie, J. Milford, R. Reitsma, T. Schwartz, J. Sullivan, and J. Abarca, *Introductory Engineering Design: A Project-Based Approach.* http://itll.colorado.edu/GEEN1400/index.cfm?fuseaction=Textbook. Copyright © 2000 Regents of the University of Colorado.
10. Johnson, David W., and Frank P. Johnson, *Joining Together: Group Theory and Group Skills,* 9th ed., Allyn and Bacon, Boston, MA, 2005.

EXERCISES

2.1. Which characteristics listed in the tables on pages 14 and 15 do you feel you now possess? Which characteristics do you feel you need to improve?

2.2. Choose three of the Seven Habits of Highly Effective People and explain how you will practice them during the coming weeks.

2.3. Discuss which of the Seven Actions for a Successful Career you believe are the most important, and explain why they are important to you. Describe how you will practice the actions most important to you.

2.4. What other examples of recent paradigm shifts can you identify?

2.5. Look around an organization of which you are a member for things that could be improved upon. Make a list of the voids that need to be filled to make the organization even better and more effective. Which of these changes would really alter the way the organization functions? What would need to be accomplished to produce a paradigm shift? How can you be a paradigm pioneer?

2.6. Identify a group of people with whom you frequently interact. Make a list of things you can do to become a better team member and to establish a creative environment.

2.7. You are in a group of four working as a team to define and solve a problem. Describe how you would handle each of the following situations:

A. Someone starts to dominate the group discussion and direction.

B. Two of the group members are good friends and seem to form a clique.

C. One member of the group is not carrying his or her load.

D. One member of the group continually makes mistakes in his or her part of the project.

2.8. Prepare a list of specific ideas that would establish a creative environment in your group.

2.9. An instructor requested that students in the class form six-person teams, attempting to maximize diversity and selecting people to work with who are new to them. A team was formed that was composed of two white men, two white women, one African American man, and one Asian American man. The group selected one of the white men as their team leader. During the first and second meetings of this team, which took place during class time and in the classroom, the instructor noted that the African American man and the white man who was not the team leader sat almost outside the circle formed by the other team participants. Moreover, the white man who was the team leader and one of the white women appeared to do all the talking and to make all the suggestions about how to proceed. The other four people on the team looked uninvolved, at least as far as the instructor could observe.

A. What might be going on in this team?

B. Should the instructor intervene? Why? How? What would you do?

C. How might your own race/ethnicity and gender affect your options and choices about intervention?

D. What preparation, training, or instruction for teamwork might have helped this team? What training or instruction might be helpful to it now?

E. What preparation or instruction in teamwork dynamics, supervision, or intervention might be helpful to you in this and similar situations?

(This exercise is adapted from the FAIRTEACH Workshop with the University of Michigan's School of Engineering Faculty, Martin Luther King, Jr., Day, 1994.)

2.10. Redo the jelly bean contest guessing problem for cylindrical gourmet jelly beans in a 1-gallon cylindrical vessel.

Enrico Fermi (1901–1954) Problems (EFP)

Enrico Fermi was an Italian physicist who received the Nobel Prize for his work on nuclear processes. Fermi was famous for his "back of the envelope order of magnitude calculation," which enabled him to obtain an estimate of the answer to a problem by applying logic and making reasonable assumptions. He used a process to set bounds on the answer by saying it is probably larger than one number and smaller than another, and arrived at an answer that was within a factor of 10 (http://mathforum.org/workshops/sum96/interdisc/sheila2.html).

2.11. *EFP 1.* How many piano tuners are there in the city of Chicago? Show the steps in your reasoning.

   A. Population of Chicago: _____

   B. Number of people per household: _____

   C. Number of households: _____

   D. Households with pianos: _____

   E. Average number of tunes per year: _____

   F. And so forth: _____

   An answer is given on the Web under Summary Notes for Chapter 2.

2.12. *EFP 2.* How many square meters of pizza were eaten by an undergraduate student body population of 20,000 during the fall term 2007?

FURTHER READING

Gunneson, Alvin. "Communicating Up and Down the Parks." *Chemical Engineering*, 98, p. 135, June 1991. Useful tips on how to improve your interactions with those employees above, at the same level, and below you in your organization.

Lumsdaine, E., and M. Lumsdaine. *Creative Problem Solving: An Introductory Course for Engineering Students.* McGraw-Hill, New York, 1990.

Mathes, J., and D. Stevenson. *Designing Technical Reports*, 2nd ed., New York, Simon and Schuster, 1991.

Phillips, Denise A., and A. E. Ladin Moore. "12 Commandments." *Chemtech*, 21, p. 138, March 1991. Rules to help improve your communication skills.

Raudsepp, Eugene. "Profits of the Effective Manager." *Chemical Engineering*, 85, p. 141, March 27, 1978. Although this article was written 15 years ago, these traits still apply to effective leadership.

Strunk, W., and E. B. White. *The Elements of Style*, 4th ed. Macmillan, New York, 2000. A concise treatise on grammar rules and writing style with many examples.

VanGundy, Arthur B., Jr. *Techniques of Structured Problem Solving*, 2nd ed. Van Nostrand Reinhold, New York, 1988.

Whimbey, A., and J. Lockhead. *Problem Solving and Comprehension: A Short Course in Analytical Reasoning*, 2nd ed. Franklin Institute Press, Philadelphia, 1980.

3 GATHERING INFORMATION ON THE PROBLEM

> The mere formulation of a problem is far more essential than its solution, which may be merely a matter of mathematical or experimental skill. To raise new questions, new possibilities, to regard old problems from a new angle requires creative imagination and marks real advances in science.
>
> —Albert Einstein

THE FIRST FOUR STEPS

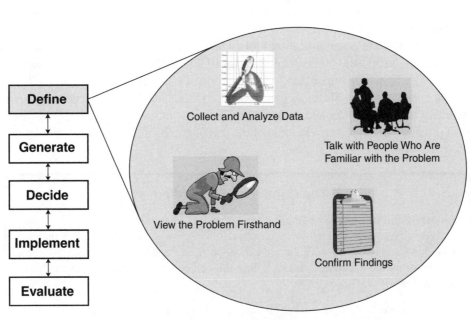

The First Four Steps

Often, one of the most difficult aspects of problem solving is understanding and defining the real problem (sometimes referred to as the underlying or root problem). In Chapter 1, we presented a number of real-world examples of incorrectly defined problem statements that demonstrated how even competent, conscientious people can define the wrong problem and waste considerable time and money looking in the wrong direction for a solution. The first task in defining the real problem is to properly gather information about the problem.

The first four steps to understand and define the real problem focus on gathering information.

1. Collect and analyze information and data.
2. Talk with people who are familiar with the problem.
3. If possible, view the problem firsthand.
4. Confirm all findings and continue to gather information.

> *"Start with an open mind."*
>
> *"Don't jump to conclusions."*
>
> *"Look at the big picture."*
>
> *"Review the obvious."*

Step 1: Collect and Analyze Information and Data

Learn as much as you can about the problem. Write down or list everything you can think of to describe the problem. Do an Internet search on all aspects of the problem. Until the problem is well defined, anything might be important. Determine which information is missing and which information is extraneous.

The information should be properly organized, analyzed, and presented so that it can serve as the basis for subsequent decision making. Make a simple sketch or drawing of the situation. Drawings, sketches, graphs of data, and other illustrations can all be excellent communication tools when used correctly. Analyze the data to show trends, errors, and other meaningful information. Display numerical or quantitative data graphically rather than in tabular form. Tables can be difficult to interpret and are sometimes misleading (see page 279). Graphing, by comparison, is an excellent way to organize and analyze large amounts of data. The Case of the Dead Fish provides an interesting example of the use of graphical data to solve problems.

The Case of the Dead Fish

Research and information gathering are great tools in problem solving. Here we consider the case of a chemical plant that discharges waste into a stream, which in turn flows into a relatively wide river. Biologists monitored the river as an ecosystem and reported the following data regarding the number of dead fish in the river and the river level:

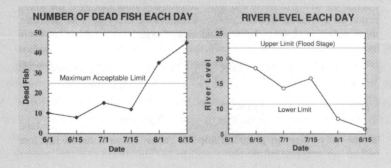

Graphs of the type shown above are called time plots and control charts. A **time plot** shows trends over a period of time (e.g., the level of a river over several days or weeks). A **control chart** is a time plot that also shows the acceptable limits of the quantity being displayed. For example, in the control chart of the river level, the upper and lower acceptable water levels would be shown. If one of the acceptable limits is exceeded, this occurrence may yield some information about the timing of the problem and its possible causes. We can then examine time plots of other pertinent quantities and look for additional clues about the problem.

From the graphs, we see that the acceptable level of dead fish was exceeded between July 15 and August 1. To investigate the source of this problem, we look for anything that might have occurred on or between July 15 and August 1. We discover that on July 29, a large amount of chemical waste was discharged into the river. Discharges of this size had not caused any problems in the past. Upon checking other factors, however, we see that there had been little rain prior to the discharge and that the water level in the river, measured on August 1, had fallen so low it might not have been able to dilute the plant's chemical waste. Consequently, the low water level, coupled with the high volume of waste, could be suggested as possible causes of the unusually large number of dead fish.

To verify our suspicion, we would have to carry the analysis further. Specifically, we would use one or more of the problem definition techniques discussed in Chapter 4.

Step 2: Talk with People Who Are Familiar with the Problem

Find out who knows about the problem and interview them. Ask penetrating questions by doing the following.

Ask insightful questions.

- Look past the obvious.
- Ask for clarification when you do not understand something.
- Ask when the problem first occurred.
- Ask how the problem occurred.
- Challenge the basic premise of any explanations given as to the cause of the problem.
- Ask where the problem is located and where everything is okay.
- Ask what was observed and whether it had been observed previously.
- Ask who else knows about the problem.
- Probe the answers you receive with follow-up questions.

Depending on the particular response you receive, additional probing with follow-up questions may prove particularly helpful. Our experience shows that seemingly naive questions (often perceived as "dumb" questions) can produce profound results by challenging established thinking patterns. This act of challenging must be an ongoing process.

You should also describe the problem to other people. Verbalizing the problem to someone else helps clarify in your own mind just what it is you are trying to do. Try to find out who the experts in the field are—and then talk to them.

When interviewing people to collect data and information, try to use as many of the types of critical thinking questions as you can (see Chapter 4). When different individuals interviewed give different interpretations of a situation, it is imperative to be aware that their individual biases can obscure or mask the actual facts. Separate the answers into those that are fact, opinionated fact, and opinion.

Fact	
Facts usually come from measurements, reports, tables, figures, firsthand observations, and other data.	"On August 16th, 45 fish were found dead in the river."
Opinionated Fact	
Opinionated facts use phrases to put a bias or spin on the factual data, in an effort to persuade others to adopt a particular point of view.	The opinionated phrase may denote the significance of the fact ("*only* 45 died"), attach value to the fact ("*surprisingly* 45 died"), suggest generalization ("*all* 45 were killed by . . ."), or advocate acceptance of the fact ("*obviously,* 45 dead fish is a serious problem").
Opinion	
Opinion is based on years of experience and can be quite useful in analyzing the problem. It can also be used to serve a person's self-interests.	"I think you need to look for another reason other than the toxic waste to explain the 45 dead fish."

Non-experts are also a rich source of creative solutions, as evidenced by the following example.

Seeking Advice

Joel Weldon, in his tape "Jet Pilots Don't Use Rearview Mirrors," described a problem encountered by a major hotel a number of years ago. The elevator capacity was inadequate for the number of guests, causing a backup on each floor and in the elevator area of the lobby. The manager and assistant manager were lamenting the problem in the lobby one day and were brainstorming about how to increase the elevator capacity. Adding additional elevator shafts would require removal of a number of rooms and a significant loss of income.

The doorman, overhearing their conversation, casually mentioned that it was too bad they couldn't just add an elevator on the outside of the building, so as not to disturb things inside. A great idea! It occurred to the doorman because he was outside the building much of the time, and that was his frame of reference. Notice, however, that the doorman's creativity alone was not enough to solve the problem. Knowledge of design techniques was necessary to implement his original idea. A new outside elevator was born, and the rest is history. External elevators have since become quite popular in major hotels. Information, good ideas, and different perspectives on the problem can come from all levels of the organization. (*Chemtech*, 13, 9, p. 517, 1983).

Go Talk to George

When equipment malfunctions, it is a must to talk to the operators because they know the "personality" of the equipment better than anyone. Most organizations have employees who have been around a long time and have a great deal of experience, as illustrated in the following example.

Remember the leaking flow meter discussed in Chapter 1? The solution that the company adopted was to replace the flow meter at regular time intervals. Let's consider a similar situation in which, immediately upon replacement, the flow meter began to leak. We list, in order, four people to whom you would talk:

- The person who installed the meter
- The technician who monitors the flow meter
- The manufacturer's representative who sold you the flow meter
- George

Who's George? Every organization has a George. George is the individual who has both years of experience to draw upon and "street smarts." George is an excellent problem solver who always seems to approach the problem from a different viewpoint—one that hasn't been thought of by anyone else. Be sure to tap into this rich source of knowledge when you face a problem. Individuals such as George can often provide a unique perspective on the situation. Strive to become the "George" of your organization.

Search out colleagues who may have useful information and pertinent ideas. Have them play the "What if . . . ?" game with you: "*What if* the flow meter leaked only five drops per day; would we need to replace it?" or "*What if* the flow meter were eliminated?" Also have them play the devil's advocate and deliberately challenge your ideas. This technique stimulates creative interactions.

Step 3: View the Problem Firsthand

While it is important to talk to people as a way to understand the problem, you should not rely solely on their interpretations of the situation and problem. If possible, inspect the problem yourself.

"You can see a lot just by looking."
—Yogi Berra

Viewing the Problem Firsthand: A Shocking Installation

Dan, a technical salesperson for an electrical contractor, received a call on a Friday morning stating that an electrical cabinet—the installation of which he had overseen the previous day—had just exploded upon initial start-up. He was informed that 10 seconds after power was supplied to the cabinet, it exploded. Dan knew that it was imperative that the issue be resolved quickly because this particular piece of equipment was critical to the operation of his customer's plant. He sat down with the engineers at his company and pored over drawings, working nearly nonstop throughout the weekend—but came up with nothing. This same cabinet had been installed in other facilities with no problem, and, as far as he knew, nothing about its design or operation had changed.

Dan took it upon himself to drive 6 hours to investigate the problem firsthand. Upon his arrival at the facility, he was led to the shattered remains of the cabinet. He quickly confirmed that the cabinet had been wired to his company's specifications. Dan then decided to take a lunch break. As he walked away from the cabinet, he saw its door leaning against the wall. He noticed that the handle installed on the door was different from any he had ever seen installed on this particular style of cabinet. Out of mere curiosity, he opened the cabinet door. To his surprise, Dan saw a 2-inch rod sticking off the back of the handle, which was partially melted. When he questioned the plant manager about the handle, he learned that it was installed by the company's maintenance crew prior to start-up so that the plant skeleton key could be used to access the cabinet.

Dan had a hunch about the handle, so he took the cabinet door with him when he left for the day. Upon arrival at his office, he took the door and compared it to one installed on an identical cabinet. His hunch was correct: The rod extending from the back of the cabinet handle that his customer had installed was just long enough to touch a positive lead on one of the electrical components in the cabinet. Dan realized that this particular component acted like a battery, storing up electrical energy. When the handle touched this component, an electrical short-circuit occurred. Dan had found his problem and saved his company from a potential lawsuit.[1]

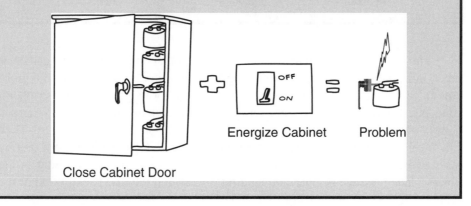

Close Cabinet Door   Energize Cabinet   Problem

Step 4: Confirm All Key Findings

Verify the information you collected. Check and cross-reference data, facts, and figures. Search for biases or misrepresentation of facts. Confirm all important pieces of information, and spot-check others. Distinguish between fact and opinion. Challenge assumptions and assertions.

Confirm All Allegations

The authors of this book were involved in a consulting project for a pulp and paper company we will call Boxright. Several years ago, Boxright had installed a new process for recovering and recycling its chemicals that were used in the paper-making process. Two years after the installation, the process had yet to operate correctly. Tempers flared and accusations flew back and forth between Boxright and Courtland Construction, the supplier of the recycling equipment. Courtland claimed the problem was that Boxright did not know how to operate the process correctly; Boxright contended that Courtland's equipment was designed incorrectly. Boxright finally decided to sue Courtland for breach of equipment performance.

Much data and information were presented by both sides to support their arguments. Courtland presented data and information from an article in the engineering literature that the company claimed proved Boxright was not operating the process correctly. At this point it looked like Courtland had cooked Boxright's goose by presenting such data. Before conceding the case, however, Boxright needed to confirm this claim. When we analyzed this key information in detail, we found in the last few pages of the article a statement that the data would not be expected to apply to industrial-size equipment or processes. When this information was presented, the lawsuit was settled in favor of the pulp and paper company, Boxright.

Throughout the problem-solving process, you should continue to gather as much information as possible by reading texts and literature related to the problem to learn about both the underlying fundamental principles and any peripheral concepts. Literature searches are particularly helpful in this regard. Perhaps a closely related problem has already been solved. George Quarderer of Dow Chemical Company appropriately describes the idea of reinventing the wheel by his statement, "Four to six weeks in the laboratory can save you an hour in the library." The message is clear: Doing a bit of research into the background of the problem may save you hours of time and effort.

The information you gather in the first four steps will be of great help to you as you "define the real problem," which is the topic of the next chapter.

SUMMARY

In this chapter we discussed methods for obtaining the information needed to define the problem. Experienced problem solvers use four steps to attack problems:

1. Collect and analyze information and data.
2. Talk with people who are familiar with the problem.
3. If possible, view the problem firsthand.
4. Confirm all findings and continue to gather information.

REFERENCES

1. Zaleski, Seth, private communication, Toledo, OH, 2006.

EXERCISES

3.1. List the three most important things you learned in this chapter. Also list the three most interesting things.

3.2. Describe a person from your past who has the characteristics of "George."

3.3. Describe a situation from your past in which you encountered a problem or situation and needed to collect information. Which of the four steps did you use?

3.4. Write out a generic procedure you will use to gather information about a project or problem.

4   PROBLEM DEFINITION

In Chapter 1, we described situations in which millions of dollars were wasted when individuals defined the *perceived problem* instead of the *real problem*. In this chapter, we address the first part of the problem-solving heuristic—problem definition. We present four techniques that will greatly enhance your chances of defining the real problem.

A study that the authors of this book conducted of experienced engineers' problem-solving methods in industry revealed some common threads that run through their problem definition techniques. We have classified these common threads into four techniques to help you understand and define the real problem instead of being sidetracked by the perceived problem.

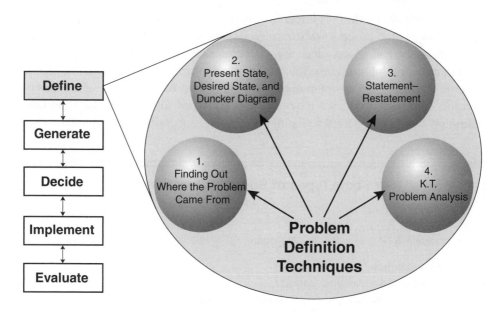

DEFINING THE REAL PROBLEM: FOUR TECHNIQUES

The four steps discussed in Chapter 3 were all related to gathering information about the problem. This information laid the groundwork that will help us use the four problem definition techniques discussed here to define the real problem.

TECHNIQUE 1: FINDING OUT WHERE THE PROBLEM CAME FROM

This technique uses a critical thinking algorithm to identify the real problem and is most effective when you are able to question other people about the problem. Our studies on problem-solving techniques in industry revealed that one of the major differences between experienced problem solvers and novice problem solvers relates to their ability to ask questions that penetrate to the heart of the problem and to interview as many people as necessary who might possess useful information about the problem. Many times you will be given a problem or problem statement by someone else rather than discovering it yourself. Under these circumstances, it is important that you make sure the problem you were given reflects the true situation. Ask as many questions as you can to ferret out the real problem.

Where did the problem originate?

Critical Thinking Algorithm

The use of critical thinking is imperative in defining and solving problems. **Critical thinking** is the process we use to recognize underlying assumptions, scrutinize arguments, and assess ideas and statements. Socratic questioning lies at the heart of critical thinking. The critical thinking algorithm applies Paul and Elder's[1] Socratic Questions to the situation to learn the real problem. While many types of Socratic Questions exist, we have selected six types to apply in the following examples. For a more complete listing, refer to the appendix to this chapter.

Some Types of Socratic Questions

Questions that clarify:
     Why do you say that?
     How does this relate to our discussion?

Questions that probe assumptions:
     What could we assume instead?
     How can you verify or disprove that assumption?

Questions that probe reasons and evidence:
     What would be an example?
     What evidence do you have to support your answer?

Questions that explore viewpoints and perspectives:
     What would be an alternative?
     What is a different way to look at it?

Questions that probe implications and consequences:
> What are the consequences if that assumption is not valid?
> How does that tie into what we learned?

Questions that revisit the original question:
> What was the point of this question?
> Why do you think I asked this question?

In the following example, we apply the critical thinking algorithm using the six types of Socratic Questions to learn the real problem.

Application of the Critical Thinking Algorithm

The Case of the Dead Fish was originally discussed in Chapter 3.

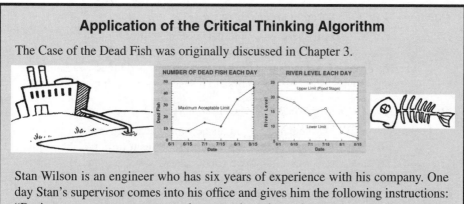

Stan Wilson is an engineer who has six years of experience with his company. One day Stan's supervisor comes into his office and gives him the following instructions: "Design a new waste treatment plant to reduce the toxic waste stream flowing into the river by a factor of 10." A quick back-of-the-envelope calculation shows that this plant could cost several million dollars. Stan is puzzled because the concentrations of toxic chemicals have always been significantly below the levels permitted by governmental regulations and company health specifications. Has Stan been given a real problem to solve or a perceived problem?

Let's apply the critical thinking algorithm to this situation.

Questions about the Question
> Q. Stan asks his supervisor where the problem originated.
> A. His supervisor says, "From bad publicity in the newspapers."

Questions for Clarification
> Q. Stan asks who posed the problem in the first place.
> A. His supervisor says, "Upper management."

Questions That Probe Assumptions

Q. Stan asks his supervisor to explain the reasoning as to how management arrived at the problem statement.

A. His supervisor explains that fish are dying because of the low water level caused by the ongoing drought. Toxic chemicals become more concentrated—and hence more toxic—when the discharge is the same but the water level is lower.

Questions That Probe Reasons and Evidence

Q. Stan asks if the concentration of chemicals in the river was approaching the LD50 level. (LD50 means that 50% of the fish will die at this concentration.)

A. Stan is informed that the concentration in the river was not measured.

Questions about the Viewpoint and Perspective

Q. Stan wonders if there is an alternative explanation for why the fish are dying; he calls a biology professor he knows.

A. The professor explains that the low water levels and higher water temperatures make fish more susceptible to disease—perhaps fungi in this case.

Questions That Probe Implications and Consequences

Q. Stan wonders whether there might be other locations in the area where fish are dead or sick, such as upstream of the plant or in the surrounding lakes and rivers where the toxic chemicals were not present. He calls the state Department of Natural Resources (DNR).

A. A government official at DNR says dead fish have been found upstream of the plant and in nearby lakes. Stan knows that there is no way the toxic chemicals could diffuse upstream of the chemical plant or get into surrounding lakes.

Questions That Probe Reasons and Evidence

Q. Stan asks DNR to test the fish for fungi.

A. The fish were infected in both the river and the lakes.

Questions about the Question

Q. Has the question been answered? Stan calls DNR and asks if it has the results of tests from the dead fish.

A. An official at DNR responds that the dead fish from both the river and the lakes were analyzed and found to contain the fungus that was causing them to die.

Epilogue

Stan was glad he found the real problem and did not go try to solve the perceived problem by designing the multimillion-dollar plant.

Keep digging to learn the motivation (who, why) for issuing the instructions to solve the perceived problem.

Scheffer and Rubenfeld[2,3] expand on the practice of critical thinking discussed by Paul and Elder by using the activities, statements, and questions shown below. Included in this table are examples applied to the Case of the Dead Fish.

Critical Thinking Actions

Predicting: Envisioning a plan and its consequences
  "I envisioned the outcome would be . . . ."
  "I was prepared for . . . ."

 Stan envisioned the proposed plant would cost millions of dollars and wanted to make sure that such an expenditure would solve the perceived problem.

Analyzing: Separating or breaking a whole into parts to discover their nature, function, and relationships
  "I studied it piece by piece."
  "I sorted things out."

Stan examined the data presented by his supervisor, and then sorted out the relevant information and facts from the perceptions.

Information Seeking: Searching for evidence, facts, or knowledge by identifying relevant sources and gathering objective, subjective, historical, and current data from those sources
  "I knew I needed to look up/study . . . ."
  "I kept searching for data."

 Stan contacted the biology professor to determine possible causes for the dead fish problem.

Applying Standards: Judging according to established personal, professional, or social rules or criteria
  "I judged it according to . . . ."

Stan attempted to find out if the concentrations of toxic chemicals in the river were higher than the LD50.

Discriminating: Recognizing differences and similarities among things or situations and distinguishing carefully as to category or rank
  "I rank ordered the various . . . ."
  "I grouped things together."

 Stan analyzed the fish kill data and grouped them according to location. He determined that the other locations where fish were dying could not be affected by his plant's discharge. He questioned whether the fish in all of the locations were dying from the same cause.

Transforming Knowledge: Changing or converting the condition, nature, form, or function of concepts among contexts

"I improved on the basics by . . . ."
"I wondered if that would fit the situation of . . . ?"

 Stan recalled news items from the past noting that fish and other forms of water life had been harmed solely by natural causes. He wondered if that might apply to the current situation. Stan again contacted the state biologist. She informed him that a fungus had, indeed, been found in several of the waters that were reporting high levels of fish dying, and that this factor, coupled with the recent weather conditions, could be killing off the fish.

Logical Reasoning: Drawing inferences or conclusions that are supported in or justified by evidence

"I deduced from the information that . . . ."
"My rationale for the conclusion was . . . ."

 Stan deduced that it was possible that the fish were dying in the river owing to a fungal infection, rather than because of high levels of toxic chemicals.

Another example of finding out where the problem came from is illustrated by the following problem, which took place at a dentist's office (a real-world problem reported by one of our students).[4]

A Real Tooth Ache

A large medical office building contains the practice of eight dentists. This practice includes three regular dentists, two orthodontists, one dental surgeon, and two dentists who do only root canals. They are complemented by a staff of 30, which includes nurses, bookkeepers, receptionists, and maintenance workers. For the past year, the practice has been having a very serious problem with employee turnover. In the previous year, 15 employees have either quit or been fired by Cindy, the office manager who was hired a year ago. The instructions given to Cindy by the dentists were "Determine what needs to be done to keep a stable work force."

A month and a half after Cindy had been working on the problem, five more employees had quit, including Penny, a nurse who had been with the practice for 17 years. The dentists held another meeting with Cindy to review her progress on the turnover issue. She proposed the following issues as the sources of the turnover problem:

1. The average age of the office staff was 45, and many of these individuals were not up to the task of learning the recently implemented computer system. For this reason, many of them had to be let go. New employees need to be more computer literate.

2. Personality conflicts exist between the new, younger employees and many of the well-established older workers, which prompted numerous employees to quit.

After presenting the doctors with this information, Cindy assured the doctors that she would solve the problem by hiring more competent and personable employees.

Application of the Critical Thinking Algorithm

Questions That Clarify

Q. Why does Cindy believe these issues are the two causes of the problem?

A. Cindy said she went about determining the causes on a case-by-case basis. She talked to several employees in the office on a regular basis about their working environment and based her report mainly on information gleaned from these conversations.

Q. Can the employees who gave Cindy the information be characterized in any way?

A. Cindy relies on two or three of the younger employees.

Challenge assumptions and reasoning.

Questions That Probe Implications and Consequences

Q. What will happen if the problem cannot be solved?

A. The dentists held a meeting, and all agreed that the quality of their patient care would be affected if the problem was not solved.

Questions That Probe Reasons and Evidence

Q. What were the reasons that caused nurse Penny to quit recently?

A. One of the dentists called Penny to determine whether her reason for her quitting corresponded to Cindy's explanation. Penny said that Cindy had been her motivation for quitting: After Cindy was promoted to office manager, she began bullying the staff, rearranging shifts with little to no notice, denying requests for vacation time with no justification, and giving unjustifiably harsh performance reviews.

Q. Was the recently implemented computer system too difficult to learn?

A. Penny said that little formal training was scheduled on how to use the new software, forcing many of the employees to take manuals home just to learn the basics.

Questions That Explore Viewpoints and Perspectives

Q. Do other former employees feel the same way that Penny does?

A. A meeting was scheduled to discuss what had been learned. The dentists asked if other employees shared Penny's sentiments about the turnover problem.

Questions about the Question

Q. Has the true cause of the turnover problem been found?

A. Over the next two weeks, the dentists spoke with many of the employees who had parted ways with their practice and many of the employees who were still working for them. The doctors soon discovered that Cindy—and her style of office management—was the true source of the turnover problem. Consequently, Cindy was fired, solving the problem of high employee turnover.

TECHNIQUE 2: USING THE PRESENT STATE/DESIRED STATE AND THE DUNCKER DIAGRAM TO DEFINE THE REAL PROBLEM

The **present state/desired state** technique is a means to determine the real problem by first describing the present state (where you are) and then describing the desired state (where you want to go). The descriptions of these states are reworked until each concern and need identified in the present state is addressed in the desired state.[5] The desired state should not contain solutions to problems that are not in the present state, however. Sometimes the statements appear to match but they don't get to the heart of the problem or they allow for many solution alternatives. You must recognize when this situation occurs and continue to rework the present state/desired state statements. This process is called cleaning up the problem statement.

When writing the desired state statement, avoid using ambiguous and vague words or phrases such as "best," "minimal," "cheapest," "within a reasonable time," and "most efficient," because these words mean different things to different people. Be quantitative where possible. For example, say that "The children's playground needs to be completed by July 1, 2007, at a cost of less than $50,000" rather than "The playground should be completed in a reasonable time at minimal cost."

This technique can be a bit confusing at first glance. To see how it works, consider the following example of the present state/desired state technique.

Missing the Mark

During World War II, a number of aircraft were shot down while engaging in bombing missions over Germany. Many of the planes that made it back to base safely were riddled with bullet and projectile holes. The damaged areas were similar on each plane.

The following instructions were given to solve the perceived problem: "Reinforce these damaged areas with thicker armor plating."

Round 1

Present State   Desired State

Many bullets/projectiles   Fewer planes being
penetrating aircraft   shot down

This is not a match because many surviving planes also have bullet holes. There is not a *one-to-one mapping* of the needs of the present state being addressed and resolved in the desired state.

Round 2

Present State   Desired State

Many bullets/projectiles   Fewer bullet holes
penetrating aircraft

These states are matched, but the distinction between the present state and the desired state is not clear enough. It may take only a single bullet hitting a critical area to down a plane.

Round 3

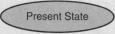   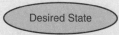

Present State   Desired State

Many bullets/projectiles   Fewer bullets/projectiles
penetrating aircraft in critical   penetrating critical areas
and noncritical areas

These two statements now match and the distinction between them is sharp, opening up a variety of solution avenues, such as reinforcing critical areas, moving critical components (e.g., steering mechanisms) to more protected locations, and providing redundant critical components.

The original instructions given to solve the perceived problem would have failed. Reinforcing the areas where returning planes had been shot would have been futile. Clearly, these were noncritical areas; otherwise, these planes would have been casualties as well.

A more appropriate problem statement can now be written as follows: "Find a way to protect the critical parts of the aircraft from being damaged by projectiles."

The Duncker Diagram

The **Duncker diagram** helps us obtain solutions that satisfy the present state/
desired state statements.[5] The unique feature of the Duncker diagram is that it
contains two major pathways (general solutions) to go from the present state (the
problem statement) to the desired state (an acceptable problem solution).

1. General solutions on the left side of the diagram show us how to move from
    the present state to achieve the desired state.
2. General solutions on the right side of the diagram show us how to make it
    okay *not* to achieve the desired state. (This idea may seem a bit contradic-
    tory—but it will be clear in a moment.)

There are two steps involved in each pathway. For each possible pathway,
we determine first functional solutions and then specific solutions. **Functional
solutions** tell us *what* we could do to move from the present state to either achieve
or not achieve the desired state. After we generate a number of functional solutions, we then generate a number of specific solutions for each functional solution. **Specific solutions** tell us *how* to implement the functional solutions.

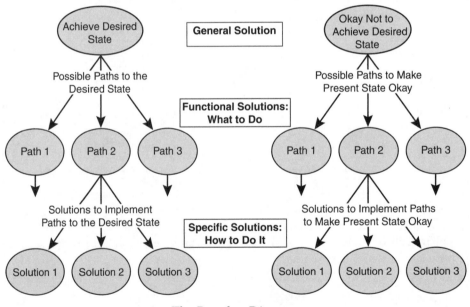

The Duncker Diagram

To help clarify the Duncker diagram, let's consider the following situation. Suppose you are unhappy in your current job at your company (this is the present state—the problem to be solved) and you want to leave your company for a new job (the desired state). The left side of the diagram is the pathway for finding a new job with a different company. Possible functional solutions on the left side of the diagram might include retraining for a different type of job or doing the same type of job but with another company. Specific solutions for obtaining the same type of job but with a different company might include networking to learn which companies have openings, searching the Web, and updating your résumé.

The right side of the diagram deals with alternatives that would make it okay to stay in your current job (that is, making it okay not to leave your current job, and not achieving the desired state as specified). A possible functional solution for the right side of the Dunker diagram might be related to achieving greater job satisfaction. Specific solutions (that is, to have greater job satisfaction) might include greater participation in decision making, more praise, or a salary increase.

Representing the problem as a Duncker diagram is a creative activity, and as such, there is no right way or wrong way to do it. After completing the Dunker diagram, you should try to write a new problem statement. Finally, you might also identify a compromise solution in which both the present state and the desired state are modified to achieve an acceptable solution.

We illustrate the use of the Duncker diagram with an example—the Kindergarten Cop.

Kindergarten Cop*

Linda Chen, who has been teaching elementary school for 25 years, has just finished a six-month leave of absence and is scheduled to return to teaching in February. She is dreading going back to work because the last few years have been extremely stressful and difficult, and she feels burned out teaching kindergarten. Students seem harder to control, which makes Linda feel more like a policewoman than a teacher.

Linda doesn't like the materials she is required to use in the classroom, and the parents of her students don't seem to take much interest in their children's education. She also enjoyed the time she had to herself during her six-month leave and strongly feels she must continue to have more time to herself as she nears retirement. Linda must wait five years to retire if she is to receive full benefits.

* Based on an actual case history.

Thus Linda's present state is to return to teaching, and her desired state is to not return to teaching. Prepare a Duncker diagram to analyze this situation.

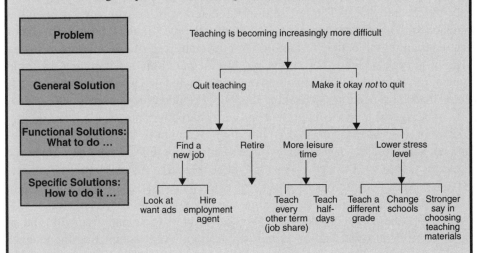

Upon analyzing her situation using a Duncker diagram, Linda discovered the real problem: The unruly classes she had the year before her six-month leave put her under a large amount of stress. Consequently, with the aid of a Duncker diagram, she arrived at the conclusion that the real problem was that she needed to find ways to lower her stress level at her workplace by teaching a different grade.

Linda's new problem statement is "If possible, find a grade to teach next year that will lower her stress at her workplace."

Let us consider another application of the Duncker diagram in the following example.

To Market, to Market

Toasty O's was one of the first organic cereals without preservatives when it first came on the market. After several months, however, its sales dropped. The consumer survey department was able to identify that customer dissatisfaction was expressed in terms of a stale taste. The company's management then issued the following instructions to solve the perceived problem: "Streamline the production process to get the cereal on the store shelves faster, thereby ensuring a fresher product."

Unfortunately, there wasn't much slack time that could be removed from the production process to accomplish this goal. Of the steps required to get the product on the shelves (production, packaging, storage, and shipping), production was one of the fastest. Thus the company considered plans for building plants closer to the major markets, as well as plans for adding more trucks to get the cereal to market faster. The addition of either new plants or more trucks would require a major capital investment to solve the problem.

Let's develop a Duncker diagram for this problem

Problem	Cereal not getting to market fast enough to maintain freshness
General Solution	Get cereal to market faster — Make it okay for cereal *not* to get to market faster
Functional Solutions: What to do …	Build more plants closer to market locations — Improve transportation system — Stop making cereal — Make cereal stay fresher longer — Convince customers that slightly stale cereal is good for you
Specific Solutions: How to do it …	Hire faster trucks and former race car drivers — Do not worry about speed limits — Charter jets to deliver product to locations farther than 1000 miles — Add a chemical to slow down the spoiling reaction — Make boxes tighter and less permeable to air and moisture

Of course, the real problem was that the cereal was not staying fresh long enough—not that it wasn't reaching the stores fast enough. Keeping the cereal fresher longer was achieved by improved packaging and the use of additives to slow the rate at which Toasty O's became stale.

The new problem statement is this: "Find how to best improve packaging to keep the cereal fresher longer."

TECHNIQUE 3: USING THE STATEMENT–RESTATEMENT TECHNIQUE

The **statement–restatement technique** developed by Parnes[6] is a method to evolve the problem statement to its most accurate representation of the problem. This technique is similar to the present state/desired state technique in that it requires us to rephrase the problem statement. With this technique, we look at the

A problem well stated is a problem half solved.
—Charles F. Kettering

fuzzy or unclear problem situation and write a statement regarding a problem to be addressed. The problem is then restated in different forms a number of times.

When restating the problem, it is important to inject new ideas, rather than simply changing the word order in the restated sentence. Using one or more of the following problem restatement **triggers** should prove helpful in arriving at a definitive problem statement.

Problem Statement Triggers

Trigger 1. Vary the stress pattern—try placing emphasis on different words and phrases.

Trigger 2. Choose a term that has an explicit definition and substitute the explicit definition in each place that the term appears.

Trigger 3. Make an opposite statement, changing positives to negatives, and vice versa.

Trigger 4. Change "every" to "some," "always" to "sometimes," "sometimes" to "never," and vice versa.

Trigger 5. Replace "persuasive words" in the problem statement such as "obviously," "clearly," and "certainly" with the argument it is supposed to be replacing.

Trigger 6. Express words in the form of an equation or picture, and vice versa.

Each time the problem is restated, we try to generalize it further to arrive at the broadest form of the problem statement.

As an illustration of the use of these triggers, consider trigger 3. Instead of asking, "How can my company make the biggest profit?" ask, "How can my company lose the most money?" In finding the key activities or pieces of equipment that, when operated inefficiently, will give the biggest loss, we will have identified those pieces that need to be carefully monitored and controlled. This trigger helps us find the **sensitivity** of the system and to focus on those variables that dominate the problem.

It is often helpful to relax any constraints placed on the problem, modify the criteria, and idealize the problem when writing the restatement sentence (see trigger 4). Also, does the problem statement change when different time scales are imposed (i.e., are the long-term implications different from the short-term implications)? As we continue to restate and perhaps combine previous restatements, we should also focus on tightening up the problem statement, eliminating ambiguous words, and moving away from a fuzzy, loose, ill-defined statement.

Using the Problem Statement Triggers

Original Problem Statement: The Toasty O's cereal is clearly not getting to market fast enough to maintain freshness.

Trigger 1
- **Cereal** not getting to market fast enough to maintain freshness. (Do other products we have get there faster?)
- Cereal not **getting** to market fast enough to maintain freshness. (Can we make the distance/time shorter?)
- Cereal not getting to **market** fast enough to maintain freshness. (Can we distribute it from a centralized location?)
- Cereal not getting to market fast enough to maintain **freshness.** (How can we keep cereal fresher, longer?)

Trigger 2
- **Breakfast food that comes in a box** is not getting to **the place where it is sold** fast enough to keep it from **getting stale.** (This restatement makes us think about the box and staleness. How might we change the box to prevent staleness?)

Trigger 3
- How can we find a way to get the cereal to market **so slowly** that it will **never** be fresh? (This restatement makes us think about how long we have to maintain freshness and what controls it.)

Trigger 4
- Cereal is not getting to market fast enough to **always** maintain freshness. (This change opens up new avenues of thought. Why isn't our cereal *always* fresh?)

Trigger 5
- The word **clearly** in the problem statement implies that if we could speed up delivery freshness would be maintained. Maybe not! Maybe the store holds the cereal too long. Maybe the cereal is stale before it reaches the store. (This trigger helps us challenge the implicit assumptions made in the problem statement.)

Trigger 6
- Freshness is inversely proportional to the time since the cereal was baked:

$$(Freshness) = \frac{k}{(Time\ since\ cereal\ baked)}$$

This restatement makes us think about other ways to attack the freshness problem. For example, what does the proportionality constant, k, depend on?

The storage conditions, packaging, type of cereal, and other factors are logical variables to examine. How can we change the value of k?

The total time may be shortened by reducing the time at the factory, the delivery time, or the time to sell the cereal (i.e., shelf time). Once again, this trigger provides us with several alternative approaches to examine to solve the problem: Reduce the time *or* change (increase) k.

Coating Aspirin:
Making an Opposite Statement

To many people, swallowing an aspirin tablet is a foul-tasting experience. A few years ago, one company that manufactured aspirin decided to do something about it. The manager gave the following instructions to his staff to solve the perceived problem: "Find a way to put a pleasant-tasting coating on aspirin tablets." Spraying the coating on the tablets had been tried in the past, but with very little success. The resulting coating was very non-uniform, which led to an unacceptable product.

Let's apply the triggers to this problem.

Trigger 1   Emphasize different parts of the statement.
            1. **Put** coating **on** tablet.

Trigger 3   Make an opposite statement.
            2. **Take** coating **off** tablet.

This idea led to one of the newer techniques for coating pills. The pills are immersed in a liquid that is then passed onto a spinning disk. The centrifugal force on the fluid and the pills as they are thrown off the spinning disk causes the two to separate, leaving a nice, even coating around the pill.

Wake Up and Smell the Coffee:
Making an Opposite Statement

High school and college students frequently have trouble getting up in the morning for their early classes. Without addressing lifestyle changes that are probably impractical (e.g., going to bed earlier), one problem statement for this situation could be as follows: "Students are having a difficult time waking up after their alarm clocks sound." This statement allows us to focus on improving the effectiveness of the alarm clock so as to wake the student more reliably.

Let's apply the triggers to this problem.

Trigger 1   Emphasize different parts of the problem statement.

    1. **Students** are having a difficult time waking up after their alarm clocks sound.
   Is it a personal issue? Are they too tired? Are they lazy?
   Add unique features to get students out of bed.

    2. Students are having a **difficult time** waking up after their alarm clocks sound.
   What could make using the alarm clock easier?
   Combine additional features other than noise.

    3. Students are having a difficult time **waking up** after their alarm clocks sound.
   Which method is used to wake them up? Should other methods be used?
   Combine additional features other than noise.

    4. Students are having a difficult time waking up after their **alarm** clocks sound.
   Is it the alarm style, volume, features, or other factor?
   Add/modify features.

Trigger 3   Make an opposite statement.

    5. How can we make students wake up immediately?
   How can we make students stay asleep?
   Require snooze use.

Use of the triggers opens new possibilities to the design of an effective alarm clock for college students.

TECHNIQUE 4: KEPNER–TREGOE PROBLEM ANALYSIS

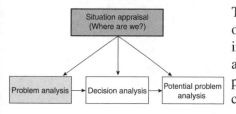

The **Kepner–Tregoe**[7] **(K.T.) problem analysis** technique is one of the four components of the K.T. strategy, which includes situation appraisal, problem analysis, decision analysis, and potential problem analysis. We will discuss problem analysis in this chapter and the other three K.T. components in Chapter 7.

The K.T. problem analysis technique displays information obtained by asking critical thinking questions in a unique way in what is called the "four dimensions of the problem." In this technique, the following distinctions are made:

- What *is* the problem versus what *is not* the problem?
- Where does the problem occur versus where is everything okay?
- When did the problem first occur versus when was everything okay?
- What is the extent of the problem?

This kind of analysis is most useful in **troubleshooting operations** where the cause of the problem or fault is not known. Problems that lend themselves to K.T. problem analysis are ones in which an undesirable level of performance can be observed and compared with the accepted standard performance.

As an example, consider the following case in which a company ordered and received a new shipment of company stationery with the logo printed at the top. A few days later, workers noticed that the logo was easily smeared. This smearing had never been observed before. In the K.T. analysis, the deviation in this case is that the printing quality is unacceptable and hence a problem must be precisely identified, described, and located.

A good problem statement often includes:
(a) What is known.
(b) What is unknown.
(c) What is sought.

The basic premise of K.T. problem analysis is that there is always something that distinguishes what the problem *is* from what it *is not*. The cause of the problem is usually a change that has taken place to produce undesirable effects. Things were okay in the past, but now they're not. Something has changed. (Recall the example in Chapter 1 dealing with printing inks: The printing company had changed to a glossier paper.) The possible causes of the problem (deviation) are deduced by examining the differences found in the problem. (It is difficult to impregnate glossy paper with ink using the current printing process.) The most probable cause of the problem is the one that best explains all the observations and facts in the problem statement. (The printing ink for the new currency notes is not penetrating the paper, so it wipes off when used.)

The Four K.T. Dimensions of a Problem

		Is	Is Not	Distinction	Cause
What	Identify	What is the problem?	What is not the problem?	What is the distinction between the **is** and the **is not?**	What is a possible cause?
Where	Locate	Where is the problem found?	Where is the problem not found?	What is distinctive about the difference in locations?	What is the possible cause?
When	Timing	When does the problem occur?	When does the problem not occur?	What is distinctive about the difference in the timing?	What is a possible cause?
		When was the problem first observed?	When was the problem last observed?	What is the distinction between these observations?	What is a possible cause?
Extent	Magnitude	How far does the problem extend?	How localized is the problem?	What is the distinction?	What is a possible cause?
		How many units are affected?	How many units are not affected?	What is the distinction?	What is a possible cause?
		How much of any one unit is affected?	How much of any one unit is not affected?	What is the distinction?	What is a possible cause?

The real challenge is to identify the distinction between the *is* and the *is not*. Particular care should be taken when filling in the "Distinction" column. Sometimes the distinction statement should be rewritten more than once to sharpen it

*Is, or is not?
That is the
question,
Watson!!!*

enough to specify the distinction exactly. For example, in one problem analyzed by the K.T. method, the statement "Two of the filaments were clear (okay) and two were black (not okay)" was sharpened to "Two filaments were clear and two were covered with carbon soot." This **sharpening** of the distinction was instrumental in determining the reason for the black filament. Think in terms of dissimilarities. What distinguishes *this* fact (or category) from *that* fact (or category)? Making such a distinction requires careful analysis, insight, and practice to ferret out the differences between the *is* and the *is not*.

From the possible causes, we try to ascertain the most probable cause. The most probable cause is the one that explains each dimension in the problem specification. The final step is to verify that the most probable cause is the true cause. This step may be accomplished by making the appropriate change to see if the problem disappears.

*When you hear
hoof beats,
don't think
zebras!*

The problem solver should also separate people's observations from their interpretations of what went wrong. A common mistake is to assume that the most obvious conclusion or the most common is always the correct one. (This point is a good place to start, but not necessarily to stop.) A famous medical school proverb that relates to the diagnosis of disease is this: "When you hear hoof beats, don't think zebras." In other words, look for simple explanations first. Finally, the problem solver should continually reexamine the assumptions and discard them when necessary.

Fear of Flying

A new model of airplane was delivered to Eastern Airlines in 1980. Immediately after the planes were put into operation, many of the flight attendants developed a red rash on their arms, hands, and faces. The rash did not appear on any other part of the body, and it occurred only on flights that went over water. Fortunately, the rash usually disappeared in 24 hours and caused no additional problems beyond that time. When the attendants flew old planes over the same routes, no ill effects occurred. The rash did not occur on all the attendants of a particular flight, but the same number of attendants contracted the rash on each flight. In addition, those flight attendants who contracted the rash felt no other ill effects.

The flight attendants' union threatened action because the attendants were upset and worried, and believed some malicious force was behind the mysterious rash. Many doctors were called in, but all were in a quandary. Industrial hygienists could not measure anything extraordinary in the cabins (*Chemtech*, 13, 11, p. 655, 1983).

Let's apply K.T. problem analysis to this situation to see if we can learn the cause of the problem.

What

The problem appears to be only a rash and not any other illness such as headache or nausea. A rash can be caused by external contact with an allergen such as poison ivy. Consequently, we can complete the first row of the K.T. table as follows:

	Is	Is Not	Distinction
What	Rash	Other illness	External contact

When

The problem occurs only when the new planes are used, but not when the old planes are used. The new planes contain new materials such as lighter composite materials and new fabric, among other things.

	Is	Is Not	Distinction
When	New planes used	Old planes used	New materials

Where

The illness occurs only in flights over water; attendants on flights over land do not develop the rash. Different crew procedures are followed on flights over water than are followed on flights over land.

	Is	Is Not	Distinction
Where	Flights over water	Flights over land	Different crew procedures

Extent

There are two categories of "extent" in this case: (1) how many units are affected and (2) how much of any one unit is affected. In terms of how many units (flight attendants) are affected, only some of the attendants are affected; not all are affected. The different attendants have different duties. How much of any one unit (attendant) is affected is defined as the fact that the rash appears only on the face, hands, and arms. The culprit must be something contacting the face, hands, and arms.

	Is	**Is Not**	**Distinction**
Extent	Only some of the attendants	All of the attendants	Different crew duties
Extent	Face, hands, and arms	Other body parts	Something contacting exposed face, hands, and arms

Let's summarize what we have learned so far:

	Is	**Is Not**	**Distinction**
What	Rash	Other illness	External contact
When	New planes used	Old planes used	New materials
Where	Flights over water	Flights over land	Different crew procedures
Extent	Face, hands, and arms	Other parts	Something contacting face, hands and arms
	Only some of the attendants	All of the attendants	Different crew duties

When we look at all of the distinctions, we see that (1) something contacting the arms and face could be causing the rash; (2) the rash occurs only on flights over water, and the use of life vests is demonstrated on flights over water; and (3) the life vests on the new planes are made of new materials or of a different brand of materials and usually three flight attendants demonstrate the use of these life vests. The new life preservers contained some material that was the rash-causing agent!

WHICH TECHNIQUE TO CHOOSE?

We do not expect you to apply every problem definition technique to every situation. In fact, when 400 problem solvers were surveyed as to which two techniques presented in this chapter were the most useful to them, their choices were virtually equally divided among those presented in this chapter. In other words, different techniques work better for different individuals and different situations, and your selection of a problem definition technique is a matter of personal choice. The main point is to be organized as well as creative in your approach to problem definition.

Spontaneous Car Starting

Molly traded in her old car for a one-year-old, high-end car that had a special key-less entry system. Everything about the car worked perfectly, with one exception: When Molly would park the car, sometimes she would come out to find its motor running. In each instance, she had turned the motor off and taken the key out before leaving the car. This problem most often occurred at the Starbucks on Washtenaw Avenue, a major thoroughfare, but seldom at the Starbucks on Liberty Street, which was a more secluded street. It also occurred a couple of times at Dunkin Donuts on Stadium Street. Even though the problem mainly occurred on Washtenaw, Molly did not want to stop going there because she enjoyed chatting with the police officers who frequented that location. The Liberty Street Starbucks seemed to have only an occasional police officer stop by. The problem arose during the midmorning hours but not over lunch or dinner time.

	Is	Is Not	Distinction
What	Spontaneous starting	Regular starting	Signal to start car

	Is	Is Not	Distinction
Where	Starbucks on Washtenaw and Dunkin Donuts on Stadium	Starbucks on Liberty	Police in Washtenaw Starbucks and Dunkin Donuts

	Is	Is Not	Distinction
When	Midmorning	Lunch	Police taking morning break
	New car	Old car used	New cars have remote entry and ignition system

	Is	Is Not	Distinction
Extent	Only in locations that the police frequent	Locations where there are no police	Police doing something like receiving/ sending calls

The newer-model keyless entry system had a remote starting capability when a signal was sent from the key chain. The frequency from the police radios matched the frequency from the key chain that started the engine.

Source: Based on a real case discussed on National Public Radio's *Car Talk*, featuring Click and Clack, the Tappet Brothers, May 13, 2006.

After the problem is defined, there is more work to be done. Nevertheless, having a well-defined problem puts us well on the way toward finding a solution.

DETERMINE WHETHER THE PROBLEM SHOULD BE SOLVED

Establish criteria to judge the solution.

Having defined the real problem, we now need to develop criteria by which to judge the solution to the real problem. One of the first questions experienced engineers ask is this: Should the problem be solved? The figure following this discussion shows how to proceed when answering this question. As you can see from the figure, the first step is to determine whether a solution to an identical problem or a similar problem is available. A literature search may determine whether a solution exists.

How do experienced engineers go about deciding whether the problem is *worth* solving? Perhaps the problem is just mildly irritating and consequently may be ignored altogether. For instance, suppose the garage door at your plant's warehouse facility is too narrow to allow easy access by some of the delivery vehicles. They can pass through, but the clearance is very tight. This is an annoying problem, but if the fix is quite costly, you could probably "live with it."

Here are some questions you should ask early in the process:

- What are the resources available to solve the problem?
- How many people can you allocate to the problem, and for how long a time?
- How soon do you need a solution? Today? Tomorrow? Next year?

These are key questions to keep in mind as you take your first steps along the way to finding a problem solution. The quality of your solution is often—but not always—related to the time and money you have to *generate it and carry it through*. In some instances, it may be necessary to extend deadlines to obtain a quality solution.

It may not be possible to completely address the cost issue until we are further along in the solution process. The cost will depend on whether the solution will be a permanent one or a temporary or patchwork solution. Sometimes *two* solutions are required: one to treat short-term symptoms so as to keep the process operating and one to solve the real problem for the long term. Be aware of these two mindsets in the problem-solving process. In some cases the "No" answers in the following figure can be changed to "Yes" by *selling* the project to management so as to get additional resources or extend the deadline. This change can be achieved by showing that the problem is an important one and is relevant to the operation of the company.

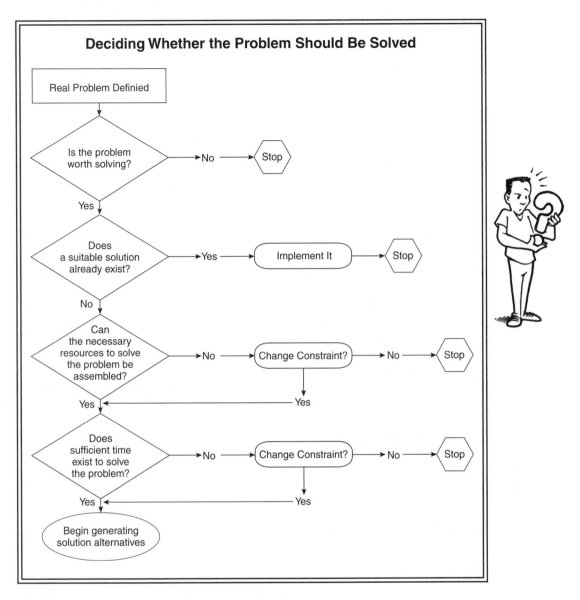

BRAINSTORM POTENTIAL CAUSES AND SOLUTION ALTERNATIVES

This brings us to the end of the first phase of the creative problem-solving process and the first step of the second phase of the process: generating solutions to problems. Techniques to generate solutions will be discussed in Chapters 5 and 6.

SUMMARY

In this chapter, we discussed the necessity for defining the real problem. Four problem definition techniques were presented to help you zero in on the true problem definition.

- **Find Out Where the Problem Came From**
  - Use the first four steps to gather information.
  - Learn who defined the problem initially.
  - Challenge reasoning and assumptions made to arrive at the problem statement given to you.

- **Present State/Desired State**
  - Write a statement of where you are and a statement of what you want to achieve, and make sure the two statements match.

- **Duncker Diagram**
  - Analyze two pathways: (1) a pathway to your desired state and (2) a pathway that makes it okay not to achieve the desired state.

- **Statement–Restatement**
  - Use the six triggers to restate the problem in a number of different ways.

- **Problem Analysis**
  - What is? What is not?
  - Where is? Where is not?
  - When is? When is not?
  - Extent is? Extent is not?

REFERENCES

1. Paul, R., and L. Elder, *The Thinker's Guide to the Art of Socratic Questioning,* Foundation for Critical Thinking, www.criticalthinking.org, 2006. This is a companion text to *The Thinker's Guide to Analytic Thinking* and *The Art of Asking Essential Questions.*
2. Scheffer, B. K., and M. G. Rubenfeld, "A Consensus Statement on Critical Thinking in Nursing," *Journal of Nursing Education,* 39, pp. 352–359, 2000.
3. Rubenfeld, M., and B. Scheffer, "Critical Thinking: What Is It and How Do We Teach It?" In: J. Dochterman and H. Y. Grace (eds.), *Current Issues in Nursing,* Mosby, St. Louis, MO, 2001, pp. 125–132.
4. Zaleski, Seth, private communication, Toledo, OH, 2006.

5. Higgins, J. S., et al., "Identifying and Solving Problems in Engineering Design," *Studies in Higher Education*, 14, 2, p. 169, 1989.

6. Parnes, S. J., *Creative Behavior Workbook*, Scribner, New York, 1967.

7. Kepner, C. H., and B. B. Tregoe, *The New Rational Manager*, Princeton Research Press, Princeton, NJ, 1981.

EXERCISES

4.1. Make a list of the most important things you learned from this chapter. Identify at least three techniques that you believe will change the ways you think about defining and solving problems. Which problem definition techniques do you find most useful? Prepare a matrix table listing all of the problem definition techniques discussed in this chapter. Identify those attributes that some of the techniques have in common and those attributes that are unique to a given technique.

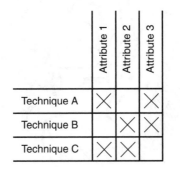

4.2. Write a sentence describing a problem you have. Apply the triggers in the statement–restatement technique to your problem.

Perceived Problem Statement: _____

_____

Restatement 1: _____

_____

Restatement 2: _____

_____

Final Problem Statement: _____

_____

Next apply the Duncker diagram to the same problem.

4.3. Carry out a present state/desired state analysis and prepare a Duncker diagram for the following problem: "I want a summer internship but no one is hiring."

4.4. You have had a very hectic morning, so you leave work a little early to relax a bit before you meet your supervisor, who is flying into a nearby airport. You have not seen your supervisor from the home office for about a year now. He has written to you saying that he wants to meet with you personally to discuss the last project. Through no fault of yours, everything went wrong: The oil embargo delayed shipment of all the key parts; your project manager had a skiing accident; and your secretary enclosed the key files in a parcel that was sent by mistake to Japan via sea mail. Your supervisor thinks that you have been so careless on this project that you would lock yourself out of your own car.

As you are driving through the pleasant countryside on this chilly late fall afternoon, you realize that you will be an hour early. You spot a rather secluded roadside park about 200 meters away. A quiet stream bubbles through the park, containing trees in all their autumn colors—such an ideal place to just get out and relax. You pull off into the park, absentmindedly get out and lock the car, and stroll by the stream. When you return, you find that you have locked the keys inside the car. The road to the airport is not the usual route; cars pass through about every 10 to 15 minutes. The airport is 9 kilometers away; the nearest house (with a telephone) is 1 kilometer away. The plane is due to arrive in 20 minutes. Your car, which is not a convertible, is such that you cannot get under the hood or into the trunk from the outside. All the windows are up and secured.

Apply the Duncker diagram and one other problem-solving technique to help you decide what to do. (Problem courtesy of D. R. Woods, McMaster University.)

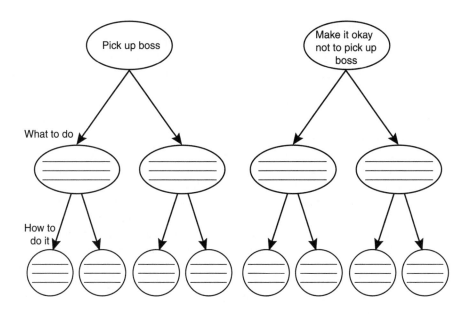

4.5. You are driving from Cambridge to London on the M11 motorway (expressway). You are scheduled to give a very important slide presentation at 1 P.M. The drive normally takes 1.5 hours, but this morning you left at 10:30 A.M. to ensure you had sufficient time. Suddenly your car stalls on the motorway halfway between Cambridge and London. What do you do? Apply two or more problem definition techniques to help answer this problem. (Problem courtesy of J. Higgins and S. Richardson, Imperial College, London.)

4.6. Sodium azide is used as the propellant in an air bag system. This chemical is mixed with an oxidizing agent and pressed into pellets, which are then hermetically sealed into a steel or aluminum can. Upon impact, ignition of the pelletized sodium azide generates nitrogen gas that inflates the air bag. Unfortunately, if the sodium azide contacts acids or heavy metals (e.g., lead, copper, mercury, or their alloys), it forms toxic and sensitive explosives. Consequently, at the end of an automobile's life, a serious problem surfaces when an automobile with an undetonated air bag is sent to the junkyard for compacting and shredding, because it might contact heavy metals during this process. The potential for an explosion during processing represents a serious danger for the people who operate the scrap recycling plant. Apply two or three problem definition techniques to this situation. (Source: *Chemtech,* 23, p. 54, 1993.)

4.7. Pillsbury, a leader in the manufacture of high-quality baking products, had its origins in the manufacture of flour for the baking industry. At the time Charles Pillsbury purchased his first mill in Minneapolis, the wheat from Minnesota was considered to be substandard compared to the wheat used in the mills in St. Louis, which was then the hub of the milling industry. Part of the problem was that winter wheat, which is commonly used in high-grade flour, could not be grown in Minnesota because of the long and cold winters there. Consequently, the Minnesota mills were forced to use spring wheat, which had a harder shell. At the time, the most commonly used milling machines used a "low grinding" process to separate the wheat from the chaff. The low grinding process refers to the use of stone wheels. A stone wheel rests directly on the bottom wheel, with the wheat to be ground placed between them. With harder wheats, a large amount of heat was generated during the grinding process, discoloring and degrading the product's quality. Thus the flour produced from the Minnesota mills was discolored and inferior, and it had less nutritional value and a shorter shelf life than flour produced in the St. Louis mills. The directions given could have been "Order more river barges to ship winter wheat up the Mississippi River from St. Louis to Minneapolis." Apply two or more problem definition techniques to this situation. (Source: Adapted from "When in Rome" by Jane Ammeson, *Northwestern Airlines World Traveler*, 25, 3, p. 20, 1993.)

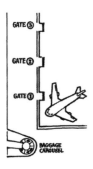

4.8. An airline at the Houston Airport tried to please its passengers by always docking its planes at gates within a one- to two-minute walk to the airport entrance and baggage claim and by having all the bags at baggage claim area within eight to ten minutes. Unfortunately, the airline received many complaints about the time it took to get the bags to the baggage claim area. The airline researched the situation and found that there was virtually no way it could unload the bags to the transport trucks, drive to the unloading zone, and unload the bags any faster. The airline didn't change the baggage unloading procedure, but it did change another component of the arrival process and the complaints disappeared. The airline did not use mirrors to solve the problem (as was the case for the slow elevators).

   A. What was the real problem?

   B. Suggest a number of things that you think the airline might have done to eliminate the complaints. Apply two or more problem-solving techniques.

   (Source: *The Washington Post,* p. A3, December 14, 1992.)

4.9. In 1991, 64% of all commercial radio stations in the United States lost money. For a radio station to remain solvent, it must have a significant revenue stream from advertisers. Advertisers, in turn, target the markets they consider desirable (i.e., based on listeners' income, spending, and interests), and for the past several years this target has been the age group from 25 to 54. Along with the revenue loss, the number of radio stations playing the Top 40 songs (i.e., the 40 most popular songs of that week) has decreased by a factor of 2 in the past three years, as did the audience for the Top 40 songs. Many stations tried playing a blend of current hits and hits from 10 to 20 years ago; however, this blend irritated the younger listeners and did not seem to solve the economic problem. Apply two or more problem definition techniques to this situation. (Source: Adapted from *The International Herald Tribune*, p. 7, March 24, 1993.)

4.10. Sara is a freshman who is away at college preparing for her first final exams. She is homesick, is stressed out, and would like to go home for the weekend to visit her parents, but her car is not working.

Sara's car is not working   At home with her parents

These states do not match, and this mismatch complicates the problem. Which problem should Sara attack? The malfunctioning car? The visit?

First Revision

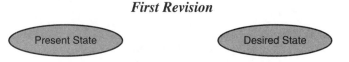

Continue in this manner until the states match.

4.11. FireKing is a small manufacturer of rich-looking fireproof filing cabinets that wants to increase its current market share of 3%. While the company's designs are elegant, the cabinets are also the heaviest ones on the market—and in customers' minds, greater weight means higher quality. However, greater weight also means higher shipping and transportation costs, which makes the cabinets very expensive. Fire-King's management asks the following question: "How can we make our product lighter so as to have a competitive price?" However, some executives believed a lighter-weight product might hurt the image of quality. Apply one or more problem definition techniques to this situation. (Problem courtesy of David Turczyn.)

4.12. Bug-B-Gone Company has developed a new method for killing roaches that is more effective than any of the other leading products. In fact, no spraying is necessary because the active ingredient is held in a container that is placed on the floor or in corners; the roach problem disappears when the container is activated. This method has the advantage that the product does all the work—the user does not need to search out and spray the live roaches. The product was test-marketed to homemakers in some southern states. Everyone who saw the effectiveness test results agreed that the new product was superior in killing roaches. Despite a massive advertising campaign, however, the standard roach sprays are still far outselling the new product. Apply one or more problem definition techniques to this situation. (Problem courtesy of David Turczyn.)

4.13. A pneumatic conveyor is a device that transports powdered solids using air in the same manner that money is transported from your car at a bank's drive-through window. In the figure below, the solids are "sucked" out of the storage hopper and conveyed by air into the discharge hopper. You are given the following instructions to solve the perceived problem: "Find an easier way to clean a pneumatic conveying system when it plugs and interrupts operation."

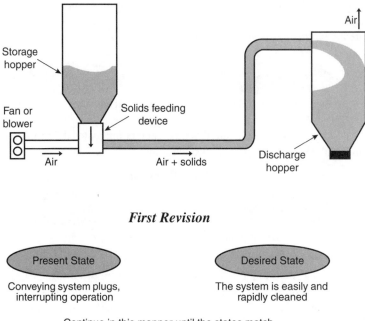

First Revision

Present State	Desired State
Conveying system plugs, interrupting operation	The system is easily and rapidly cleaned

Continue in this manner until the states match.

4.14. A major American soap company carried out a massive advertising campaign in an attempt to expand its sales in Poland. The television commercials featured a beautiful woman using the company's soap during her morning shower. Thousands of sample cakes were distributed door to door throughout the country. Despite these massive promotional efforts, the campaign was entirely unsuccessful. Polish television had been used primarily for Communist Party politics, and commercials were relatively rare. What was aired on television was usually party-line politics. Apply one or more problem definition techniques to this situation. (Problem courtesy of Christina Nusbaum.)

4.15. Employees of a certain store are allowed to take merchandise out of the department store on approval. The original procedure required each employee to write an approval slip identifying the merchandise taken. Some employees are abusing the system by taking the clothing and destroying the slip, thereby leaving no record of the removed merchandise. Apply one or more problem definition techniques to this situation. (Problem courtesy of Maggie Michael.)

Problem Analysis

4.16. After Crest toothpaste had been on the market for some time, Procter & Gamble, its manufacturer, decided to offer a mint-flavored version in addition to the original, wintergreen-flavored product. In the course of developing the new mint-flavored product, a test batch of mint-flavored product was produced by the same pilot unit used to produce wintergreen-flavored product. The pilot equipment used a tank and impeller device to mix the mint flavor essence with the rest of the ingredients to form the finished product (which is a very viscous solution). Some of the pilot plant product was packed into the familiar collapsible tubes for further testing. Tubes used in testing the mint flavor were identical to those used for the wintergreen-flavored product. In the packing operation, toothpaste was pumped through lines into the as-yet-unsealed ends of brand new tubes. After filling, the open tube ends were heat-sealed. The packing operation is illustrated in the figure.

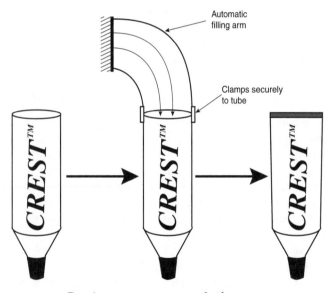

Continuous movement of tubes

To assess storage stability, some of the filled tubes were randomly separated into several groups and each group was stored in a constant-temperature room. Storage temperatures varied from 40 °F to 120 °F.

Early sampling of the mint-flavored product showed nothing unusual. However, several months into the test, a technician preparing to test the product from one of the stored tubes noted that the first 0.25 inch of paste squeezed onto a toothbrush was off-color. The rest of the product in the tube met the color specification. Nothing like this had ever been seen with the original formula. Further testing showed that a person had to squeeze more product out of those tubes that had been stored at higher temperatures and/or stored for longer times before a product that met the color specifications would exit the mouth of the toothpaste tube. Tubes stored for a period of time at 40 °F contained no off-color product, whereas tubes stored for the same length of time at higher temperatures produced off-color paste.

The only exception to these results was a single tube, which had been stored at a temperature above 40 °F. A leakage of off-color product was found around the base of the cap on this tube, but the product inside the tube met the color specifications.

While other tests showed the off-color product to be safe and effective in cleaning teeth, consumers certainly would not accept a color change in a product expected to have the same color from the first squeeze to the last. Moreover, such a change could have been an early warning of more serious problems to come. This phenomenon had to be understood and eliminated before the new flavor could be marketed. Accordingly, various possible remedies were tested: caps and tubes made of different materials, different mixing methods, and so forth. None of these changes had any effect on the off-color problem. All raw materials, including the new mint flavor essence, were checked and found to meet specifications. A subsequent batch of the wintergreen product was made and tested for storage stability and, as usual, no off-color problems occurred.

Carry out a K.T. problem analysis to learn the cause of the off-color toothpaste.

4.17. Chocolate butter paste is the primary ingredient used by a number of major bakeries for a wide variety of pastries. The paste is a very viscous liquid that is manufactured by Cocomaker Industries in a major populous city in the Midwest. Cocomaker supplies customers as close as Dolton and as far away as Chicago (which is a long drive from its plant). The paste flows from the production line into five-gallon drums, which are placed immediately into refrigerated trucks for shipment to the respective customers. Until February, all the trucks had been the same size and the drums were stacked in rows three drums wide, four drums high, and eight drums deep. Now two rather small customers, Bell Bakery and Clissold Bakery, each requiring 20 drums per day, have been added in the Chicago area. Supplying these new customers, along with an increased order by the Chicago customer Hoyne Industrial Bakers, necessitated the purchase of a larger truck. The new truck could fit five drums across, four drums high, and eight drums deep. The truck would stop at Bell and Clissold just before and just after stopping at Hoyne in Chicago proper. With the increased market in the Chicago area, Cocomaker's plant is running at close to maximum capacity. Because the ingredients of the paste are mixed by static mixers, the pumps are currently operating at their maximum capacity and the plant is operating 20 hours per day.

In November, Cocomaker successfully lured two nearby customers, Damon Bakery and Oakley Bakery, away from one of its competitors. By increasing plant operation to 24 hours per day, all orders could be filled. As the Christmas season approached, however, the usual seasonal demand for chocolate butter paste posed a problem for Cocomaker: It needed to meet demands not encountered in previous years. The company decided that if the processing temperature was increased by 20 degrees, the paste would be sufficiently less viscous, and production demands could be met with the current pump limitations. Unfortunately, the increased capacity began to generate problems as Christmas approached. The pumps began failing on a regular basis; a strike at the supplier of the shipping containers caused Cocomaker to buy containers from a new supplier, which claimed to carry only sturdier containers at a 10% increase in price; the safety officer had an emergency appendectomy; and—most troubling—Hoyne called about an unacceptable bacteria count in shipments for the last five days. As a result of the bacteria, people who bought Hoyne's products have been getting ill.

An immediate check of the bacteria levels shows that they are at the same acceptable levels they have always been when leaving Cocomaker's plant. You call Hoyne and tell them that the plant levels show that the paste is within bacteria specifications. Two days later, you receive a call from Hoyne, saying that the bakery had hired an independent firm, which reported that the bacteria levels for the chocolate butter paste are well above an acceptable level. You call the Damon, Bell, Clissold, and Oakley bakeries and ask them to check their bacteria counts; they report back that everything is within the specifications most often reported. A spot check of other customers shows no problems. Now you receive a call from Hoyne, saying the bakery is initiating legal and governmental actions to close your plant down.

Carry out a K.T. problem analysis to learn the cause of the problem.

4.18. Sparkling mineral water is the primary product of Bubbles, Inc. This firm, which is based in France, serves three major markets—Europe, North America, and Australia. It collects water from a natural spring; the water is then filtered through a parallel array of three filter units, each containing two charcoal filters. The filtration process removes trace amounts of naturally occurring contaminants. The filtered water is stored in separate tank farms, one for each market, until it is transported by tanker truck to one of the three bottling plants that serve the company's markets. When the water arrives at the bottling plant, it is temporarily placed in 3500 m^3 storage tanks until it can be carbonated to provide the effervescence that is the trademark of the producer. Some of the water is also flavored with lemon, cherry, and raspberry additives.

Next, the sparkling water is packaged in a variety of bottle sizes and materials, ranging from 10-ounce glass bottles to 1-liter plastic bottles. The European market receives its shipments directly by truck, usually within three days. Products bound for North America or Australia are shipped first by truck to the waterfront and then by freighters to their overseas destinations.

Business has been good for the last several months, with the North American and European markets demanding as much sparkling water as can be produced. This situation has required that Bubbles contract with additional plastic bottle suppliers to keep up with the increased demand. It has also forced regularly scheduled maintenance for the Australian and North American tank farms to be delayed and rescheduled because of the high demand for the product. There is also, of course, a larger demand placed on the spring that supplies the mineral water for the process.

Unfortunately, the news is not all good for Bubbles. The bottling plant for the Australian market is currently several weeks behind schedule owing to a shipment that was lost at sea. This catastrophe has required that water from the company's reserve springs, which are located many miles from the bottling plant, be used to augment the water supplied by the regular spring so that the bottling plant can operate at an even higher level of production. The availability of water from the reserve springs is hindered by their remote locations, but the water from these springs does not require filtration. In addition, contract negotiations are going badly and it appears there will be a strike at all of the bottling plants. Recent weather forecasts indicate that relief from the ongoing drought, which has already lasted three months, is not likely. Worst of all, customers in the North American and Australian markets are complaining that all shipments of the sparkling water in the last six weeks have contained benzene in unacceptably high concentrations. You know that benzene is often used as an industrial solvent but is also found naturally.

A quick survey of the bottling plant managers shows that the North American-bound products that are currently packaged and awaiting shipment have benzene concentrations in excess of acceptable concentrations. However, the managers of the bottling plants that service the Australian and European markets report that no significant level of benzene was detected in the bottles that are currently stored. Authorities in the North American and Australian markets have already begun recalling the product, with authorities in the European market pressuring Bubbles for a quick solution and threatening to recall products as a precautionary measure.

Carry out a K.T. problem analysis to learn the cause of the problem. (Source: Adapted from *Chemtech,* "When the Bubble Burst," p. 74, February 1992.)

4.19. Currently, many drilling platforms in the Gulf of Mexico collect oil from a number of oil wells, which they then pump through a single pipeline from the platform to shore. Most of these wells have always been quite productive. Consequently, the oil flows through the pipeline lying on the ocean floor at a reasonable rate.

When the oil comes out of the wells, it is at a temperature of approximately 145 °F; by the time the oil reaches shore, the temperature in most pipelines is approximately 90 °F. The temperature of the water on the ocean floor for the majority of the platforms within two miles of shore is approximately 45 °F. However, the water depth increases as you move away from shore and the temperature of the water on the ocean floor decreases to 39 °F.

Recently, two new platforms (A and B) were erected in the Gulf Coast farther out from shore than the other drilling platforms. About a year and a half after both came on stream, a disaster occurred on Platform A, such that no oil could be pumped to shore through the pipeline from this platform. Platform B continued to operate without any problems. When the crude composition at the well head was analyzed, it was found to have exactly the same chemical composition (e.g., asphaltenes, waxes, gas) as that found in the well heads on all other platforms. The only difference between Platform A and Platform B was that the production rate of Platform A was much lower than that of Platform B. Nevertheless, the production rate from Platform A was still greater than many of the platforms near the shoreline.

Carry out a K.T. problem analysis to learn the reason for the plugging of pipeline A.

4.20. Research or create a statement of a perceived problem and then apply one or more of the following problem definition techniques to that problem statement:

A. Find out where the problem came from

B. Present state/desired state and Duncker diagram

C. Statement–restatement technique

D. Problem analysis

(*Hint:* See the problems in Chapter 11.)

FURTHER READING

Copulsky, William. "Vision Innovation." *Chemtech,* 19, p. 279, May 1989. Interesting anecdotes on problem definition and vision related to a number of popular products.

De Bono, Edward. *Serious Creativity.* Harper Business (a division of Harper Collins), New York, 1993. Summary of 20 years of creativity researched by de Bono. Many useful additional problem definition techniques are presented.

The following books are all published by the Foundation for Critical Thinking (P.O. Box 220, Dillon Beach, CA 94929, www.critical thinking.org):

Richard Paul and Linda Elder, *The Miniature Guide to Critical Thinking Concepts and Tools,* 4th ed. (2004).

Linda Elder and Richard Paul, *The Miniature Guide to Analytic Thinking* (2003).

Richard Paul, Robert Niewoehner, and Linda Elder, *The Miniature Guide to Engineering Reasoning* (2006).

Linda Elder and Richard Paul, *The Miniature Guide to Asking Essential Questions* (2002).

Richard Paul and Linda Elder, *The Thinker's Guide to the Art of Socratic Questioning* (2006).

Richard Paul and Linda Elder, *The Thinker's Guide to Critical and Creative Thinking* (2004).

APPENDIX
Questions for a Socratic Dialogue

Recently, R. W. Paul's six types of Socratic Questions were expanded to nine types. These questions are reproduced with permission from the Foundation for Critical Thinking. For a more complete description of Socratic Questioning, see *The Thinker's Guide to the Art of Socratic Questioning* (2006), by Richard Paul and Linda Elder. Details may be found at www.criticalthinking.org.

Questions of Clarification

- What do you mean by _____ ?
- What is your main point _____ ?
- How does _____ relate to _____ ?
- Could you put that another way?
- What do you think is the main issue here?
- Is your basic point _____ or _____ ?
- Could you give me an example?
- Would this be an example: _____ ?
- Could you explain that further?
- Would you say more about that?
- Why do you say that?
- Let me see if I understand you; do you mean _____ or _____ ?
- How does this relate to our discussion/problem/issue?
- What do you think John meant by his remark? What did you take John to mean?
- Jane, would you summarize in your own words what Richard has said? Richard, is that what you meant?

Questions That Probe Purpose

- What is the purpose of _____ ?
- What was your purpose when you said _____ ?
- How do the purposes of these two people vary?
- How do the purposes of these two groups vary?
- What is the purpose of the main character in this story?
- How did the purpose of this character change during the story?
- Was this purpose justifiable?
- What is the purpose of addressing this question at this time?

Questions That Probe Assumptions

- What are you assuming?
- What is Karen assuming?

- What could we assume instead?
- You seem to be assuming _____. Do I understand you correctly?
- All of your reasoning depends on the idea that _____. Why have you based your reasoning on _____ rather than _____ ?
- You seem to be assuming _____. How would you justify taking this for granted?
- Is it always the case? Why do you think the assumption holds here?

Questions That Probe Information, Reasons, Evidence, and Causes

- What would be an example?
- How do you know?
- What are your reasons for saying that?
- Why did you say that?
- What other information do we need to know before we can address this question?
- Why do you think that is true?
- Could you explain your reasons to us?
- What led you to that belief?
- Is this good evidence for believing that?
- Do you have any evidence to support your assertion?
- Are those reasons adequate?
- How does that information apply to this case?
- Is there reason to doubt that evidence?
- What difference does that make?
- Who is in a position to know if that is the case?
- What would convince you otherwise?
- What would you say to someone who said _____ ?
- What accounts for _____ ?
- What do you think is the cause?
- How did this come about?
- By what reasoning did you come to that conclusion?
- How could we go about finding out whether that is true?
- Can someone else give evidence to support that response?

Questions about Viewpoints or Perspectives

- You seem to be approaching this issue from _____ perspective. Why have you chosen this perspective rather than that perspective?
- How would other groups or types of people respond? Why? What would influence them?
- How could you answer the objection that _____ would make?
- Can/did anyone see this another way?

- What would someone who disagrees say?
- What is an alternative?
- How are Ken's and Roxanne's ideas alike? Different?

Questions That Probe Implications and Consequences

- What are you implying by that?
- When you say _____ , are you implying _____ ?
- But if that happened, what else would also happen as a result? Why?
- What effect would that have?
- Would that necessarily happen or only probably happen?
- What is an alternative?
- If this and this are the case, then what else must be true?

Questions about the Question

- How can we find out?
- Is this the same issue as _____ ?
- How could someone settle this question?
- Can we break this question down at all?
- Is the question clear? Do we understand it?
- How would _____ put the issue?
- Is this question easy or difficult to answer? Why?
- What does this question assume?
- Would _____ put the question differently?
- Why is this question important?
- Does this question ask us to evaluate something?
- Do we need facts to answer this?
- Do we all agree that this is the question?
- To answer this question, what other questions would we have to answer first?
- I'm not sure I understand how you are interpreting the main question at issue. Could you explain your interpretation?

Questions That Probe Concepts

- What is the main idea we are dealing with?
- Why/how is this idea important?
- Do these two ideas conflict? If so, how?
- What was the main idea guiding the thinking of the character in this story?
- How is this idea guiding our thinking as we try to reason through this issue? Is this idea causing us problems?
- What main theories do we need to consider in figuring out _____ ?
- Are you using this term " _____ " in keeping with educated usage?

- Which main distinctions should we draw in reasoning through this problem?
- Which idea is this author using in her or his thinking? Is there a problem with it?

Questions That Probe Inferences and Interpretations

- Which conclusions are we coming to about _____ ?
- On what information are we basing this conclusion?
- Is there a more logical inference we might make in this situation?
- How are you interpreting her behavior? Is there another possible interpretation?
- What do you think of _____ ?
- How did you reach that conclusion?
- Given all the facts, what is the best possible conclusion?
- How shall we interpret these data?

5   BREAKING DOWN THE BARRIERS TO GENERATING IDEAS

> For every failure, there's an alternative course of action. You just have to find it. When you come to a roadblock, take a detour.
> —Mary Kay Ash
> (Founder of Mary Kay Cosmetics)

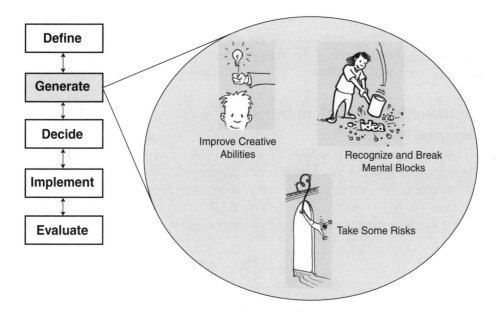

Define

Generate

Decide

Implement

Evaluate

Improve Creative Abilities

Recognize and Break Mental Blocks

Take Some Risks

Once you have defined the problem, you want to make sure you generate the best solution. Sometimes problems may seem unsolvable; at other times, they may appear to have only one less-than-ideal solution. In such a situation, you can use the idea generation techniques described in this chapter to lead you to the best solution. Perseverance is perhaps the most notable characteristic of successful problem solvers, so don't become discouraged when solutions aren't immediately evident. Many times mental blocks may hinder your progress toward a solution. The first step in overcoming these blocks is to recognize them. You can then use blockbusting techniques to move forward toward the best solution.

What is the nature of these mental blocks and what causes them? Some common causes of blocks have been summarized by Higgins et al.:[1]

Common Causes of Mental Blocks

- Defining the problem too narrowly
- Attacking the symptoms, rather than the real problem
- Assuming there is only one right answer
- Getting "hooked" on the first solution that comes to mind
- Getting "hooked" on a solution that almost works (but really doesn't)
- Being distracted by irrelevant information, called "mental dazzle"
- Getting frustrated by a lack of success
- Being too anxious to finish
- Defining the problem ambiguously

There is a direct correlation between the time people spend "playing" with a problem and the diversity of the solutions they are able to generate. Don't be afraid to "play" with the problem.

RECOGNIZING MENTAL BLOCKS

Conceptual Blocks

Let's look at how easy it is to have a conceptual block to a problem. Try this exercise *before* you read the solutions provided on page 92.

Before turning the page, draw four or fewer straight lines (without lifting the pen from the paper) that will cross through all nine dots (Adams, pp. 16–20).[2] Next, draw three straight lines that pass though all the dots.

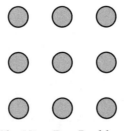

The Nine Dot Problem

This puzzle is very difficult to solve if you do not cross the imaginary boundary created by the eight outer dots. Another common assumption that is not part of the problem statement is that the lines must go through the centers of the dots. Possible solutions are provided on page 92.

Conceptual blockbusting[2] focuses on the cultivation of idea-generating and problem-solving abilities. The first step to becoming a better problem solver is to understand what conceptual blocks are and how they interfere with problem solving. A **conceptual block** is a mental wall that prevents the problem solver from correctly perceiving a problem or conceiving its solution. The most frequently occurring conceptual blocks are perceptual blocks, emotional blocks, cultural blocks, environmental blocks, intellectual blocks, and expressive blocks.

Perceptual Blocks

Perceptual blocks are obstacles that prevent the problem solver from clearly perceiving either the problem itself or the information needed to solve it. A few types of perceptual blocks are described here.

- **Stereotyping.** Survival training teaches individuals to make full use of all the resources at their disposal when they face a life-threatening situation. For example, if you were stranded in the desert after the crash of your small airplane, you would have to make creative use of your available resources to survive and be rescued. Consider the flashlight that was in your toolkit. The stereotypical uses for it would be for signaling, finding things in the dark, and so on. But how about using the batteries to start a fire, the casing for a drinking vessel for water that you find in the desert cacti, or the reflector as a signaling mirror in the daylight?
- **Limiting the Problem Unnecessarily.** The nine dot problem is an example of limiting the problem unnecessarily. You must explore and challenge the boundaries of the problem if you hope to find the best solution.
- **Saturation or Information Overload.** Too much information can be nearly as big a problem as not enough information. You can become overloaded with minute details and be unable to sort out the critical aspects of the problem. Air traffic controllers have learned to overcome this kind of perceptual block. They face information overload regularly in the course of their jobs, particularly during bad weather. They are skilled in sorting out the essential information to ensure safe landings and takeoffs for thousands of aircraft daily.

Emotional Blocks

Emotional blocks interfere with your ability to solve problems in many ways. They decrease the amount of freedom with which you explore and manipulate ideas, and they interfere with your ability to conceptualize fluently and flexibly. Emotional blocks also prevent you from communicating your ideas to others in a

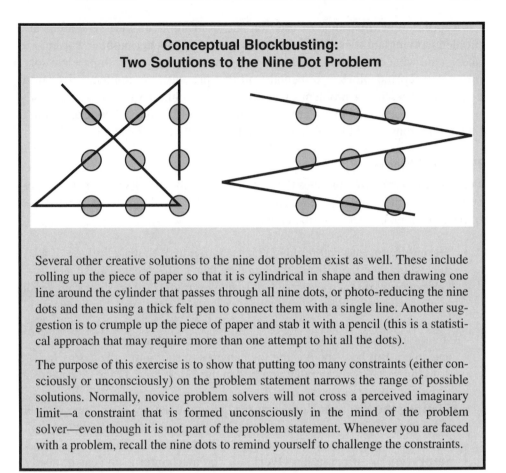

**Conceptual Blockbusting:
Two Solutions to the Nine Dot Problem**

Several other creative solutions to the nine dot problem exist as well. These include rolling up the piece of paper so that it is cylindrical in shape and then drawing one line around the cylinder that passes through all nine dots, or photo-reducing the nine dots and then using a thick felt pen to connect them with a single line. Another suggestion is to crumple up the piece of paper and stab it with a pencil (this is a statistical approach that may require more than one attempt to hit all the dots).

The purpose of this exercise is to show that putting too many constraints (either consciously or unconsciously) on the problem statement narrows the range of possible solutions. Normally, novice problem solvers will not cross a perceived imaginary limit—a constraint that is formed unconsciously in the mind of the problem solver—even though it is not part of the problem statement. Whenever you are faced with a problem, recall the nine dots to remind yourself to challenge the constraints.

manner that will gain their approval. Some types of emotional blocks are described here:

*Failure is not failure, but an opportunity to begin again, more intelligently.
—Henry Ford*

- **Fear of Risk Taking.** This block usually stems from childhood. Most people grow up being rewarded for solving problems correctly and punished for solving problems incorrectly. Implementing a creative idea is like taking a risk. You take the risk of making a mistake, looking foolish, losing your job, or (in a student's case) getting an unacceptable grade. Some ideas for overcoming the fear of risk taking will be discussed later in this chapter.
- **Lack of Appetite for Chaos.** Problem solvers must learn to live with confusion. For example, the criteria for the best solution may seem contradictory. What may be best for the individual may not be best for the organization or group.
- **Judging Rather Than Generating Ideas.** This block can stem from approaching the problem with a negative attitude. Judging ideas too quickly

can discourage even the most creative problem solvers. Wild ideas can sometimes trigger feasible ideas that lead to innovative solutions. This block can be avoided by approaching the problem with a positive attitude.

- **Lack of Challenge.** Sometimes problem solvers don't want to get started because they perceive the problem as being too trivial and easily solved. They believe that the problem is not worthy of their efforts.
- **Inability to Incubate.** Rushing to solve the problem just to get it off your mind can create blocks.

Cultural Blocks

Cultural blocks are acquired by exposure to a given set of cultural patterns, whereas environmental blocks are imposed by our immediate social and physical environment. One type of cultural block is the failure to consider an act that causes displeasure or disgust to certain members of society. To illustrate this type of block, Adams cites the following problem:[2]

Rescuing a Ping Pong Ball[2]

Two pipes, which serve as pole mounts for a volleyball net, are embedded in the floor of a gymnasium. During a game of ping pong, the ball accidentally rolls into one of the pipes because the pipe cover was not replaced (see below). The inside pipe diameter is 0.06 inch larger than the diameter of the ping pong ball (1.50 inches), which is resting gently at the bottom of the pipe. You are one of a group of six people in the gym, along with the following objects:

A 15-foot extension cord	A bag of potato chips
A file	A chisel
A wire coat hanger	A carpenter's hammer
A monkey wrench	A flashlight

Being aware of potential conceptual blocks is the first step to overcoming them.

List as many ways as you can think of (in five minutes) to get the ball out of the pipe without leaving the gym or damaging the ball, pipe, or floor.

A common solution to this problem is to smash the handle of the hammer with the monkey wrench and to use the splinters to obtain the ball. Another less obvious solution is to urinate in the pipe. Many people do not think of this solution because of a cultural block, because urination is considered a "private" activity in many countries.

Environmental Blocks

Environmental blocks are distractions (phones, interruptions) that inhibit deep, prolonged concentration. Working in an atmosphere that is pleasant and supportive most often increases the productivity of the problem solver. Conversely, working under conditions where there is a lack of emotional, physical, economical, or organizational support to bring ideas into action usually has a negative effect on the problem solver and decreases the level of productivity. Ideas for establishing a working environment that enhance creativity were presented in Chapter 2.

Intellectual Blocks

Intellectual blocks can occur as a result of inflexible or inadequate uses of problem-solving strategies. A lack of the intellectual skills necessary to solve a problem can certainly be a block, as can a lack of the information necessary to solve the problem. For example, attempting to solve complicated satellite communications problems without sufficient background in the area would soon result in blocked progress. Additional background, training, or resources may be necessary to solve a problem. Don't be afraid to ask for help.

Expressive Blocks

Expressive blocks—that is, the inability to communicate your ideas to others, in either verbal or written form—can also hinder your progress. Anyone who has played a game of charades or Pictionary can certainly relate to the difficulties that this type of block can cause. Make sketches and drawings, and don't be afraid to take the time to explain your problem to others.

As we have just seen, many types and causes of mental blocks exist. If you find your problem-solving efforts afflicted by one of them, what can you do? Try one of the blockbusting techniques that we present next!

BLOCKBUSTING

A number of structured techniques are available for breaking through mental roadblocks.[3] Collectively, they are referred to as blockbusting techniques. Goman identifies a number of blocks to creativity and offers some suggestions on how to overcome these blocks.[4] The following table summarizes these blocks and block-busters.

Goman's Blockbusters

Block	Blockbuster
1. Negative Attitude Focusing attention on negative aspects of the problem or possible unsatisfactory outcomes hampers creativity.	**1. Attitude Adjustment** List the positive outcomes and aspects of the problem. Realize that with every problem there is not only danger of failure but also an opportunity for success.
2. Fear of Failure One of the greatest inhibitors to creativity is the fear of failure and the inability to take a risk.	**2. Risk Taking** Outline what the risk is, why it is important, what the worst possible outcome would be, what your options are with the worst possible outcome, and how you would deal with this failure.
3. Following the Rules Some rules are necessary, such as stopping at a red light. Others, such as the idea that you must take the familiar (or most efficient, or shortest) route to work, hinder innovation.	**3. Breaking the Rules** Remove unnecessary constraints imposed by the solution requirements.
4. Over-reliance on Logic A need to proceed in a step-by-step fashion may relegate imagination to the background.	**4. Creative Internal Climate** Turn the situation over to your imagination, your feelings, and your sense of humor. Play with insights and possibilities.
5. Belief That You Aren't Creative Believing that you are not creative is a serious hindrance to generating creative solutions. Believing that you can't do something is a self-fulfilling prophesy.	**5. Creative Beliefs** Encourage your creativity by asking "what if" questions, daydreaming, and making up metaphors and analogies. Try different ways of expressing your creativity.

In regard to Goman's fifth blockbuster, there are definitely ways you can increase your creativity by learning new attitudes, values, and ways of approaching and solving problems and by heeding the guidelines presented in the next section.

IMPROVING YOUR CREATIVE ABILITIES

Dr. Edward de Bono, an international creativity authority, is serious about the need for creative thinking.[5] In his book *Serious Creativity*, de Bono, the father of lateral thinking, takes the opportunity to summarize 25 years of research into creative thinking techniques.

Although one of the first steps in the problem-solving process recommended by experienced engineers is the gathering of information, de Bono cautions problem solvers in this regard. For example, when you begin working on a new problem or research topic, it is normal to read all the information available on the problem. Failing to do so may mean "reinventing the wheel" and wasting much time. However, during the course of gathering this information, you may destroy your chances of obtaining an original and creative solution if you are not careful. As you read, you will be exposed to the existing assumptions and prejudices that have been developed by previous workers or researchers. Try as you may to remain objective and original, your innocence will have been lost. De Bono recommends reading just enough to familiarize yourself with the problem and get a "feel" for it. At this point you may wish to stop and organize some of your own ideas before proceeding with an exhaustive review of the literature. This strategy allows you to preserve your opportunities for creativity and innovation.

Have you ever heard the old saying, "If it ain't broke, don't fix it"? De Bono claims the attitude reflected by this statement was largely responsible for the decline of U.S. industry in the past few decades. American managers operated in a strictly reactive mode, merely responding to problems as they arose. Meanwhile, their Japanese counterparts were fixing and improving things that weren't problems. Soon, the American "problem fixers" were left behind. To survive in today's business culture, proactive thinking—as opposed to reactive thinking—is required. This shift in thinking patterns requires creativity.

Raudelsepp[6] has suggested a variety of techniques that can be used to improve your creativity. They are listed in the following table.

Improving Your Creative Abilities[6]

Keep track of your ideas at all times.	
	Many times ideas come at unexpected times. If an idea is not written down within 24 hours, it will usually be forgotten.
Pose new questions to yourself every day.	
	An inquiring mind is a creatively active one that enlarges its area of awareness. If you are doing a homework problem, ask yourself how to make the problem more difficult or more exciting.
Learn about things outside your specialty.	
	Use cross-fertilization to bring ideas and concepts from one field or specialty to another.
Avoid rigid, set patterns of doing things.	
	Overcome biases and preconceived notions by looking at the problem from a fresh viewpoint, always developing at least two or more alternative solutions to your problem.

Continues

Improving Your Creative Abilities[6] (Continued)

Be open and receptive to ideas (yours and others).

Rarely does an innovative solution or idea arrive complete with all its parts ready to be implemented. New ideas are fragile; keep them from breaking by seizing the tentative, half-formed concepts and possibilities and developing them.

Be alert in your observations.

This principle is a key to successfully applying the Kepner–Tregoe approaches discussed in Chapter 7. Keep alert by looking for similarities, differences, and unique and distinguishing features in situations and problems. The larger the number of relationships you can identify, the better your chances of generating original combinations and creative solutions.

Learn to know and understand yourself.

Deepen your self-knowledge by learning your strengths, skills, weaknesses, dislikes, biases, expectations, fears, and prejudices.

Keep abreast of your field.

Read the magazines, trade journals, and other literature in your field to make sure you are not using yesterday's technology to solve today's problems.

Keep your sense of humor.

You are more creative when you are relaxed. Humor aids in putting your problems (and yourself) in perspective. Many times it relieves tension and makes you more relaxed.

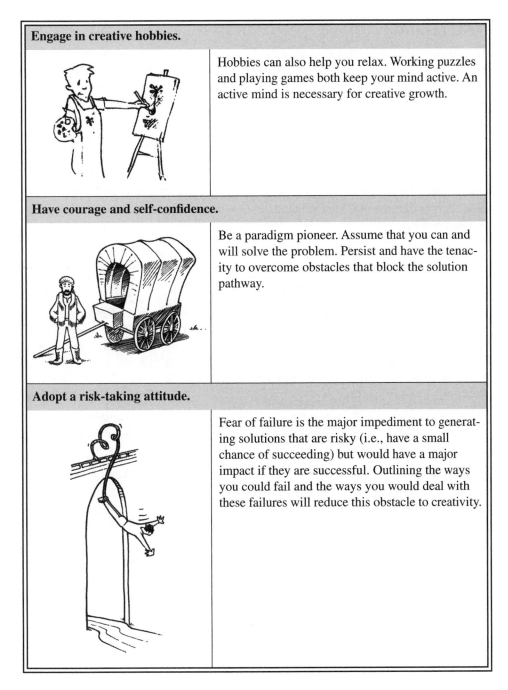

Engage in creative hobbies.

Hobbies can also help you relax. Working puzzles and playing games both keep your mind active. An active mind is necessary for creative growth.

Have courage and self-confidence.

Be a paradigm pioneer. Assume that you can and will solve the problem. Persist and have the tenacity to overcome obstacles that block the solution pathway.

Adopt a risk-taking attitude.

Fear of failure is the major impediment to generating solutions that are risky (i.e., have a small chance of succeeding) but would have a major impact if they are successful. Outlining the ways you could fail and the ways you would deal with these failures will reduce this obstacle to creativity.

RISK TAKING

We just saw that risk taking is important for improving your creativity. What are risks? **Risks** are actions, with no certainty of succeeding, that require significant effort, resources, and/or time. If the actions are successful, however, they will have a major impact. Truly innovative solutions that make a significant difference in your life, organization, or community are almost never found without some risk taking. Of course, the risk taking we encourage you to engage in is not risk taking for the sake of taking a risk. Rather, it is *measured risk taking*. Know the consequences if your risk fails! The consequences of both positive and negative outcomes must be weighed and assessed. And recognize that whenever you take a risk, there will most likely be someone out there to criticize it. Don't be too sensitive to criticism.

Management Takes a Risk

In 1959, Xerox completed the first prototype of a photocopier and initiated plans to send the new device into mass production. The company soon discovered that mass-producing dependable, high-quality machines would require a major financial investment. Consequently, it hired Arthur D. Little, a consulting firm, to carry out a financial and marketing analysis of the proposed project.

The analysis concluded that no more than 5000 units of the photocopiers would sell, which might not justify such a large capital investment. The project looked like it would end before it began. Fortunately, Xerox's management took a risk and went ahead with the project.

Epilogue: Ten years later Xerox passed the billion-dollar mark in sales of copiers as a result of its revolutionary office copiers.

Source: Adapted from Smith, Douglas K., and Robert C. Alexander, *Fumbling the Future*, William Morrow, New York, 1988.

Management Fails to Take a Risk

In 1973, Xerox developed the Alto System, the first personal computer (PC), the first handheld mouse and the first word processing system. A survey showed there was no market for PCs, however, so the company decided not to take the risk and as a result did not market the Alto.

Epilogue: Xerox was the first firm to develop the PC, yet it remains a "copier company" to many people. By contrast, the revenues from Apple's and IBM's PCs measured in the billions of dollars by 1981.

Source: Adapted from Smith, Douglas K., and Robert C. Alexander, *Fumbling the Future,* William Morrow, New York, 1988.

Coca-Cola's Failure in Indonesia

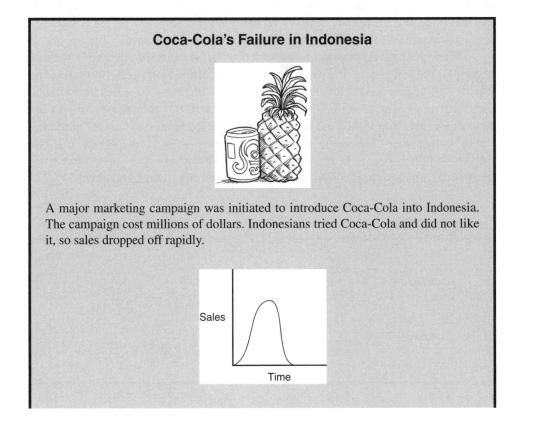

A major marketing campaign was initiated to introduce Coca-Cola into Indonesia. The campaign cost millions of dollars. Indonesians tried Coca-Cola and did not like it, so sales dropped off rapidly.

Coca-Cola failed! But did the company quit? No! It investigated *why* the sales dropped off. During its research, the company found that Indonesians were used to tea, coffee, and tropical soft drinks and were unaccustomed to carbonated drinks. In response, Coca-Cola phased in carbonation by introducing it into strawberry-, pineapple-, and banana-flavored soft drinks.

Epilogue: The sales of Coca-Cola in Indonesia now surpass the sales of local tropical drinks.

Source: Adapted from Mattimore, Bryan W., *99% Inspiration*, Amacom, USA, 1994, p. 29.

We have just seen three case histories in which companies faced the prospect of taking a risk. The one case when management chose *not* take a risk resulted in the loss of billions of dollars in potential revenues. So why don't more companies and individuals take risks? The reason is generally fear of failure.

Many people and companies believe that the ideal learning curve is the one shown on the left below. It's a smooth upward journey to success. In reality, the journey to success is more likely to be peppered with setbacks or negative events, as shown on the figure on the right. These are not failures; **they are events on the learning curve**. You should use the knowledge gained from these events constructively so that your chances of success will be even greater on the next try. The only time failure occurs is when there is a negative event and you do not learn anything. To make a breakthrough, you must be willing to make mistakes.

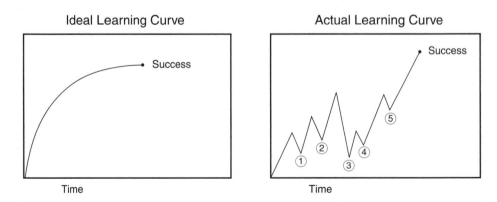

Progress as a Function of Time

In 1958, Tom Monaghan opened a pizza store in Ypsilanti, Michigan. After a year and a half, it went out of business. Was this a failure? It would have been if Tom had not tried to learn the reason his store went belly-up. Instead, Tom researched the reason for the closing and, after some careful planning, opened another store in 1960. This store was the first in what went on to become a world-wide pizza chain, Domino's. To Monaghan, the closing of his first pizza store was not a failure, but rather an event on the learning curve.

In the past, the University of Michigan's business school offered a course called Failure 101.[7] The basic premise of this course is to encourage risk taking by teaching the students not to be afraid to fail with the ideas they have generated. The course provided many opportunities for students to fail on a number of projects in the marketing area. The class discussed numerous examples of first failures that eventually developed into major successful ventures, such as Tom Monaghan's pizza shop. The first car rental agency opened by Warren Avis did not succeed. Glue developed by the 3M Company didn't stick well enough and was nearly abandoned until someone used it to develop Post-it notes. The first two comic strips created by Bill Waterston failed before *Calvin and Hobbes* took off. When the Petrossian brothers, who fled from Russia in 1917, introduced caviar at the Ritz Hotel in Paris, the French made ready use of the nearby spittoons. The brothers were quite discouraged and might easily have given up on the idea. Fortunately, they persisted and overcame this first rejection, and today Petrossian Caviar is sold throughout France at prices of as much as $1000 per pound.

The instructor of the Failure 101 course also gave the students projects that at first seemed nearly impossible. Consider the following projects:

- Design and prepare a marketing campaign for reversible baby diapers.
- Plan a marketing campaign to open a maternity shop in a retirement center.

The students enthusiastically tackled these opportunities to fail. For example, they suggested manufacturing baby diapers that are blue on one side and pink on the other side.

If major breakthroughs are to be made, risks must be taken. Failures resulting from these risks will occur but should not deter any future risk taking. The knowledge gained from these failures should be used constructively so that the chances of success will be even greater on the next try.[7] The following table shows what we should do to help overcome the fear of failure.

Overcoming Fear of Failure

1. Outline what the risk is and explain why the risk is important for you to take.

2. Describe the worst possible outcome if you take the risk and fail.

3. Describe your options given the worst possible outcome.

4. Describe what you could learn from the worst possible outcome.

As we have just seen, risk taking is essential if major breakthroughs are to be made. The question for you is this: "Will you be able to have or develop a mindset that will allow you to take risks, or will you be like the manager at Xerox who did not market the Alto?" To help develop a risk-taking mindset, practice taking small risks whenever possible, such as volunteering to speak at a conference or meeting, challenging established patterns of doing business in your organization, or trying a new sport.

Cautions

Do not take risks just for the sake of saying that you are a risk taker! You must be willing to live with the consequences if what you hope for doesn't come through.

The Risk of Risk Taking

A young man just out of college had saved up $15,000 during his first two years of working and was looking for an investment opportunity. He saw himself as rather conservative, but wanted to change and become more of a risk taker. He saw an advertisement for a coffee company based in Florida that was offering franchises that would make investors thousands of dollars in their spare time. The company distributed single-pot servings of ground-flavored coffee in individual packets, and it claimed that some of the flavorings for the coffee could not be found anywhere else.

When the young man contacted the company, he learned that for $10,000 he could buy a franchise for his area. With that initial investment, he would receive $4000 worth of coffee bags and 20 display cases for the coffee. The next step was for the investor to contact local stores to place the coffee, giving 20% of the profits to each storeowner. For an extra $3000, the company owner in Florida promised to fly to his area for 3 days to help him place the coffee in at least 12 stores. After placing the cases, all that the new franchise owner had to do was to check each store on a regular basis, replenish the coffee packets that had been sold, and collect his profits. When his supply of the coffee bought for $4000 was depleted, the company owner would sell him another batch of coffee. According to the company, such a franchise was a surefire way to double the investor's money in a year.

The young man decided to take the plunge and buy a franchise. He paid $13,000 to the company owner and, within the next month, the display cases with the coffee were placed in 12 stores in the area. After a week, the new franchise owner went to check his coffee stations and replenish the coffee that had been purchased in each of the stores. To his surprise, not nearly as much coffee had been purchased during the first week as he was led to believe would happen. When the young man returned to the stores a week later, he found that even less coffee was purchased in the second week than in the first. He then went back a month after the initial placement, but found that less than half of the coffee he had originally placed had been sold. The franchise owner still had a closet full of coffee from the initial amount supplied by the owner.

This trend continued for several months, but it became apparent that the franchise owner was unlikely to recover even 80% of his investment. Shortly thereafter, the young man stopped checking the stores to replenish the coffee. He wound up giving away the remaining coffee, which filled his closet. He had taken a risk and lost about $12,000 of his investment.

In this case, the young man had not anticipated that the coffee franchise company was inflating the possibility for profit and was not prepared to support his effort. He did not recognize that this investment would not be a good match given the time and energy he was willing to commit. More research and thoughtful consideration upfront might have prevented this loss.

The prudent use of risk taking can be a powerful tool for successful problem solving. In Chapter 7, we will discuss a technique called potential problem analysis that can be used to identify the possible downside to problem solutions that may involve risk.

SUMMARY

This chapter presented techniques to help you overcome mental blocks, improve your creative abilities. and adopt an attitude of being willing to take risks. Here are some ways to help you develop more creative solutions:

- Be able to recognize the different mental blocks when they appear (i.e., perceptual, emotional, cultural, environmental, intellectual, and expressive blocks).
- Use Goman's blockbusters.
- Practice the 12 ways to increase your creative ability.
- Develop a more positive attitude toward risk taking. Before taking on risk, however, make sure you have identified all potential negative outcomes and would be willing to live with those consequences.
- Recognize that "failure" is simply an event on the learning curve *unless* you do not learn from the event—then it is a failure.

REFERENCES

1. Higgins, J. S., et al., "Identifying and Solving Problems in Engineering Design," *Studies in Higher Education,* 14, 2, p. 169, 1989.
2. Adams, James L., *Conceptual Blockbusting: A Guide to Better Ideas,* 3rd ed. © 1986. Reprinted by permission of Da Capo Press, a member of Perseus Books Group.
3. Van Gundy, A. B., *Techniques of Structured Problem Solving,* 2nd ed., Van Nostrand Reinhold, New York, 1988.
4. Goman, Carol K., *Creativity in Business: A Practical Guide for Creative Thinking,* Crisp Publications, 1200 Hamilton Ct., Menlo Park, CA, 94025, 800-442-7477. 1989.
5. De Bono, Edward, *Serious Creativity,* Harper Business, a division of HarperCollins Publishers, New York, 1993.
6. Raudelsepp, E., "Taking This Test to Measure Your Creativity," *Chemical Engineering,* 85, p. 95, July 2, 1979.
7. Matsen, J., "How to Fail Successfully," Dynamo Publishing, Houston, TX, 1990.

EXERCISES

5.1. List the five most important things you learned from this chapter. Also list the five most interesting things you learned.

Mental Blocks

5.2. A. Make a list of the worst business ideas you can think of (e.g., a maternity shop in a retirement village, a solar-powered night-light, reversible diapers).

   B. Take the list you generated in part (a) and turn it around to make the ideas viable concepts for entrepreneurial ventures, (e.g., reversible diapers—blue on one side and pink on the other).

5.3. A. Rearrange four pencils to make six equal triangles.

   B. Remove six pencils to leave two perfect squares and no odd pencils.

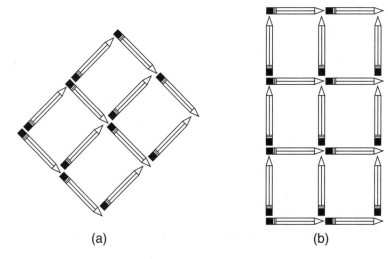

(a)   (b)

5.4. A. Rearrange three balls so that the triangle points up instead of down.

   B. Moving one black poker chip only, make two rows of four.

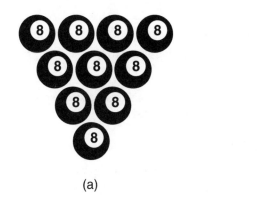   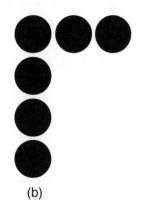

(a)   (b)

5.5. Fifty-seven sticks are laid out to form the equation. Remove eight sticks to make the answer correct. Do not disturb any sticks other than the eight to be removed. First list any perceived constraints that you initially thought could be blocks to solving this problem. (Source: *Brain Busters* by Phillip J. Carter and Ken A. Russel, Sterling Publishing, New York, 1992.)

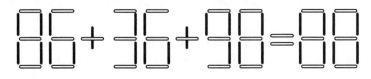

5.6. A prize is hanging by a string from a 10-foot ceiling. You are seated in an immovable chair 6 feet away. In your possession are 10 pieces of paper, a pair of scissors, a reel of tape, paper clips, a box of matches, and a ball of string. Suggest ways of obtaining the prize while remaining seated.

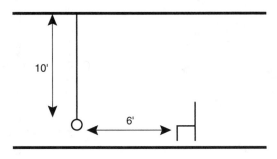

5.7. Identify the mental blocks you encountered in Exercises 5.3 through 5.6.

5.8. Give a specific example for each of the following:

    A. Each of Adams's perceptual blocks

    B. Each of Adams's emotional blocks

    C. Each of Higgins's hindrances to generating alternatives

    D. Each of Goman's five blocks

5.9. Apply Goman's blockbusters to yourself by making a list of specific things you could do when faced with each of the five blocks.

Improving Your Creative Ability

5.10. Pick three of the 12 techniques listed in the table on improving your creative abilities to work on in the next month. Outline the first steps on how you will do this.

5.11. Which of the 12 techniques on improving your creative abilities do you believe are your current strengths? Your current weaknesses?

5.12. Create a scenario on how Coca-Cola or Xerox might have used techniques from the table on improving creative ability to develop their products.

Risk Taking

5.13. Identify a small, medium, and large risk you should take in the not too distant future. Describe your fear of failure for each risk. Apply each of the items in the table on overcoming fear of failure.

5.14. Develop a scenario for what Xerox's Alto System might have looked like if the company had decide to use the items in the table on overcoming fear of failure when deciding on this product's future.

5.15. What lesson can you take away from the example of the young man who invested in the coffee business?

5.16. Describe some creative risks that you can take the next time that you search for a new job.

5.17. Discuss some of the points you would consider as you decide whether a risk you are contemplating is appropriate.

5.18. Think of a situation where you took a risk. Describe the fears that you had to overcome to be able to take the risk. What were the negative consequences that you had to consider might occur as a result of your decision to proceed? How would you have dealt with those consequences if the risk had not been successful?

FURTHER READING

Adams, James L. *Conceptual Blockbusting: A Guide to Better Ideas*, 3rd ed. Addison-Wesley, Stanford, CA, 1986.

Von Oech, Roger. *A Whack on the Side of the Head: How You Can Be More Creative*, revised edition. Warner Books, New York, 1990.

6 GENERATING SOLUTIONS

> Nothing is more dangerous than an idea, when it is the only one you have.
>
> —Emile Chartier

This chapter focuses on a variety of idea generation techniques, which are shown in the diagram below.

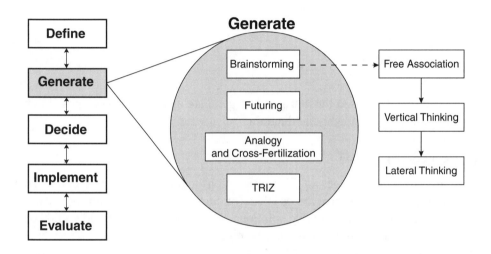

BRAINSTORMING

Brainstorming—one of the oldest techniques to stimulate creativity—is a familiar and effective technique for generating solutions. It provides an excellent means of getting the creative juices flowing. Recent surveys of people working in industry show that brainstorming is routinely used as an effective tool not only for two or three individuals discussing a problem in an informal setting, but also in more formal, large-group problem-solving sessions.

We begin our process with free association—that is, by writing down as many suggestions as we can without judgment of the feasibility. At first the flow of suggestions will be very high; however, after a while you will observe that the rate at which new ideas or suggestions are produced becomes quite slow. At this point we need to use triggers to rejuvenate the rate of suggestions. Some of the most commonly used triggers are vertical thinking, lateral thinking, TRIZ, cross-fertilization, and futuring.

The following figure shows the overall scheme of the brainstorming process. We begin with free association. It is followed by vertical thinking using Osborn's checklist, which reviews and builds on and expands the initial list of ideas. We then move to lateral thinking using random stimulation and other people's views. Finally, we engage in futuring, analogy and cross-fertilization, and TRIZ.

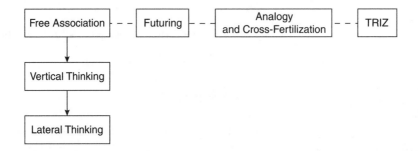

After we have used these triggers to generate as many ideas as possible we organize our ideas in a fishbone diagram.

FREE ASSOCIATION

Typically, the initial stages of idea generation begin with an unstructured **free association** of ideas to solve the problem (brainstorming). During this activity, the group creates lists of all possible solutions. These lists should include wild solutions or unusual solutions without any regard to their feasibility. When brainstorming in groups, people can build upon one another's ideas or suggestions. This triggering of ideas in others is key to successful group brainstorming.

You can use brainstorming to improve your creativity in technical areas. When you finish a homework problem, brainstorm all the ways you could have worked the problem incorrectly, with more difficulty, more easily, or in a more exciting way. Brainstorm a list of all the things you learned from the problem or ways you could extend the problem. Ask "What if?" questions. For example, what if someone suggested doubling the size of the equipment? Brainstorm all the advantages and disadvantages of making such a change.

Another critical component of group brainstorming is maintaining a positive group attitude. No negative comments or judgments are allowed during this stage of the solution process: Reserve your evaluation and judgment until later. The more ideas that are generated, the better chance that the group will devise an innovative, workable solution to the problem at hand. Nothing kills a brainstorming session faster than negative comments. These comments must be kept in check by the group leader or the session will usually be reduced to one of "braindrizzling."

Comments That Reduce Brainstorming to Braindrizzling

- That won't work.
- It's against our policy.
- It's not our job.
- We haven't done it that way before.
- We don't have enough time.
- That's too expensive.
- That's too much hassle.
- That's not practical.
- That's too radical.
- We can't solve this problem.

We have conducted numerous brainstorming exercises with groups of students. An example of an unstructured session is shown next.

Brainstorming Activity

Problem Statement

Suggest uses of old cars as equipment for a children's playground.

Ideas Generated by Free Association

- Take the tires off and roll them along the ground.
- Get on the roof and use the car as a slide.
- Take the seats out and use them as a bed on which to rest between activities.
- Teenagers could take the engine apart and put it back together.
- Cut the car apart and turn it into a 3-D puzzle.
- Make a garden by planting flowers inside.
- Use the tires to crawl through as an obstacle course.
- Make the car into a sculpture.
- Take the doors off and use them as goals for hockey.

As mentioned earlier, typically the ideas flow quickly at first and then slow abruptly after several minutes. That is, the process hits a "roadblock." These roadblocks hinder our progress toward a solution. Luckily, we can use some other blockbusting techniques to help overcome these mental blocks and generate additional alternatives.

VERTICAL THINKING

Vertical thinking can build on the ideas already generated (piggybacking) or it can look at the different parts of the problem in an effort to generate new ideas. One of the vertical thinking techniques is Osborn's checklist. This checklist is shown in an abbreviated format in the following table.

Osborn's Checklist for Adding New Ideas[1]

Adapt? .... How can this (product, idea, plan, etc.) be used as is? What are other uses it could be adapted to?

Modify? .... Change the meaning, material, color, shape, odor?

Magnify? .... Add a new ingredient? Make it longer, stronger, thicker, higher?

Minify? .... Split up? Take something out? Make it lighter, lower, shorter?

Substitute? .... Who else, where else, or what else? Another ingredient, material, or approach?

Rearrange? ... Interchange parts? Other patterns or layouts? Transpose the cause and effect? Change positives to negatives? Reverse roles? Turn it backward or upside down? Sort it?

Combine? ...... Combine parts, units, ideas? Blend? Compromise? Combine from different categories?

Example of Vertical Thinking

Continuing with the playground equipment example . . .

Adapt: Take the hood off the car, and use it as a toboggan in winter.

Modify: Remove the engines and side panels, and make go-carts.

Magnify: Over-inflate the inner tubes from the tires, and use them to create a "romper room"/jumping pit.

Minify: Crush the cars into cubes, and allow the kids to climb on the blocks.

Substitute: Use the cars' seats in swings.

Rearrange: Turn the car upside down, and use it as a teeter-totter.

Combine: Use the side panels or roof of the car to make a huge canopy or fort.

LATERAL THINKING

Edward de Bono developed the **lateral thinking** techniques of random stimulation and using other people's views to generate ideas during brainstorming. Lateral thinking provides two different ways to come at the problem direction and get "unstuck." It ensures that ideas are generated that never would be generated by free association or vertical thinking.

Lateral Thinking Using Random Stimulation

Random stimulation is a technique that is especially useful if we are stuck or in a rut.[2,3] It is a way of generating totally different ideas than previously considered. As a result, it can "jump-start" the idea generation process and free it from whatever current rut it may be in.

The introduction of strange or "weird" ideas during brainstorming should not be shunned but rather encouraged. Random stimulation makes use of a random piece of information (perhaps a word culled from the dictionary or a book (e.g., the eighth word down on page 125) or one of the words in the sample list picked by a random finger placement. This word serves as a trigger or switch to change the patterns of thought when a mental roadblock occurs. The random word can be used to generate other words that can stimulate the flow of ideas.

A Short List of Random Stimulation Words

all, albatross, airplane, air, animals, bag, basketball, bean, bee, bear, bump, bed, car, cannon, cap, control, cape, custard pie, dawn, deer, defense, dig, dive, dump, dumpster, ear, eavesdrop, evolution, eve, fawn, fix, find, fungus, food, ghost, graph, gulp, gum, hot, halo, hope, hammer, humbug, head, high, ice, icon, ill, jealous, jump, jig, jive, jinx, key, knife, kitchen, lump, lie, loan, live, Latvia, man, mop, market, make, maim, mane, notice, needle, new, next, nice, open, Oscar, opera, office, pen, powder, pump, Plato, pigeons, pocket, quick, quack, quiet, rage, rash, run, rigid, radar, Scrooge, stop, stove, save, saloon, sandwich, ski, simple, safe, sauce, sand, sphere, tea, time, ticket, treadmill, up, uneven, upside-down, vice, victor, vindicate, volume, violin, voice, wreak, witch, wide, wedge, X-ray, yearn, year, yazzle, zone, zoo, zip, zap

In using the random simulation technique, we randomly put our finger on one of the words in this short list. Suppose it fell upon the word "document." This word makes us think of the word "paper," which made us think of "art" and the progression shown below.

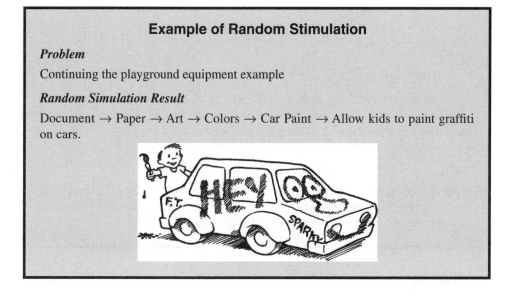

This kind of pattern change allows us to view the problem from new perspectives that we had not previously considered.

Lateral Thinking Using Other People's Views

When approaching a problem that involves the thoughts and feelings of others, a useful thinking tool is **other people's views (OPV)**.[2] The inability to see the problem from various viewpoints can be quite limiting. By contrast, imagining yourself in the role of the other person allows you to see complications of the problem that you had not considered previously. For example, automotive engineers must be aware of many perspectives if they hope to design a successful vehicle. In particular, they must consider the views of the consumers, their company's marketing personnel, management, the safety department, the financial people, and the service personnel. Failure to take any of these groups' views into account could result in a failed product.

Consider an argument between a newly hired store manager and an employee. The issue at hand is the employee's desire to take a two-week vacation during the store's busiest period, the Christmas season. The manager's main concern is having enough help to handle the sales volume. The employee, however, has made reservations for an Antarctic cruise, one year in advance (with the former manager's approval), and stands to lose a lot of money if he has to cancel them. This problem does not have a solution yet, but by using OPV each person can see what the other person stands to gain or lose from the vacation, and each will have a better understanding of the types of compromises the other person might be willing to make. Examples using this technique are shown below.

Example of Other People's Views

Problem

Continuing the playground example

Think about viewing the car from a child's viewpoint. Think about walking around on your knees. How would this change your perspective? That is, imagine the playground from a child's height. What was your favorite toy? How could this be mimicked with used auto parts?

Example

From a child's point of view, the intact car would be an exciting chance to pretend to be a grownup. Just take off the door, remove other dangerous equipment, and let the kids pretend to drive. Just leave the car as it is.

FUTURING

Futuring is a blockbusting technique that focuses on generating solutions that currently may not be technically feasible but might become practical in the future. In futuring, we ask questions such as "What are the characteristics of an ideal solution?" and "What currently existing problem would make our jobs easier when solved, or would solve many subsequent problems, or would make a major difference in the way we do business?" One of futurist Joel Barker's key ideas is that you should be bold enough to suggest alternatives that promise major advances, yet may have only a small probability of success.

The rules for futuring are relatively simple: Try to imagine the ideal solution without regard to whether it is technically feasible. Then begin by making statements such as "If [this] happened, it would completely change the way I do business." For example, the University of Michigan's College of Engineering Commission on Undergraduate Education used futuring exercises to help formulate the goals and directions of its engineering education program for the 1990s and into the twenty-first century. The members of the commission were asked, "What do you see the student doing in 2009?" Their answers included these responses:

- "I see students using interactive computing to learn all their lessons. There are animations of processes where the students can change operating parameters and get instant visual feedback on their effect."
- "I see lecture halls where the lecturer is a hologram of the most authoritative and dynamic professor in the world on that particular topic."

In futuring, you visualize the idealized situation that you would like to have and then work on devising ways to attain it. Here's the futuring process in a nutshell:

The Futuring Process

1. Examine the problem carefully to make sure the real problem has been defined.
2. Imagine yourself at some point in the future after the problem has been solved. What are the benefits of having a solution?
3. "Look around" in the future. Try to imagine an ideal solution to the problem at hand without regard to its technical feasibility. Remember, in the future, anything is possible.
4. Make statements such as "If only [this] would happen, I could solve [this problem]."
5. Dare to change the rules! The best solutions to some problems are contrary to conventional wisdom.

Futuring in Action:
Useful Products from Cheese Waste

The waste products from cheese and yogurt plants are quite acidic, so they cannot be discharged directly into lakes or rivers. Instead, these wastes must be treated so that they can be safely discharged from the plant. One suggestion is to build a waste treatment facility that will neutralize the acid and kill the bacteria in the waste. It is important to keep both the cost of the treatment materials and the capital cost of the facility at a minimum so that we do not severely erode the profits of the yogurt and cheese making. Let's try an exercise in futuring.

Let's imagine ourselves in the future, with a booming yogurt- and cheese-making business. Why is our plant doing so well? It is highly successful because there are no wasted materials in our operation. All of the waste streams that might potentially damage our environment are being put to good use. What are we using them for? The main waste stream contains sugar and protein. What could we be using those materials for? Protein is an essential dietary requirement. We could separate out the protein and use it for human consumption (food additives) or animal feed supplements (more likely). What about the sugar? Could we sell it to someone as a raw material for another process? What kind of process? Sugars can be fermented, can't they? Perhaps we could use the sugar to produce ethanol for a profit. What's left after removing the protein and the sugar? Could this material be landfill? Landfilling is placing the material in the ground—could we place it in the ground for a profit? What about placing the leftover material on the surface of the ground? Could it be used as a fertilizer? Or as a biodegradable de-icing product for use on the roads? (*Note:* The de-icing idea is already being used in some cities.)

SUMMARY

Define the Real Problem: The problem is not how to treat the waste but more generally what to do with it.

Imagine the Future: The plant is profitable and has no adverse environmental impact.

Generate Solutions: Our success due to the fact that we have no waste production. All of our plant's byproducts are recycled or sold.

ORGANIZING BRAINSTORMING IDEAS: THE FISHBONE DIAGRAM

Fishbone diagrams are a graphical way to organize and record brainstorming ideas. These diagrams look like a fish skeleton (hence their name). To construct a fishbone diagram, we follow this procedure:

1. Write the real problem you want to solve by generating ideas in a box or a circle to the right of the diagram. Next, draw a horizontal line (the backbone) extending from the left side to the box:

2. Categorize the potential solutions into several major categories (e.g., whole car, parts, painting) and list them along the bottom or top of the diagram. Extend diagonal lines from the major categories to the backbone. These lines form the basic skeleton of the fishbone diagram.
3. Place the potential solutions related to each of the major categories along the appropriate line (or bone) in the diagram.

A fishbone diagram for organizing the ideas for the cars as playground equipment problem is shown below. The most difficult task in constructing such a diagram is deciding which major categories to use for organizing the options. In this example, we have selected "Painting," "Whole Car," and "Parts." The ideas that were generated fall neatly into these categories. Other categories often used in fishbone diagrams include personnel, equipment, method, materials, and the environment. This activity of sorting and organizing the information is a very valuable component of the solution process.

By reviewing the fishbone diagram, we can evaluate the solutions that have been generated. We have put a structure to the solutions, organizing them and allowing us to "attack" the problem from a number of different fronts if we choose. Clearly, fishbone diagrams can be very helpful in visualizing all the ideas that you have generated.

Painting
- Let kids paint graffiti on the cars
- Paint targets and let kids throw balls at them
- Paint the car as a covered wagon and let the kids play cowboys

Whole Car
- Turn the car into a teeter-totter (upside down)
- Turn the car into a go-cart
- Crush the car and make blocks from it
- Let kids drive the car as is
- Open the car's doors and use them as goals for field hockey

Parts
- Use the seats in swings
- Use the roof and doors as part of a fort
- Use the tire inner tubes as part of an obstacle course (to jump on)
- Use the car's hood as a toboggan
- Use the car's springs for a wobble ride

We now choose the best idea on each of the major bones of the fish:
>Painting → Graffiti
>Parts → Tire Inner Tubes
>Whole Car → As Is

We could go even further and choose the best of the major branches:
>Whole Car → As Is

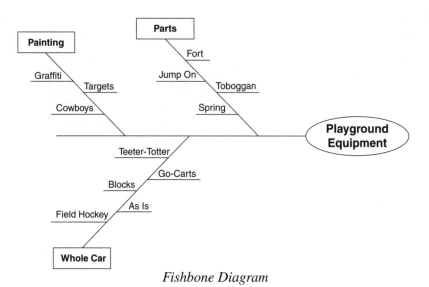

Fishbone Diagram

Cautions

Another step, which has been omitted in this example, is actually necessary before we choose the solutions to put on the fishbone diagram. That step is evaluating the suggestions generated. In the preceding example, we should have addressed a pressing issue—namely, the children's safety—for each of the ideas generated. We could address this safety issue by using the Kepner–Tregoe approach of potential problem analysis.

BRAINWRITING

Two or more individuals are required to carry out an interactive brainstorming session. If you have no one to interact with, however, you can use another technique to generate ideas: **brainwriting.** In brainwriting, you follow the same procedure as brainstorming (e.g., free association, Osborn's checklist, random stimulation, futuring). Write down your ideas as fast as you generate them, without pausing or stopping to evaluate the ideas. Also, keep a notebook handy to write down ideas whenever they occur to you, because they often come at unusual times. After you have completed your list, organize your ideas (solutions) into a fishbone diagram.

Mind mapping[4] is a technique that is used to represent ideas linked to and arranged radially around a central key word or idea. This technique helps you create nonlinear graphical relationships between your ideas. Typically the mind maps take up one side of a piece of paper, with the central idea being located in the middle of the page. Other ideas or elements that relate to the central idea are arranged radially around the central idea. Connections to the central idea are made using different-style lines or different colors. This kind of graphical representation (which is not unlike a graphical outline) of your ideas can be very powerful in visualizing and establishing relationships and associations between seemingly disparate elements or ideas. Computer software is commercially available that can help you easily construct mind maps.

ANALOGY AND CROSS-FERTILIZATION

It is well documented that a number of the most important advances in science, engineering, art, and business have come from cross-fertilization and analogies with other disciplines. In this process, ideas, rules, laws, facts, and conventions from one discipline are transferred to another discipline.

Generating ideas by **analogy** is an approach that works quite well for many individuals. With this strategy, we look for analogous situations and problems in both related and unrelated areas. To use this technique effectively, of course, it is important that you read and learn about things outside your area of expertise. Consider the Shockblockers Shoes developed by the U.S. Shoe Corporation (*Washington Post,* p. A47, December 18, 1992). This company wanted to develop shoes that would absorb the shocks associated with walking. It looked around to find out what other paraphernalia were used to protect the body from external contact. Ultimately, the company's research and development team studied the materials used inside a professional football helmet. The U.S. Shoe Corporation eventually decided to include the same shock-absorbing foam in the soles of its new line of "Shockblocker" shoes.

Another example of using this technique is the problem encountered in the 1960s when scientists recognized that there was no available material that would survive the high temperatures generated on a space capsule's surface during reentry to the Earth's atmosphere. Consequently, a government directive was issued: "Find a material able to withstand the temperatures encountered on reentry." By the early 1970s, no one had produced a suitable material that satisfied the directive, yet we had sent astronauts to the Moon and back. How had this achievement been possible?

The real problem was "How can we protect the astronauts upon reentry"—not "Find a material that can withstand such high temperatures." Once the real problem was determined, a solution soon followed. One of the scientists working on the project asked a related question: How do meteors eventually reach the Earth's surface without disintegrating completely? Upon investigation of this problem, he found that although the surface of the meteor vaporized while passing through the atmosphere, the inside of the meteor was not damaged. This analogy led to the idea of using materials on the outside of the capsule that would vaporize when exposed to the high temperatures encountered during reentry. Consequently, the heat generated by friction with the Earth's atmosphere during reentry would be dissipated by the vaporization of a material that coated the outside of the space capsule. By sacrificing this material, the temperatures of the capsule's underlying structural material remained at a tolerable level to protect the astronauts. Once the real problem was uncovered, the scientists solved the problem by using analogies and transferring ideas from one situation to another.

To solve problems by analogy, you should follow four steps.[5]

---

1. State the problem.
2. Generate analogies (this problem is like . . .).
3. Solve the analogy.
4. Transfer the solution to the problem.

When generating analogies, apply the same rules you did in brainstorming. For example, in the case of the stale cereal (from Chapter 4), we could say, "Keeping the cereal fresh is like preserving raw fish in the tropics without a refrigerator and without cooking." How could we preserve fish in those circumstances? We could add lemon or lime juice to make ceviche (pickled fish). So what could we add to the cereal to keep it fresh?

A Cold Winter's Day

A large office building in the city is not as energy efficient as the building's owners would like. To keep their heating bills down, the building is kept colder than the occupants prefer, and many complaints have been received.

Step 1. State the Problem. (What is the situation?)

The occupants of building are too cold. Utilities bills are too high. Too many complaints are being received.

Step 2. Generate Analogies. (What else is like this situation?)

Generate as many possibilities as you can, then choose one to work with: Being cold in the office is like . . .

> Being too cold at a football game.
> Being too cold on a camping trip.
> Being too cold in a car that hasn't warmed up in the winter.
> Being too cold in bed at night.

Step 3. Solve the Analogy.

When you are too cold on a camping trip, you build a campfire, which serves as a source of both heat and light.

> **Step 4. Transfer the Solution to the Problem.**
>
> Instead of building a campfire in the office, rent or buy portable space heaters. Use a readily available source of heat and light to solve the building's energy problems. Install a heat recovery system to recover waste heat from the fluorescent lights to warm the offices and improve the energy efficiency. (*Note:* This practice is used in modern energy-efficient office buildings.)

To practice generating ideas by **cross-fertilization,** you might ask what each of the following pairs would learn if they went to lunch or dinner together that would improve themselves and/or the way they perform their jobs:

A beautician and a college professor
A police officer and a software programmer
An automobile mechanic and an insurance salesperson
A banker and a gardener
A choreographer and an air traffic controller
A maitre d' and a pastor

Dinner at Antoine's

Let's consider a dinner meeting between a beautician and a college professor. The beautician could provide the professor with tips on the importance of having and maintaining an attractive physical appearance. Beauticians are typically good conversationalists and listeners, so the beautician could also share these skills to help the professor establish a more effective rapport with the students. Thanks to these insights, the professor would be better able to understand and respond to student concerns and problems. The professor might also pick up some tips on managing a small business, which would be helpful in organizing and managing a research group.

College professors, by contrast, are usually involved in research and keep up-to-date on the latest developments in their chosen fields. The beautician could benefit from a discussion of these topics and be encouraged to obtain the newest beauty information and perhaps experiment with some new ideas. For example, new chemical/color treatments could be studied or explored using discarded hair samples. The beautician could learn how to carry out an experiment by treating samples of hair with a new curling product for varying lengths of time to determine the optimal treatment procedure for different types of hair.

Many other combinations of professions would also provide growth experiences for both participants. The cross-fertilization of ideas from one group to another is a powerful method for adapting ideas from one discipline or profession to solve problems in another discipline or profession. Many times managers will bring together a small group of people from diverse (ethnic, cultural) backgrounds to interact and look at a problem and solution from many vantage points.

INCUBATING IDEAS

The incubation period is very important in problem solving. Working on a solution to a problem and being forced to meet a deadline often causes you to pick the first solution that comes to mind and then "run with it," instead of stopping to think about alternative solutions. Many times it is advantageous to take a break when working on a problem to let your ideas incubate while your subconscious works on it. Of course, you shouldn't turn the responsibility over to your subconscious completely by saying, "Well, my subconscious hasn't solved the problem yet."

Once the generation of ideas has halted (or you collapse from the effort), an incubation period may be in order. Little is truly understood about mental incubation, but the basic process involves stopping active work on the problem and letting your subconscious continue the work "behind the scenes." Everyone has, at one time or another, been told to "sleep on a problem," in hopes that the solution will be apparent in the morning. This incubation—that is, subconscious work—has been described as a mental scanning of the billions of neurons in the brain in search of a novel or innovative connection to lead to a possible solution.[6]

When members of the National Academy of Engineering were asked, "What do you do when you get stuck on a problem?" some of their responses were as follows:

- "Communicate with other people. Read articles. Try new techniques *after a period of digestion*. Follow a lead if it looks promising. Keep pursuing."
- "Ask questions about all the circumstances. *Go home and think*. Go to your arsenal of past experiences. Identify factors related to the problem. Read, write, and exchange ideas."
- "I write down everything that I must know to have a solution and everything that I know about the problem so far. Then I usually *let it sit overnight,* and think about it from time to time. While it is sitting, I often review the recent literature on similar problems and get an idea on how to proceed."
- "When I can afford the liberty of doing so, I will *put the problem down and do something else for a while*. My mind keeps working on the problem, and often I will think of something while not trying to."

The common thread that runs through these responses is the notion of an incubation period. If the solution to the problem is not an emergency, incubation is a useful (in)activity to consider.

TRIZ

TRIZ, which stands for "Teoriya Resheniya Izobreatatelskikh Zadatch" and is Russian for "Theory of Inventive Problem Solving (TIPS)," is the brainchild of Russian engineer and scientist Genrich Altshuller.[7-11] Altshuller has studied tens of thousands of patents, looking for similarities and innovations in the patents. The TRIZ process recognizes that technical systems evolve so as to increase ideality by overcoming contradictions mostly with minimal introduction of resources. Thus, for creative problem solving, TRIZ provides a dialectic way of thinking—that is, it seeks to understand the problem as a system, to imagine the ideal solution first, and to resolve contradictions.

You can think of TRIZ as another way of lateral thinking. It is based on two basic principles, as described by Domb:[8]

- Someone, someplace, has already solved your problem or one similar to it. Creativity means finding that solution and adapting it to the current problem.
- Don't accept contradictions. Resolve them.

The first principle essentially tells us, "Don't reinvent the proverbial wheel." The second principle focuses on contradictions. Contradictions include situations in which one object or system has contradictory or opposing requirements, or in which when one feature of the system improves, another worsens. Everyday examples abound:

- Wireless Internet access should be readily available to students on campus (good), but increased access makes it difficult to protect personal information (bad).
- MP3 players should have vast storage capabilities for audio and video (good), but increased storage may increase size and power consumption (bad).
- A product gets stronger (good), but its weight increases (bad). For example, bulletproof vests should be strong (good), but can be bulky and uncomfortable to wear (bad).
- When hard disk space for file storage is increased (good), it becomes more difficult to locate the correct file because the disk is so large (bad).
- Automobile air bags deploy quickly to protect the passenger (good), but the more rapidly they deploy, the more likely they are to injure or kill small or out-of-position people (bad).

- Cell phone networks should have excellent coverage so users have strong signals (good), but cell phone towers are not very nice to look at (bad).
- The email spam filter should be efficient enough to remove all my junk emails (good), but then it is more likely to screen some emails that I actually want to receive (bad).

The first step in the TRIZ process is to state the problem and the contradictions you are trying to resolve. To resolve the contradictions, we identify which features would improve the solution (good) and which features would worsen the solution (bad). Altshuller assembled a list of 39 features that were common to the thousands of patents he analyzed. A complete description of each of these features can be found on the TRIZ Web site (http://www.triz-journal.com/archives/1998/11/d/ default.asp).

---

39 TRIZ Features[9]

1. Weight of moving object	21. Power
2. Weight of stationary object	22. Loss of energy
3. Length of moving object	23. Loss of substance
4. Length of stationary object	24. Loss of information
5. Area of moving object	25. Loss of time
6. Area of stationary object	26. Quantity of substance
7. Volume of moving object	27. Reliability
8. Volume of stationary object	28. Measurement accuracy
9. Speed of object	29. Manufacturing precision
10. Force (intensity)	30. Object-affected harmful
11. Stress or pressure	31. Object-generated harmful
12. Shape	32. Ease of manufacture
13. Stability of the object	33. Ease of operation
14. Strength	34. Ease of repair
15. Durability of moving object	35. Adaptability or versatility
16. Durability of nonmoving object	36. Device complexity
17. Temperature	37. Difficulty of detecting
18. Illumination intensity	38. Extent of automation
19. Use of energy by moving object	39. Productivity
20. Use of energy by stationary object	

This list is used to formulate a 39×39 contradiction matrix by listing each of the features along the side and the top of the matrix. The features along the top are those that make the product or situation worse (bad); those along the side improve the product or situation (good).

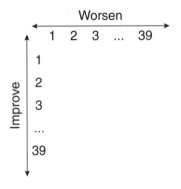

In TRIZ, first we identify the contradictions. Next we use the 39×39 contradiction matrix to suggest which of the Altshuller's 40 principles (discussed later in this section) might be useful to explore in solving the problem and resolving the contradiction. We formulate the contradiction by specifying which features are improving and which features are worsening. For example, if we were trying to develop a new structural material to be used in airplanes, we could say that we want more strength (improving feature) without more weight (worsening feature). In this case, strength (feature 14) is improving, but the weight of a moving object (feature 1) is worsening. We then locate the improving feature in the first column (vertical) of the matrix and the worsening feature in the first row (horizontal). In our example, the intersection is found in row 14, column 1 of the following abbreviated (14×6) contradiction matrix. An interactive form of the full 39×39 TRIZ contradiction matrix is available at http://www.triz40.com/.

TRIZ Contradiction Matrix[9]

		1. Weight of moving object	2. Weight of stationary object	3. Length of moving object	4. Length of stationary object	5. Area of moving object	6. Area of stationary object
Improving Feature		**Worsening Feature**					
	1. Weight of moving object	*	—	15, 8 29, 34	—	29, 17 38, 34	—
	2. Weight of stationary object	—	*	—	10, 1 29, 35	—	35, 30 13, 2
	3. Length of moving object	8, 15 29, 34	—	*	—	15, 17 4	—
	4. Length of stationary object	—	35, 28 40, 29	—	*	—	17, 7 10, 40
	5. Area of moving object	2, 17 29, 4	—	14, 15 18, 4	—	*	—
	6. Area of stationary object	—	30, 2 14, 18	—	26, 7 9, 39	—	*
	7. Volume of moving object	2, 26 29, 40	—	1, 7 4, 35	—	1, 7 4, 17	—
	8. Volume of stationary object	—	35, 10 19, 14	19, 14	35, 8 2, 14	—	—
	9. Speed of object	2, 28 13, 38	—	13, 14 8	—	29, 30 34	—
	10. Force (intensity)	8, 1 37 18	18, 13 1, 28	17, 19 9, 36	28, 10	19, 10 15	1, 18 36, 37
	11. Stress or pressure	10, 36 37, 40	13, 29 10, 18	35, 10 36	35, 1 14, 16	10, 15 36, 28	10, 15 36, 37
	12. Shape	8, 10 29, 40	15, 10 26, 3	29, 34 5, 4	13, 14 10, 7	5, 34 4, 10	—
	13. Stability of the object	21, 35 2, 39	26, 39 1, 40	13, 15 1, 28	37	2, 11 13	39
	14. Strength	1, 8 40, 15	40, 26 27, 1	1, 15 8, 35	15, 14 28, 26	3, 34 40, 29	9, 40 28

The four numbers in this intersection box are 1, 8, 15, and 40. These numbers refer to four of the 40 Altshuller principles that may help us solve the problem. For the weight versus strength contradiction, we can use 1 (segmentation), 8 (anti-weight), 15 (dynamics), and 40 (composite material films) to brainstorm solutions to resolve our contradiction and solve our current problem (e.g., developing a better airplane material). Altshuller developed these 40 principles in an effort to summarize solution techniques that have already been identified for other problems (i.e., someone, someplace, has already solved a similar problem). Explanations of each of the 40 principles are available on TRIZ40 Web site.[9]

Altshuller's 40 Principles of TRIZ[9]

1. Segmentation	21. Skipping
2. Taking out	22 "Blessing in disguise"
3. Local quality	23. Feedback
4. Asymmetry	24. "Intermediary"
5. Merging	25. Self-service
6. Universality	26. Copying
7. "Nested doll"	27. Cheap short-living
8. Anti-weight	28. Mechanics substitution
9. Preliminary anti-action	29. Pneumatics and hydraulics
10. Preliminary action	30. Flexible shells and thin films
11. Beforehand cushioning	31. Porous materials
12. Equipotentiality	32. Color changes
13. The other way around	33. Homogeneity
14. Spheroidality	34. Discarding and recovering
15. Dynamics	35. Parameter changes
16. Partial or excessive actions	36. Phase transitions
17. Another dimension	37. Thermal expansion
18. Mechanical vibration	38. Strong oxidants
19. Periodic action	39. Inert atmosphere
20. Continuity of useful action	40. Composite material films

Example Application of TRIZ:
A New Structural Material for Bulletproof Garments

Problem Statement

Bulletproof vests should be strong, but not heavy.

Step 1. ***Identify the Contradiction(s)***

Strength (improves) versus weight (worsens)

Step 2. ***Look at the List of Features and Identify Those Important to Your Contradiction***

Strength: Feature 14
Weight: Feature 2

Step 3. ***Identify Which Are Improving Features and Which Are Worsening Features***

Strength (feature 14) improves; weight (feature 2) worsens

Step 4. ***Refer to the TRIZ Contradiction Matrix to Learn Which of Altshuller's Principles May Be Useful for the Problem***

Row 14 (strength) and column 2 (weight) of the contradiction matrix indicate the following principles may be useful: 40, 26, 27, 1 (see shaded box on page 134). We now look at the principles list to learn that these numbers correspond to

> 40. Composite materials
> 26. Copying
> 27. Cheap short-living
> 1. Segmentation.

Next, we brainstorm how we could use these four principles to solve our problem.

40. Composite materials

The explanation of this principle from the TRIZ Web site is

• Change from uniform to composite (multiple) materials such as reinforced polymers.

For lighter-weight, stronger vests, the use of composites is an active area of research. Polymers (Kevlar) reinforced with carbon nanofibers are currently being investigated as a strong, lightweight alternative to steel for structural materials.

26. Copying

The explanation of this principle from the TRIZ Web site is

- Instead of an unavailable, expensive, fragile object, use simpler and inexpensive copies.
- Replace an object or process with optical copies.
- If visible optical copies are already used, move to infrared or ultraviolet copies.

We could copy the design of abbreviated SCUBA diving wet suits for use as bulletproof garments.

27. Cheap short-living objects

The explanation of this principle from the TRIZ Web site is

- Replace an inexpensive object with a multiple of inexpensive objects, comprising certain qualities (such as service life, for instance).

This principle does not appear to be readily applicable to this problem. This is not necessarily unusual, because Altshuller's principles are merely general suggestions intended to help us focus our thinking in areas that have proven fruitful in previous problems.

1. Segmentation

The explanation of this principle from the TRIZ Web site is

- Divide an object into independent parts.
- Make an object easy to disassemble (replace worn or damaged parts).
- Increase the degree of fragmentation or segmentation.

Perhaps we could consider several different coverings for different parts of the body (e.g., pants, vest) rather than a one-piece suit. Perhaps we could use different materials to cover the critical areas such as chest and head, each of which takes advantage of specific properties that would be customized for its particular application.

Thus, by identifying problem contradictions, we can use the TRIZ process to help us reach a solution. In this case, we were able to generate two additional ideas using the TRIZ method.

If the tools of TRIZ are used in an effective manner, the major challenges of today will be resolved more rapidly to produce the success stories of tomorrow.[10], *

---

* The authors would like to thank Glenn Mazur for educating us on this topic.

SUMMARY

This chapter has presented techniques to help you generate creative solutions. Many times it is advantageous to take a break when working on a problem to let your ideas incubate while your subconscious works on it. But don't turn the entire responsibility over to your subconscious. Instead, use the following techniques to help spur your creativity:

- Use brainstorming to generate solutions to the problem.
  - Use free association to generate the initial set of ideas.
  - Use vertical thinking (Osborn's checklist) to build on previous ideas and generate new ideas: adapt, modify, magnify, minify, rearrange, combine.
  - Use lateral thinking—random stimulation and other people's views—to generate new ideas when you are stuck in a rut.
- Use futuring to remove all technical blocks to envision a solution in the future.
- Use a fishbone diagram to help organize the ideas and solutions you generate.
- Use analogies and cross-fertilization to bring ideas, phenomena, and knowledge from other disciplines to bear on your problem.
- Use TRIZ to resolve contradictions.

REFERENCES

1. Felder, R. M., "Creativity in Engineering Education," *Chemical Engineering Education*, 22, p. 3, 1988.
2. De Bono, E., *Lateral Thinking*, Harper & Row, New York, 1970.
3. De Bono, Edward, *Serious Creativity*, Harper Business, a division of HarperCollins Publishers, New York, 1993.
4. Buzan, T., *The Mind Map Book.* Penguin, New York, 1991.
5. Van Gundy, A. B., *Techniques of Structured Problem Solving*, 2nd ed., Van Nostrand Reinhold, New York, 1988.
6. Reid, R. C., "Creativity?", *Chemtech*, 17, p. 14, January 1987.
7. Altshuller, G. S., and R. V. Shapiro, "About a Technology of Creativity," *Questions of Psychology*, 6, pp. 37–49, 1956.
8. Domb, Ellen, "Think TRIZ for Creative Problem Solving," *Quality Digest,* 2003, http://www.qualitydigest.com/aug05/articles/03_article.shtml.
9. http://triz.org, Technical Innovation Center, *40 Principles Extended Edition.* ISBN: 08640740-5-2.
10. Mazur, Glenn H., Executive Director of QFD Institute, Ann Arbor, MI, www.mazur.net.
11. http://www.triz-journal.com/archives/1998/11/d/default.asp

EXERCISES

6.1. List the five most important things you learned from this chapter. Also list the five most interersting things.

6.2. Keep a journal of all the good ideas you generate.

6.3. A. Make a list of the worst business ideas you can think of (e.g., a maternity shop in a retirement village, a solar-powered night-light, reversible diapers).

B. Take the list you generated in part (a) and turn it around to make them viable concepts for entrepreneurial ventures (e.g., reversible diapers—blue on one side and pink on the other).

6.4. Apply Goman's four steps (Chapter 5) for generating solutions to solving problems by analogy for a problem you have.

A. State the problem: _____

B. Create analogies: This situation is like _____

C. Solve the analogy: _____

D. Transfer the solution: _____

6.5. Rent a video. Watch half of the movie with a friend(s). Stop the movie. Have each of you "create" your own ending. Watch the rest of the movie and discuss the results. Whose ending was better? Why?

6.6. Write a paragraph discussing how you can improve your ability to generate ideas. Compare and contrast the various idea generation techniques. Is there a common thread that runs through all of these techniques? Identify situations in which each technique might best apply.

6.7. Suggest 50 ways to increase spectator participation at (a) professional basketball games. [Examples: Have a drawing at each game in which the people in the randomly selected seats get to play for 2 minutes. Give the fans one arrow each to shoot at the basketball in midair to try to block the shot.] Now suggest 25 ways for spectator participation in (b) football, (c) baseball, and (d) hockey.

6.8. You are a passenger in a car that lacks a speedometer. Describe 25 ways to determine the speed of the car.

6.9. An epidemic on a chicken farm created 1000 tons of dead chickens. The local landfill would not accept the dead chickens for disposal. It is also against the law to bury the chickens. The local authorities are insisting that the matter be dealt with immediately. Suggest ways to solve the farmer's problems. (Problem adapted from *Chemtech*, 22, 3, p. 192, 1992.)

6.10. A reforestation effort in Canada is running into trouble in a particular region. In one nursery alone, 10 million seedlings were eaten by voles. The voles even consumed the varieties chosen for the unpalatable phenol/condensed tannin secondary metabolite they contain. The voles overcame this unpalatability by cutting the branches, stripping the bark, and then leaving the branches for a few days before eating them. This process caused the unpleasant components to decline to acceptable levels. Suggest 15 ways to solve the reforestation problem in this nursery. (Problem adapted from *Chemtech,* 21, p. 324, 1991.)

6.11. Kite flying is a growing hobby around the world. (Kites are very entertaining—it is not unusual to find kites that fly at altitudes of more than 2000 feet.) Suggest 25 ways that kites can be used for purposes other than entertainment.

6.12. The use of a steam cycle is a popular means of generating electricity for industrial and domestic use. Unfortunately, the current theoretical maximum efficiency of a steam plant is approximately 40% and the effects on the environment of emissions from these plants are of growing concern. How do you envision energy being produced and consumed in the future?

6.13. Choose two people from different professions (e.g., repair person, florist, dentist, accountant, police officer, hockey coach, car designer, custodian, bellhop, cruise ship activity director, Cub Scout leader) and make lists similar to the ones below suggesting what these individuals could learn from each other that would enrich each other's lives. (Problem courtesy of Matt Latham and Susan Stagg Williams.)

Pastor Gives to a Maitre d'

A. Ideas to rapidly assess people's needs

B. Suggestions on how not to take every problem she hears personally (thick-skinned)

C. The importance of a well-groomed physical appearance

D. Suggestions on how far you can push people (in terms of views and ideals)

E. Ideas on offering suggestions and advice

F. Ideas on how to be more self-reliant (scheduling)

Maitre d' Gives to a Pastor

A. Knowledge to calm upset individuals or perform crowd control

B. Understanding and dealing with people; approachability

C. Memory techniques to remember frequent customers

D. An appreciation of having a boss and someone watching what you do

E. Ideas on how to learn to be happy with your job and yourself

6.14. Read the article by J. M. Prausnitz (Professor at the University of California–Berkeley) entitled "Toward Encouraging Creativity in Students" in *Chemical Engineering Education* (Winter 1985, p. 22).

A. Discuss the ideas presented on problem recognition.

B. How are creativity and synthesis defined?

C. Discuss two examples used to illustrate "the tying together of two separate ideas."

    D. What does the article suggest about creativity and the cross-fertilization of ideas from one area to a completely different area?

    E. What is the single most important point the author is making about problem solving?

6.15. Make a list of several ways you can improve your creative abilities. Describe how you would implement some techniques from the table on page 98.

6.16. Carry out a futuring exercise to visualize the following items:

    A. A telephone call in the year 2020

    B. Eating a meal with your family in the year 2050

    C. A homework assignment in the year 2025

    D. A homework assignment in the year 2125

6.17. Describe the most creative television advertisement you have seen (Super Bowl commercials are a good source), and explain why it was so creative.

6.18. Use the TRIZ method to generate possible solutions for these problems:

    A. Wireless Internet access should be readily available to students on campus, yet secure enough to protect personal information.

    B. The email spam filter should be efficient enough to remove all of your junk emails (good), but then it is more likely to screen some emails that you actually want (bad).

    C. Increase the level of services provided by the U.S. Postal Service without increasing the cost.

    D. Figure out a way for me to lose 10 pounds, without having to be hungry all the time.

6.19. Carry out a TRIZ analysis for the following problems:

    A. Automobiles should be strong and sturdy enough to provide adequate crash protection, yet light enough to allow for good gas mileage.

    B. Bulletproof vests should be strong (good), yet not too bulky and uncomfortable to wear (bad).

    C. Increased hard disk space allows for more file storage (good), but creates difficulty in locating the correct file because the disk is so large (bad).

    D. Automobile air bags deploy quickly to protect the passenger (good), but the more rapidly they deploy, the more likely they are to injure or kill small or out-of-position people (bad).

    E. Cell phone networks should have excellent coverage so that users have strong signals (good), but cell phone towers are not very nice to look at (bad).

FURTHER READING

Adams, James L. *Conceptual Blockbusting: A Guide to Better Ideas*, 3rd ed. Addison-Wesley, Stanford, CA, 1986.

Mihalko, Michael. *Cracking Creativity: The Secrets of Creative Genius*. Ten Speed Press, Berkeley, CA, 2001.

———. *Thinkertoys*, 2nd ed. Ten Speed Press, Berkeley, CA, 2006.

Von Oech, Roger. *A Whack on the Side of the Head: How You Can Be More Creative*, revised edition. Warner Books, New York, 1990.

7   DECIDING THE COURSE OF ACTION

> In a moment of decision, the best thing you can do is the right thing to do. The worst thing you can do is nothing.
>
> —Theodore Roosevelt

Once the real problems have been defined and some potential solutions have been generated, it is time to apply the third step in our heuristic: decide. Specifically, we must do the following:

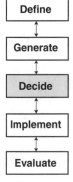

- Decide which problem to address first and which actions we need to take to address this problem.
- Select the best solution from our possible alternatives.
- Decide how to avoid additional problems as we implement our chosen solution.

An organized process for making these essential decisions is the Kepner–Tregoe (K.T.) approach, which is described in *The New Rational Manager* and depicted in the diagram.[1,2]

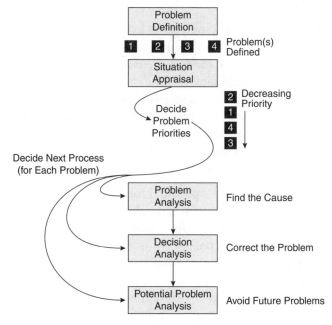

Components of the Kepner–Tregoe Approach

K.T. SITUATION APPRAISAL

After we define the problems, we move through the K.T. approach by starting with K.T. situation appraisal, which helps us when we are faced with multiple problems at the same time. During situation appraisal, we do two things:

- We analyze the problems that we are facing to determine their importance and set their priority (based on several criteria that we will describe).
- We classify each problem based on the type of action that will be required for its solution.

Deciding the Priority

In many situations, a number of problems may arise at the same time. In some cases, these problems are interconnected; in other cases, they are totally unrelated, and it is "just one of those days." When these situations occur, **K.T. situation appraisal** can prove useful in deciding which problem should receive the highest priority.

With this technique, we first make a list of all of the problems and then try to decide which problem in this group should receive our initial attention. Each problem is measured against the following criteria: timing, trend, and impact. These criteria are rated as warranting either a high degree of concern (H), a moderate degree of concern (M), or a low degree of concern (L).

Evaluation Criteria

Timing. How urgent is the problem? Is a deadline involved? What will happen if nothing is done for a while? For example, suppose you are the manager of a bakery and one of the five ovens in a bakery is malfunctioning, but the other four ovens could pick up the extra load. It may be possible to wait to solve this problem and instead address more urgent problems, so we would give the problem an L rating (low degree of concern). If the other four ovens are operating at maximum capacity and a major order must be filled by the evening, however, the rating assigned to the problem for timing would be H (high degree of concern) because the problem must be solved now.

Trend. What is the problem's potential for growth? In the bakery example, suppose the malfunctioning oven is overheating—it's getting hotter and hotter—and cannot be turned off. Consequently, the trend is getting worse, and you have a high degree of concern (H rating) about a fire starting. You also could have a high degree of concern if you are getting increasingly further behind on your customers' orders. If the oven is off and you can keep up with the orders with the four correctly functioning ovens, then the trend would be rated as generating a low degree of concern (L).

Impact. How serious is the problem? What are the effects on the people, the product, the organization, and its policies? In the bakery example, suppose you cannot get the oven repaired in time to fill the order of a major client. If you could subsequently lose the client's business as a result of this failure, then the impact warrants a high degree of concern (H). If you can find a way to fill all the orders for the next few days, then the impact of one malfunctioning oven would generate a moderate degree of concern (M).

Deciding Which Action to Take

In the second part of the K.T. situation appraisal, we ask the following questions to determine which action we should take:

- Do we need to learn the cause of the problem? This question would prompt us to use problem analysis (PA). In the PA technique, the cause of the problem or the fault is unknown and we have to find it. What happened in the *past* that is causing the trouble *now?* This algorithm for finding the root cause was discussed in Chapter 4.

Once the problem is known, we need to make a decision of what to do about the problem so we move to decision analysis.

- Do we need to make a decision among possible alternatives? For this question, we would use decision analysis (DA). In the DA technique, the cause of the problem has been found and now we need to decide what to do about it. The decision at the present time is how to correct the problem.

Once the decision is made, we move to potential problem analysis, where we take steps to ensure the success of our decision.

- Do we need to analyze the potential problems that might arise from our solution alternatives, and make some contingency plans to ensure the success of our solution? To address this issue, we would use potential problem analysis (PPA). In the PPA technique, we want to ensure the success of our decision and anticipate and prevent problems from occurring in the future.

We now consider two other examples and solutions to help illustrate the K.T. approach to prioritizing problems.

K.T. Situation Appraisal:
You Know It's a Really Bad Day When . . .

First let's consider the problem of the man pictured below. Here we see a dog hanging on to the homeowner's leg as he clings to the briefcase containing very important papers while his house burns. His car is not working and it appears that in the distance a tornado is approaching.

We see that we have five problems to address in filling out our situation appraisal table:

Problem	Timing (H, M, L)	Trend (H, M, L)	Impact (H, M, L)	Next Process (PA, DA, PPA)
1. Get dog off leg				
2. Repair car				
3. Put out fire				
4. Protect papers in briefcase				
5. Prepare for touchdown of tornado				

Let's discuss each problem and evaluate the criteria for each.

1. It is necessary to get the dog off your leg now (high priority). The trend is getting worse because wounds from the bite are becoming more serious (high priority); the impact is that you can do nothing else until the dog is off your leg (high priority). The process is to decide how to get the dog off your leg (DA).

2. Repairing the car can wait (low priority), as this problem is not getting worse (low priority). If the car is not repaired soon, however, it could have an impact on your job—you would not be able to visit clients (moderate priority). The problem is to find out what is wrong with the car (PA).

3. Putting out the fire receives high priority in all three categories. The problem is to decide (DA) how to do it: Get the hose or fire extinguisher; call the fire department; and/or make sure everyone is out of the house.

4. If you rush off to handle the other projects in this list, you need to make sure your work of the last few months, which includes signed documents in your briefcase, is protected. This PPA process entails making sure your signed papers (which your clients now wish they had not signed) are in a safe place.

5. While the tornado looks somewhat close in the picture, it may simply indicate that a tornado is in the area, and thus may be just a tornado warning. This hazard might merit use of the DA/PPA processes.

Problem	Timing (H, M, L)	Trend (H, M, L)	Impact (H, M,L)	Next Process (PA, DA, PPA)
1. Get dog off leg	H	H	H	DA
2. Repair car	L	L	M	PA
3. Put out fire	H	H	H	DA
4. Protect papers in briefcase	M	M	H	PPA
5. Prepare for touchdown of tornado	M	H	H	DA/PPA

We have two problems that have high (H) ratings in all categories; now we must decide which one to tackle first. To do so, we perform a pairwise comparison of these two problems in each category. In the timing category, the man cannot really move to put out the fire or call the fire department because of the dog; hence the dog removal project gets the vote in the timing category. In terms of impact, the dog's teeth are sinking deeper and deeper into the leg and the pain is such that the man cannot really think about anything else; hence the dog gets the top vote in this category as well. The dog also gets top vote in the impact category because the man cannot move to do anything else. Clearly, the first task is to decide how to get the dog off the man's leg.

K.T. Situation Appraisal: First Day on the Job—Trial by Fire

Sara Brown has just become manager of Brennan's Office Supply Store. The Brennan Company owns 10 such stores in the Midwest. Sara's store, which is located in the downtown area on a busy street, has an inventory of more than $1 million and more than 20,000 square feet of floor space.

On her first day of work, Sara is inundated with problems. A very expensive, custom-ordered desk that was delivered last week suffered a number of scratches while it was being unpacked, and the stockroom manager wants to know what he should do. Sara has just discovered that the store has not yet paid the utility bills that were due at the end of last month, and she realizes that the store has been habitually late in paying its bills. The accounts receivable department tells her that it has had an abnormally high number of delinquent accounts over the past few months, and the accounting personnel want to know which action they should take. A large stack of boxes in the storeroom that were delivered last week have yet to be opened and inventoried. The impression Sara has been getting all morning from the 30 employees is that they are all unhappy and dislike working at Brennan's.

To top things off, shortly after lunch, a large delivery truck pulls up to the front of the store and double-parks, blocking traffic. The driver comes into the store and announces that he has a shipment of 20 new executive desks. Where does Sara want them placed? The employees tell Sara that this shipment was not due until next week and there isn't any place to put them right now. Outside the store, Sara can hear the horns of the angry drivers as the traffic jam grows.

What should Sara do?

Problem	Subproblem	Timing (H, M, L)	Trend (H, M, L)	Impact (H, M,L)	Next Process (PA, DA, PPA)
1. Space	Unopened boxes	L	L	L	DA
2. 20 new desks	Traffic jam	H	H	H	DA
3. Personnel	Employee morale	M	M	H	PA
4. Finances	Money owed	M	M	H	DA
	Money due	M	M	M	PA
5. Quality	Scratched desk	L	L	M	DA/PPA

1. While boxes on the floor may be an eyesore and awkward to step around, Sara does not have to do anything about them immediately (timing = L). The situation will not get worse as the result of their presence (trend = L), and the impact of not having the boxes opened and their contents on the shelves is low. The process to address this subproblem is decision analysis (DA): Sara has to decide who is to open the boxes and when to do it.

2. What to do about the 20 new desks has to be decided (DA) immediately (timing = H). The implications of not accepting or accepting and storing such a large order also produce a high degree of concern (impact = H). Finally, a traffic jam is beginning to form and is getting worse while Sara is deciding what to do (trend = H).

3. The employee morale issue needs to be addressed in the very near future, albeit not immediately (timing = M). It is believed that lack of care and sloppiness were factors in damaging the custom-ordered desk, so its impact is the source of a high degree of concern (impact = H). The morale, while low, could get worse; therefore the trend is cause for a moderate (M) degree of concern. Sara doesn't know why the morale is low, so she needs to carry out a problem analysis (PA) to learn more about the problem.

4. Sara needs to pay the utility bills fairly soon (timing = M) or the electrical power to the store could be shut off; that possibility is reason for a high degree of concern (impact = H). Sara needs to find out why the money due the store has not been paid (PA).

5. Nothing needs to be done with the scratched desk immediately, but Sara does need to decide what to do in the not too distant future (DA). She also needs to plan how to unpack the desks and other items more carefully (PPA).

Comparing the ratings, we see the first thing that Sara needs to do: make a decision about whether to find space for the desks in the store or send them to the company warehouse.

K.T. PROBLEM ANALYSIS

After completing the situation appraisal, we will either begin working on the problem to be solved (PA), making a decision (DA), or deciding how to ensure the success of the alternative we have chosen (PPA). We discussed the strategy of **K.T. problem analysis** in Chapter 4. In problem analysis, we investigate the four

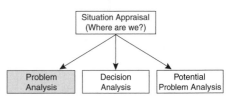

dimensions of the problem: *what, where, when,* and *extent.* We also need to list *what is* and *what is not* the problem, and draw a distinction between the two.

K.T. DECISION ANALYSIS

In this section, we will discuss how to choose the best solution from a number of alternative solutions that have been formulated to solve the problem. **K.T. decision**

analysis is a logical algorithm for choosing between different alternative solutions to find the one that best fulfills all the objectives.

1. Write a concise **decision statement** about what it is you want to decide and then use the first four steps discussed in Chapter 3 to gather information. Identify what you are trying to accomplish and which resources are available.

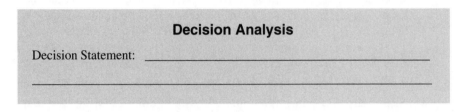

2. List all the objectives to be achieved by the decision, and then divide these objectives into two categories: **musts** and **wants.** The musts are mandatory to achieve a successful solution; they have to be measurable and realistic. The wants are desirable but not mandatory.

	MUSTS	
1.		
2.		
3.		
	WANTS	
1.		
2.		
3.		

3. Develop a list of alternatives or options (A, B, C) from which to choose.

Alternative Solution:	A	B	C

4. Evaluate each alternative solution against each of the musts. If the alternative solution satisfies all the musts, it is a "go" and you should continue to evaluate that alternative; if it does not satisfy any one of the musts, it is a "no go" and should not be considered further. In the following example, Alternative B did not satisfy Must 2. Consequently, there is no need to consider this alternative further and you do not need to evaluate the wants for Alternative B.

Decision Analysis

Decision Statement: _____

_____

Alternative Solution		A		B		C	
Musts	1. 2.	Go Go		Go No Go		Go Go	
Wants	Weight	Rating	Score	Rating	Score	Rating	Score
1. 2.					No Go		
		Total A =		Total B =		Total C =	

5. Examine the list of the objectives you want to satisfy. The wants are desirable but not mandatory; they give you a comparative picture of how the alternatives perform relative to each other. Make a list of all the characteristics that the ideal solution should have and then rank-order them, putting the most important want first and the least important want last. Next, assign a *weight* (ranging from 1 to 10) to each want to indicate how important that characteristic (or want) is. Assigning weights is a subjective task. If a want is extremely important, you should give it a high weight (9 or 10). If it is only moderately important, you should assign it a lower weight (6 or 7).

Decision Analysis

Decision Statement: _____

_____

Alternative Solution		A		C	
Musts	1. 2.	Go Go		Go Go	
Wants	Weight	Rating	Score	Rating	Score
1. 2.	8 7				
		Total A =		Total C =	

6. Evaluate each alternative against the wants and give it a *rating* (ranging from 0 to 10) as to how well it satisfies the want. If the alternative fulfills all possible aspects of a want, it would receive a rating of 10. If it only partially fulfills that want, it might receive a rating of 4 or 5.

7. Multiply the weight of the want by its rating to arrive at a *score* for the want for that alternative. For Want 1 in the preceding table, the weight is 8 (it is a fairly important want) and Alternative A does not do a very good job of filling this want. Thus it is given a rating of 3. The score for Alternative A for Want 1 is $8 \times 3 = 24$. Perform a similar evaluation for every want and then add up the scores for each alternative. The alternative with the highest total score is your tentative first choice.

While identifying weights and calculating scores may at first seem somewhat subjective, it is an extremely effective technique for people who can dissociate themselves from their personal biases and seek to arrive at a logical evaluation of each alternative. If the alternative you "feel" should be the proper choice turns out to have a lower score than your tentative first choice, then you should reexamine the weight you have assigned to each want. Analyze your instincts to better understand which wants are really important to you. After rescoring the options, if your favorite alternative still scores lower than the others, perhaps your "gut feeling" is incorrect.

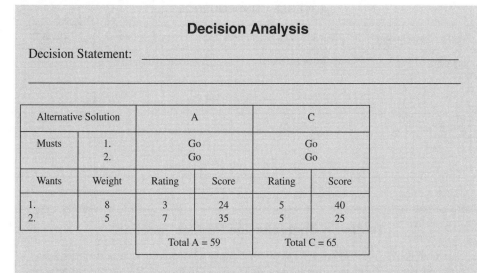

Decision Analysis

Decision Statement: _____

_____

Alternative Solution		A		C	
Musts	1. 2.	Go Go		Go Go	
Wants	Weight	Rating	Score	Rating	Score
1.	8	3	24	5	40
2.	5	7	35	5	25
		Total A = 59		Total C = 65	

Our tentative solution to this unknown problem is Alternative C. Before making this solution our final choice, however, we should carry out an Adverse Consequences Analysis.

ADVERSE CONSEQUENCES OF THE ALTERNATIVE SOLUTIONS

The last step in the decision-making process is to explore the risks associated with each alternative solution. In this phase, we take the top-scoring potential solutions and make a list of all the things that could possibly go wrong if we were to choose each alternative. We then try to evaluate the *probability* (0–10) that the adverse consequence will occur and the *seriousness* (0–10) of the consequence if it were to occur. The product of these two numbers can be thought of as the **threat** to the success of the mission.

It is important not to let the numerical scores in the decision analysis table obscure the seriousness of an adverse consequence. In some cases, the second highest scoring alternative might be selected simply because the potential adverse consequences of selecting the highest scoring alternatives are too dire. Alternatively, rather than calculating a numerical score for the threat level, we could use the same evaluation system that we used in situation analysis: low degree of concern (L), moderate degree of concern (M), or high degree of concern (H).

ADVERSE CONSEQUENCES

Adverse Consequences	A. Probability of Occurrence	B. Seriousness If It Occurs	Threat
Alternative A 1. 2. 3.	(0–10) or (L, M, H)	(0–10) or (L, M, H)	A × B
Alternative C 1. 2. 3.			

Decision Analysis: The Perfect Vacation

Lara and Tom Anderson are a 23-year-old couple who want to take a summer vacation and escape from their hectic schedules. The Andersons live in the suburbs of Chicago and commute 45 minutes each way on crowded trains to downtown Chicago. They are eager to get away from the hustle and bustle and experience a change of scenery. They have set aside $2000 for the vacation, which is the maximum amount they can spend. Both love learning new things, seeing interesting sites, and eating good food, though Tom is currently on a diet. Tom likes to do outdoor sporting activities, whereas Lara likes to visit art museums and is happy to just sit outside and read. The main goal for both is to come back refreshed. The Andersons have brainstormed and identified three vacation possibilities.

Lara tells Tom about three museums she would like to visit in New York. While the airfare is cheap, the New York hotels are expensive; thus the couple would have to get a hotel outside the city and commute to stay within their budget.

Tom is agreeable to that plan—he enjoys theater and there are certainly excellent restaurants in New York—but also suggests a second alternative. If the couple went to northern Michigan, he could golf, sail, and visit Mackinac Island, which has a lot of rich history, fun restaurants, and hiking trails. Upper Michigan is also home to the Mackinac Bridge, world-class golf courses in Traverse City, and Sleeping Bear Sand Dunes, where the Andersons could hike and travel across the dunes in a dune buggy.

Now Lara shows Tom a brochure about Cancun, Mexico, where the pair could spend a week in the sun sailing and lying on the beach—all for $895 per person (airfare, lodging, and meals are included in the same price). Cancun is not known for its food, and Tom doesn't like spicy cuisine. Lara points out that guided tours of the Mayan ruins can be found only two hours away.

Lara and Tom agree to do a K.T. decision analysis on their options. Their musts are staying within their budget, enjoying new sights, and experiencing no stress. All vacation alternatives will cost less than $2000, so consequently all are a "go" on this criterion. Tom and Lara have never been to any of these locations, so all are a "go" for this must as well. In terms of the third must (no stress), New York is a "no go" because the Andersons would have the same stressful commute each day as they currently have in Chicago and would not come back refreshed.

Tom and Lara narrowed their wants list down to three: nice views and scenery, good food, and learning new things. The views of the clear Gulf of Mexico water and sandy beaches in Cancun are wonderful (rating = 10). The meeting of the Great Lakes (Lake Michigan and Lake Huron) and the Mackinac Bridge is a wonderful sight, as is Mackinac Island. This island doesn't allow cars, so walking, bicycles, and horses are the only modes of transportation (rating = 10).

There are excellent restaurants in northern Michigan, such as Tapawingo, which is listed in the *Zagat Guide* (rating = 8). Tom does not like spicy food, and the restaurants in Cancun—while good—are not at the same level as those found in northern Michigan (rating = 3).

Learning is the couple's most important want. In Cancun, learning about Mayan history would be quite rewarding (rating = 8). In northern Michigan, the Andersons could visit Fort Mackinac (which dates from the Revolutionary War) and Fort Michilimackinac (which dates from the French–Indian War in 1715); both are rich in history (rating = 7).

Decision Statement

Where should we go on vacation to learn new things, see new sights, eat good food, and get away from any stress?

K.T. DECISION ANALYSIS TABLE

	A. Cancun	B. New York	C. Northern Michigan
Musts			
Cost limit	Go	Go	Go
New sights	Go	Go	Go
No stress	Go	No Go	Go
Wants			
Learn 10	× 8 = 80		× 7 = 70
Food 8	× 3 = 24		× 8 = 64
View 5	× 10 = 50		× 7 = 35
	154		169

The best tentative decision is for the Andersons to vacation in northern Michigan. Before Lara and Tom can make this their final choice, however, they must consider the adverse consequences of each solution that is deemed to be a "go."

Adverse Consequences

Lara and Tom now brainstorm the major things that could go wrong if they were to choose either of these solutions and then assess the probability (P: 1–10) that it could go wrong and how serious (S: 1–10) the consequences would be if that event did occur. The threat (T) to the choice of each alternative solution is then the product of these two numbers: $T = P \times S$.

Bad weather could be a factor for both of the Andersons' final choices. The probability of bad weather in northern Michigan this time of year is (2/10). Their vacation would fall during hurricane season in the Gulf Coast and the probability of a hurricane is relatively high, but the storm might not hit Cancun, so they estimate the overall probability of a hurricane hitting Cancun as (4/10). Of course, a hurricane hitting Cancun would have very serious consequences (9/10) if it were to occur. Crowds in northern Michigan could make it difficult for the Andersons to get into restaurants and museums; the probability of this problem occurring is (4/10) and its seriousness is (5/10) if it were to occur. A guide strike in Cancun would prevent the Andersons from visiting the Mayan ruins, but the probability of such an occurrence is low (1/10). If it did occur, a guide strike would be very serious (8/10).

Alternative	Probability (P)	Severity (S)	Threat (P × S)
Northern Michigan			
Bad weather	2	5	10
Crowds	4	5	20
Total			30
Cancun, Mexico			
Bad weather	4	9	36
Guide strike	1	8	8
Total			44

There are insufficient adverse consequences to change the Andersons' initial decision. Their best choice is still a vacation in northern Michigan.

The following case is an industrial example using decision analysis.

Choosing a Paint Gun

A new auto manufacturing plant is to be built, and you have been asked to choose the electrostatic paint spray gun to be used on its assembly line. The industry standard gun is Paint Right. While experience has shown that Paint Right performs adequately, its manufacturer is located in Europe, which means that servicing of the paint gun is slow and difficult. The paint gun must provide a precise flow rate of paint to avoid both excessive waste from high flow rates and longer application times with low flow rates. It must also deliver a uniform size of spray droplets so that the paint is applied evenly and produces a nice finished appearance.

The desirable traits of the gun are durability, ease of service in the event of a malfunction, low cost, and familiarity to the operators. While the European company, Paint Right, currently has the largest market share, the price of its paint spray gun is significantly inflated. Two U.S. companies are eager to enter the market with their products: New Spray and Gun Ho.

Decision Statement

Choose an electrostatic paint spray gun. The paint guns available are manufactured by Paint Right, New Spray, and Gun Ho.

Course of Action

The first step is to break down the important qualities of paint guns, and to decide what you must have and what you want to have. From your experience and discussions with other paint personnel, you determine that you have two musts: (1) adequate control over the paint flow rate and (2) acceptable paint appearance. You have also identified four wants: (1) easy service, (2) low cost, (3) long-term durability, and (4) familiarity to plant personnel.

First, you need to determine whether each of the alternatives satisfy the two musts. Plant records show that Paint Right is able to meet both of these criteria. Next, laboratory experiments are performed with New Spray and Gun Ho to determine whether each will be able to meet both musts. The results show that New Spray meets the standards but Gun Ho cannot control the flow of paint at the level required. As a result, it is eliminated from consideration.

The four wants are then weighted, and ratings are assigned for each gun that satisfies the musts (as carefully as possible). The first want—ease of service—is an important issue and receives a weight of 7. Because the paint gun's parent company, Paint Right, is located in Europe, it is difficult to get rapid service, so the company's rating for this want is 2. Thus the Paint Right gun has a score of $7 \times 2 = 14$ on this want. Durability is of moderate importance and receives a weight of 6. Paint Right's gun is very durable and receives a rating of 8, giving it a score of 48 on this want. The familiarity and low cost wants are of lesser importance, so each option receives a weight of 4. Because the plant personnel are currently using the Paint Right gun, it receives a rating of 9, giving it a score of $4 \times 9 = 36$.

We continue in this manner until the entire decision analysis table is filled out.

Solution

Musts		Paint control		New Spray		Gun Ho	
Adequate flow control		Go		Go		No Go	
Acceptable appearance		Go		Go		Go	
Wants	**Weight**	**Rating**	**Score**	**Rating**	**Score**	**Rating**	**Score**
Easy service	7	2	14	9	63		
Durability	6	8	48	6	36		
Low cost	4	3	12	7	28	**No Go**	
Familiarity	4	9	36	2	8		
Total			**110**		**135**		

After applying an Adverse Consequences Analysis, New Spray's electrostatic spray paint gun was still chosen over Paint Right's model for the new plant.

Decision Analysis Example: Choosing Your First Job

Several years ago, a graduating senior from the University of Michigan used K.T. decision analysis to help him decide which industrial job offer he should accept. John had a number of constraints that needed to be met. Specifically, his fiancée (now his wife) was also graduating in chemical engineering at the same time, and both wanted to remain reasonably close to their hometown in Michigan. In addition, as a part of a dual-career family, John needed a guarantee that the company would not transfer him. After interviewing with a number of companies, he narrowed his choices to three companies: Dow Corning, ChemaCo, and TrueOil.

The first thing John did was to identify the musts that each offer had to satisfy; these criteria are shown in the K.T. decision analysis table. Upon evaluating each company to learn whether it satisfied all the musts, he found that TrueOil did not satisfy the "no transfer" must. Consequently, John eliminated this company from further consideration. Next, he identified the wants and assigned a weight to each criterion. The remaining two companies were then evaluated against each want and a total score was obtained for each company. Dow Corning scored 696 points, and ChemaCo scored 632 points; the apparent best choice was Dow Corning.

K.T. DECISION ANALYSIS: JOB OFFER							
Objectives		**Dow Corning**		**ChemaCo**		**True Oil**	
Musts							
In Midwest		Midland, Michigan	Go	Toledo, Ohio	Go	Detroit, Michigan	Go
Located within 40 miles of spouse's position		Another major company also in Midland	Go	Industrialized Northern Ohio	Go	Major metropolitan area	Go
No-transfer policy		Major plant in Midland	Go	Major plant in Toledo	Go	Must transfer	No Go
Wants	**Weight**		**Rating**	**Score**	**Rating**	**Score**	
Plant safety	10	Good (silicone)	7	70	Mainly oil derivatives (okay)	5	50
Education assistance program	10	Tuition aid	8	80	Tuition aid	8	80
Encourage advanced degree	10	Very positive	9	90	Positive	8	80
Type of position	10	Process engineer	9	90	Pilot plant design and operation	10	100
Salary and benefits	9	Good	6	54	Very good	8	72
Near hometown (Traverse City, Michigan)	8	150 miles	10	80	400 miles	5	40
Advancement policy	7	From within	10	70	From within	10	70
Large company	6	Medium size	6	36	Small size	3	18
Attitude of interviewer	5	Knowledgeable and positive	8	40	Knowledgeable and positive	8	40
Company image	4	Known	5	20	Unknown	3	12
Stability of industry	4	Silicone (very good)	9	36	Oil (excellent)	10	40
Return on stockholder's investment	3	Excellent (#2 in nation)	10	30	Excellent (#4 in nation)	10	30
Total				696		632	No Go

Before making the final decision, John needed to evaluate the adverse consequences of his first and second choices. The results of these adverse consequence analysis are shown in the following table. The adverse consequences analysis ranked both choices in the same order as before; as a result of this analysis, the apparent first choice was confirmed as the final choice.

ADVERSE CONSEQUENCES ANALYSIS: JOB OFFER

Alternative	Probability (P)	Severity (S)	Threat (P × S)
Dow Corning			
Midland is not very exciting	6	3	18
High rent	4	6	24
Total			**42**
ChemaCo			
Toledo is not very exciting	6	8	48
High rent	5	6	30
Total			**78**

Both John and his wife are working at Dow Corning in Midland, Michigan. (Only the names of the other companies have been changed in this real-life example.)

Cautions

The assigning of weights and scores is, indeed, very subjective. We could easily abuse this decision-making process by giving higher weights—and thus higher scores—to a predetermined favorite project. Such a biased weighting would skew the numbers and sabotage the decision-making process. You are urged to refer to Kepner and Tregoe's book,[1,2] which highlights the danger signals that guarantee acceptance of a certain alternative and that blackball all other choices. This bias could result from the construction of "loaded" want objectives, the inclusion of too many unimportant details that obscure the analysis, or a faulty perception of which objectives can guarantee success. Consequently, it is very important to keep an open mind when making your evaluation.

Missing Information

The most difficult decisions are those where you don't have all the necessary information available upon which to base your decision. Under these conditions, it might prove helpful if, after you have prepared a K.T. decision analysis table, you look at the extremes of the missing information and perform a "What if?" analysis.

As an example, let's revisit the job offer scenario. Suppose that Dow Corning had not yet decided the type of position John would have with the company. John could assume the best case (i.e., his desired position of process engineer), which he would rate at 9; he would assign a low rating of 1 to the worst case (i.e., traveling sales representative on the road full-time). With this assumption, the total score for Dow Corning would drop to 616—lower than the score for ChemaCo. This "want" requires a key piece of information, so John must obtain more information from Dow Corning before he can accept the company's offer. If Dow Corning cannot tell John which type of job he would have, it might at least be able to tell him which type of job he might *not* have (e.g., traveling sales representative). If the company could not provide at least the latter information, John could have been "forced" to choose ChemaCo. Of course, if all other factors are positive, John could still decide to take a risk and choose Dow Corning with the chance he will be able to secure the desired position upon hiring or shortly after being hired.

Is the Decision Ethical?

This question is extremely important, and we will delay our discussion of ethics until Chapter 9, where we present some thoughts that we hope will help you answer this question.

K.T. POTENTIAL PROBLEM ANALYSIS

Having made a decision, quite naturally we want to plan to ensure its success. We need to look into the future to learn what could go wrong and make plans to avoid these pitfalls. To aid us in our planning, Kepner and Tregoe have suggested an algorithm that can be applied not only when we are trying to increase the likelihood that our decision will be a successful one, but also when we are analyzing problems involving safety. The **K.T. potential problem analysis** (PPA) approach can decrease the chance of a disastrous outcome. As with the other K.T. approaches, we construct a table as part of this analysis: The K.T. PPA table delineates the potential problems and suggests possible causes, preventive actions, and contingent actions.

K.T. POTENTIAL PROBLEM ANALYSIS

Potential Problem	Possible Causes	Preventive Action	Contingent Actions
A.	1. 2.		
B.	1. 2.		

In analyzing potential problems, we identify how serious each problem would be if it were to occur and how likely it is to occur. Would the problem prove fatal to the success of the decision (a must), would it hurt the success of the decision (a want), or would it simply be annoying? First, brainstorm (see Chapter 6) to identify the *potential problems*, and list your results in the K.T. PPA table. Be especially alert for potential problems when (1) deadlines are tight; (2) you are trying something new, complex, or unfamiliar; (3) you are trying to assign responsibility; and (4) you are following a critical sequence. Next, brainstorm and list all *possible causes* that could bring about each problem. Now, develop *preventive actions* for each cause. Finally, develop a *contingent action* (last resort) to be undertaken if your preventive action fails to prevent the problem from occurring. Establish early warning signs to trigger the contingency plan. Do not, however, proceed with contingency plans; instead, focus on preventive actions.

As an example of potential problem analysis, we will use a situation that most of us have faced at one time or another: buying a used car. First, we brainstorm the potential problems that could exist with a used car.

> Concealed damage
> Wheels not aligned
> Suspension problems
> Leaking fluids
> Odometer incorrect

Next, we list the possible causes for each potential problem. Let's look at possible causes of concealed damage:

> The car was in a flood.
> The car was in an accident.

Now, we list the preventive actions we could take so that we could determine if the car was in a flood:

> Take a deep whiff inside the car and trunk. Does it smell moldy?
> Look for rust in the spare tire well.

Finally, we list the contingent action we would take if the car was in a flood:

Don't buy the car.

The following table gives the complete K.T. PPA for buying a used car.

K.T. POTENTIAL PROBLEM ANALYSIS: BUYING A USED CAR (NOT A LEMON)

Potential Problem	Possible Causes	Preventive Action	Contingency Plan
1. Concealed damage; body condition is not what it appears to be	Car was in a flood; window/trunk leak	Take a deep whiff inside the car and trunk. Does it smell moldy? Look for rust in the spare tire well.	Don't buy the car.
	Car was in an accident; car rusted out	Use a magnet along the rocker panels, wheel wells, and doors to check for painted plastic to which the magnet won't stick. Look under the insulation in the doors and trunk for signs the car was a different color.	Offer a much lower price.
2. Car has improperly aligned front and back wheels	Car was in an accident	Pour water on dry pavement and drive through it to determine whether the front and rear wheel tracks follow the same path or are several inches off.	Don't buy the car.
3. Car has suspension problems	Hard use; poor maintenance	Check the tire treads for peaks and valleys along the outer edges.	Require that the suspension be fixed before buying the car.
4. Leaking fluids	Poor maintenance	Look under the hood and on the ground for signs of leaking fluids.	Require seals be replaced before buying the car.
5. Odometer not correct	Tampered with; broken	Check the windows and bumpers for decals or signs of removed decals indicating a lot of traveling. Look for excessive wear on the accelerator and brake pedals. Check the title.	Offer a much lower price.
6. Car ready to fall apart	Car not maintained during previous ownership	Check the fluid levels (oil, coolant, transmission, brake). Check whether the battery terminals are covered with sludge. Check for cheap replacement of oil filters, battery, and other parts.	Don't buy the car.

K.T. Potential Problem Analysis:
Marketing and Selling the New Ragin' Cajun Chicken Sandwich

Wes Thompson is the manager of a Burgermeister (not the real name of the chain) restaurant, which specializes in fast-food hamburgers. He has just been notified by the corporation that a new chicken sandwich, called the Ragin' Cajun Chicken, will be introduced into Burgermeister restaurants in two weeks. This information surprised Wes because he had never heard anything about the new sandwich from the company or from advertisements. The memo says that plans for a national advertising campaign have unfortunately been delayed until after the introduction of the sandwich.

According to the memo, next week Wes's restaurant will receive a shipment of 500 Ragin' Cajun Chicken sandwiches. These sandwiches will be shipped frozen and have a shelf life of three months in the freezer. The notification also stresses the importance of proper handling of the uncooked chicken. To prevent cross-contamination by *Salmonella* (the bacteria present in some raw chicken), specially marked tongs will be used solely to handle the uncooked chicken.

Along with the shipment of the chicken, Wes's restaurant will receive a new broiler to be used exclusively for preparation of the new sandwich. It is important that the broiler operate at least at 380 °F to ensure that the chicken will be fully cooked during its five-minute preparation time.

Wes thought that it was very important that the transition run smoothly when Ragin' Cajun Chicken sandwiches were added to the menu in two weeks. To prevent any problems, he carried out a brainstorming session using the techniques discussed in Chapter 6 and identified four potential problems (e.g., bacteria in food) and the corresponding consequences (e.g., illness) that were deemed the most logical outcomes of those problems. Next, Wes and his team brainstormed all causes (e.g., employees don't handle the raw chicken properly) that could produce each of the potential problems. Unfortunately, many causes could produce each potential problem (e.g., chicken stored too long). For each cause, Wes's team listed a preventive action (e.g., train the employees on proper food handling). Finally, the group identified a contingency action if training the employees to handle the food properly does not work. In this case, the contingency action will be a periodic inspection of the chicken and the chicken-handling procedures.

The complete PPA table is shown here.

MARKETING AND SELLING THE NEW RAGIN' CAJUN CHICKEN SANDWICH

Potential Problem	Consequence	Possible Cause	Preventive Action	Contingent Action
People don't buy sandwich	Restaurant loses money	Customers don't know about sandwich	Make own signs for sandwich	Have cashiers suggets chicken to customers
		Too expensive	Compare unit cost with competition	Run promotional specials
		Food too spicy	Inform customers of mild variety	Run promotional specials
Bacteria in food	Illness, lawsuits	Employees don't handle raw chicken properly	Train employees	Perform periodic inspections
		Improper use of broiler	Train employees	Perform periodic inspections
		Chicken stored too long	Set up dating system	Inspect and discard chicken if necessary
		Freezer not cold enough	Perform temperature checks	Inspect and discard chicken if necessary
Substandard sandwich quality	Customers complain; no return business	Wrong items on sandwich	Have cashiers double-check accuracy	Provide free remade sandwiches for affected customers
		Sandwich sits too long under heat lamps	Mark discard time on sandwich	Inspect sandwiches before serving
Substandard service time	Customers complain; no return business	Sandwich preparation takes too long	Always have chicken precooked	Have sandwiches pre-made

Of the 10 possible causes of potential problems noted in the table, four actually occurred. Wes noticed the following problems:

- Most customers were unaware of the new menu item. Wes made signs announcing the new sandwich and asked his cashiers to suggest the chicken sandwich (i.e., "Would you care to try our new Ragin' Cajun Chicken today?"). Sales of the sandwich increased dramatically because of this in-store promotion.
- Wes held a special training session for all employees to explain how critical the proper handling and preparation of the chicken was. Afterward, Wes also performed periodic inspections and noticed that employees weren't following his instructions (e.g., use special tongs and wash your hands after handling raw chicken). After a week of inspections, all employees were following the new operating procedures. Fortunately, no cases of food poisoning were reported.

- At the training session, Wes also explained the procedure for operating the broiler. Once the Ragin' Cajun Chicken was placed on the menu, Wes observed how employees operated the new broiler. Thanks to his observation, an explosion that might have been caused by improper lighting of the broiler was avoided.
- Early on, customers made several complaints about improperly made sandwiches. This problem was solved by having cashiers double-check the accuracy of the order before serving the sandwich. This double-checking helped improve the communication between cashiers and cooks, and higher accuracy in preparation was noticed for all sandwiches.

Because Wes already had a strategy in place for handling these issues, possible disaster was averted.

Source: Developed in collaboration with Michael Szachta, University of Michigan, 1993.

SUMMARY

Once the real problems have been defined and some potential solutions have been generated, we must do the following:

- Decide which problem to address first and which actions we need to take to address this problem.
- Select the best solution from our possible alternatives.
- Decide how to avoid additional problems as we implement our chosen solution.

An organized process for making these decisions is the Kepner–Tregoe (K.T.) approach. One of the unique features of each of the K.T. strategies is the way they are able to display the data. In each case (situation appraisal, problem analysis, decision analysis, potential problem analysis), you fill out a table and then analyze the data in that table to reach a decision.

SITUATION APPRAISAL

Problems	Timing (H, M, L)	Trend (H, M, L)	Impact (H, M,L)	Next Process (PA, DA, PPA)
1. 2. 3.				

PROBLEM ANALYSIS

	Is	Is Not	Distinction	Probable Cause
What				
Where				
When				
Extent				

DECISION ANALYSIS

Alternative Solution		A		B		C	
Musts	1. 2.	Go Go		Go No Go		Go Go	
Wants	Weight	Rating	Score	Rating	Score	Rating	Score
1. 2.					No Go		
		Total A =		Total B =		Total C =	

POTENTIAL PROBLEM ANALYSIS

Potential Problems	Possible Causes	Preventive Actions	Contingent Plan
A.	1. 2.		
B.	1. 2.		

REFERENCES

1. Kepner, C. H., and B. B. Tregoe, *The Rational Manager,* Kepner–Tregoe, Princeton, NJ, 1976.
2. Kepner, C. H., and B. B. Tregoe, *The New Rational Manager,* 2nd ed., Princeton Research Press, Princeton, NJ, 1981.

EXERCISES

Situation Appraisal

7.1. It is 12:45 A.M. on March 24, 1989. You have just been alerted that the *Exxon Valdez* tanker has run aground on the Bligh Reef and is spilling oil at an enormous rate. By the time you arrive at the spill, 6 million gallons of oil have been lost and the oil slick extends over an area of more than 1 square mile.

A meeting with the emergency response team is called. At the meeting, someone suggests that a second tanker be dispatched to remove the remaining oil from the *Exxon Valdez.* Unfortunately, the number of damaged compartments from which oil is leaking is not known at this time and there is concern that if the tanker slips off the reef, it could capsize if the oil is removed from only the compartments on the damaged side.

Someone else suggests using chemical dispersants (i.e., soap-like substances), which would break up the oil into drops and cause it to sink. However, it is not known if sufficient chemical is available to cover a spill of this magnitude. A marine biologist at the meeting also objects to the use of dispersants, stating that once these chemicals are in the water, they would be taken up by the fish and thus be extremely detrimental to the fishing industry.

The use of floatable booms to surround and contain the oil also inspires a heated discussion. Because of the size of the spill, there is not enough boom material even to begin to surround the slick. The Alaskan governor's office says the available material should be used to surround the shore of a small village on a nearby island. The Coast Guard argues that the slick is not moving in that direction, insisting that the boom material should be used to contain or channel the slick movement in the fjord. The Department of Wildlife says the first priority is the four fisheries, which must be protected by the boom or else the fishing industry will be depressed for years—or perhaps even generations—to come. A related issue is that millions of fish were scheduled to be released from the fisheries into the oil-contaminated fjord two weeks from now. Other suggestions as to where to place the boom material were also put forth at the meeting.

Carry out a K.T. situation appraisal for the *Exxon Valdez* spill.

7.2. The four members of the Adams family live east of Los Angeles in a middle-class community. Tom Adams commutes to work in downtown Los Angeles; his commute is 45 miles each way, and he is not in a car or van pool. Tom has been thinking about looking for a job closer to his home. However, he has been working for more than a year on a project that, if successfully completed, could lead to a major promotion at his current company. Unfortunately, there is a major defect in the product; this error has yet to be located and corrected. Tom must solve the problem in the very near future because the delivery date promised to potential customers is a month away.

Tom's financial security is heavily dependent on this promotion because of rising costs at home. Both of the Adams children need braces for their teeth, Tom needs a new car (it broke down twice on the freeway this past fall), the house is in need of painting, and there is a water leak in the basement that he has not been able to repair.

Sarah, Tom's wife, is a mechanical engineer. She has been considering getting a part-time job, but there are no engineering jobs available in the community. Full-time positions are available in northern Los Angeles, but accepting one would pose major problems with respect to chauffeuring and managing the children. There are a few day-care centers in the community, but rumor has it they are very substandard. In addition, last year the Adams's son Alex was accepted as a new student by the premier piano teacher in the area and there is no public transportation from their home to his studio. Melissa, the Adams's daughter, is very sad at the thought of giving up her YMCA swimming team and her Girl Scout troop, both of which meet after school.

Carry out a K. T. situation appraisal for the Adams family's predicament.

7.3. Use the techniques in Chapter 6 to make up a situation similar to those presented in Exercises 1 and 2 and carry out a K.T. situation appraisal for it.

Decision Analysis

7.4. You have decided you can spend up to $16,000 to buy a new car. Prepare a K.T. decision analysis table to decide which car to buy. Use your local newspaper to collect information about the various models, pricing, and options and then decide on your *musts* (e.g., air bag) and your *wants* (e.g., quadraphonic stereo, CD player). How would your decision be affected if you could spend only $10,000? What about $25,000?

7.5. You need one more three-hour nontechnical course to fulfill your degree requirements. Upon reviewing the course offerings, and the time you have available, you note the following options:

Music 101:	Music Appreciation (2 hours)
Art 101:	Art Appreciation (3 hours)
History 201:	U.S. History—Civil War to Present (3 hours)
Art 203:	Photography (3 hours)
Geology 101:	Introductory to Geology (3 hours)
Music 205:	Piano Performance (2 hours)

Music 101 requires that students spend a significant amount of time outside of class listening to classical music. The student reaction to the class has been mixed: Some students learned what to listen for in a symphony; others did not. The teacher for this class is knowledgeable but boring.

Art 101 has the students memorize the names of the great masters and learn how to recognize their works. The lecturer is extremely boring, and you must go to class to see the slides of the great art works. While the course write-up looks good, it misses the mark in developing a real appreciation of art. Nevertheless, it is quite easy to get a relatively good course grade.

History 201 features an outstanding lecturer who makes history come alive. The instructor is a hard grader, however—C is certainly the median grade in this course. In addition, the outside reading and homework loads are enormous. While some students say the workload is equivalent to a five-hour course, most report that they learned a great deal from the course and plan to continue the interest in history they developed during this course.

Art 203 teaches the fundamentals of photography. Unfortunately, the equipment and film required for this course are quite expensive. Most of the time spent on the course occurs outside of class, while students are looking for artistic shots. The instructor is very demanding and bases his grade on artistic ability. Some students say that no matter how hard you work, if you don't develop a "photographic eye" you might not pass the course.

Geology 101 has a moderately interesting lecturer and a normal level of homework assignments. Its two major out-of-town field trips will require you to miss a total of one week of class during the term. The average grade is B, but there is nothing conceptually difficult or memorable about the course.

Music 205 requires that you pass a tryout to be admitted to the class. While you will spend only one-half hour each week with your professor, many, many hours of practice are required. You must have significant talent to get a C or better.

Prepare a K.T. decision analysis table to decide which course to enroll in.

7.6. Centralia, Pennsylvania, a small community situated in the Appalachian mountain range, was once a prosperous coal-mining town. In 1962, in preparation for the approaching Memorial Day parade, the town's landfill was deliberately set on fire in an attempt to eliminate odors, paper buildup, and rats. Unfortunately, the fire burned down into the passageways of the abandoned mine shafts under the town. Although repeated efforts were made to stop the blaze, the fire could not be extinguished. By 1980, after burning for 18 years, the fire had grown in size to nearly 200 acres, with no end in sight.

Mine fires are especially difficult for firefighters because they are located far below the surface of the earth, burn very hot (between 400 °F and 1000 °F), and give off toxic and explosive gases as well as large volumes of steam when the heat reaches the water table. Anthracite coal regions have very porous rock; consequently, a significant amount of combustion gas can diffuse directly up through the ground and into people's homes. Subsidence—that is, shifting of the earth—is another serious condition arising from such a fire. When the coal pillars supporting the ceilings of mines' passageways burn, large sections of earth may suddenly drop 20 or 30 feet into the ground.

Clearly, the Centralia mine fire has very serious surface impact and must be dealt with effectively. Several potential solutions to end the mine fire are described below. Perform a K. T. decision analysis to decide which option is the most effective method to deal with the fire. Consider such issues as cost, relocation of the town of Centralia, and potential success of extinguishing the fire.

Solution Options

A. *Completely excavate the fire site.* Strip-mine the entire site to a depth of 435 feet, digging up all land in the fire's impact zone. This would require partial dismantling of Centralia and nearby Byrnesville for more than 10 years, but available reclamation techniques could restore the countryside after this time. This method guarantees complete extinction at a cost of $200 million. This cost includes both the relocation of families and the restorative process.

B. *Build cut-off trenches.* Dig a trench to a depth of 435 feet, and then fill it with a clay-based noncombustible material. Behind the trench, the fire will be allowed to burn unchecked, but inside the trench it is contained by the barrier. The cost of implementation would be about $15 million per 1000 feet of trench, and total containment of the fire would require approximately 7000 feet of trench. Additionally, partial relocation of Centralia would be required for three years, costing about $5 million.

C. *Flood the mine.* Pump 200 million gallons of water per year into the mine at a cost of $2 million annually for 20 years to extinguish the fire. Relocation of the townspeople will not be necessary, but subsidence and steam output should be considered, as well as the environmental impact and trade-offs of the large quantities of acidic water produced by this technique.

D. *Seal the mine entrances to suffocate the fire.* Encase the entire area in concrete to seal all mine entrances, and then allow the fire to suffocate naturally from a lack of air. This option would require short-term relocation of the towns and outlying areas, and the suffocation itself would probably take a few years owing to the large amount of air in the shafts and in the ground. Although this method has never been attempted, the cost is estimated to be about $100 million.

E. *Use fire-extinguishing agents.* Pump halons (gaseous fluorobromocarbons) into the mine to extinguish the blaze. The cost for this method would be on the order of $100 million. Relocation may be necessary.

F. *Do nothing.* Arrange a federally funded relocation of the entire area and allow the fire to burn unchecked. Approximately $50 million would be required to relocate the town.

(This problem developed by Greg Bennethum, A. Craig Bushman, Stephen George, and Pablo Hendler, University of Michigan.)

7.7. When painting a new automobile, it is essential that the exterior surface be clean before the painting begins. Any impurities present when the paint is applied will severely degrade the quality of the paint finish. Consequently, line operators use solvent-moistened wipes to clean the surface of each vehicle body before it enters the paint booth.

Current body wipe operations at one of the Big Three auto companies in the United States can be summarized as follows: The operator soaks a new, dry body wipe (a white synthetic cloth about 1 foot square) in an open bath of solvent. After wringing out any excess solvent, the operator wipes down the exterior of the vehicle body. The operator then disposes of the wipe in a drum and moistens a new wipe for the next vehicle. Because the wipes in the drum contain significant amounts of solvent (a hazardous and possibly toxic substance), the drum is sealed when it becomes full and is sent to a hazardous waste landfill for disposal.

This cleaning operation must be applied to each vehicle body as it moves along a conveyor belt from the assembly shop into the paint booth. Depending on demand, the production rate may require painting as many as 80 bodies per hour. When defects in the paint job are found, the body must be taken offline for spot repairs or complete repainting. If a large percentage of bodies have paint defects, then production of the entire plant can be reduced as repaint jobs back up at the paint shop.

Upper-level management has decided to open another plant that will also require body wipe operations. Owing to the more stringent environmental regulations for new plants, the emission of solvent during the painting process must be reduced. If possible, management would also like to make other improvements to the current method of cleaning.

What is the best body wipe method to adopt in the new plant? Engineering has proposed four alternative methods:

A. *Use each wipe on more than one vehicle.* This alternative requires less effort by the operators because they do not need to moisten a wipe as often. Less solvent is applied per vehicle. Not only are the additional operational costs of this alternative negligible, but raw material costs, waste solvent, and waste wipes are also significantly decreased. There is a small chance that reusing wipes would leave impurities on the vehicle and cause the paint coat to crater.

B. *Recycle.* This option requires (expensive) additional equipment to wash the wipes and recover solvent. The amount of solvent applied to each vehicle would remain the same, but consumption of virgin raw materials and total solvent emissions would decline moderately. Disposal of waste wipes and solvent would be decreased moderately as well. Unfortunately, the recycled wipes would likely deteriorate and leave lint on the vehicle, thereby causing paint defects.

C. *Incinerate used body wipes.* With this option, the energy value of the spent wipes can be recovered. In addition, the need for disposing of hazardous waste is totally eliminated. It is possible—albeit unlikely—that the ash will need to be sent to a landfill as nonhazardous waste. With incineration, there are no changes in the actual wiping process; the option is completely "end-of-pipe." Therefore solvent emissions will be unaffected. Incineration is moderately expensive.

D. *Use a closed-top bath.* The solvent bath would be covered with a lid that the operator would remove each time he or she soaks a rag. This approach would cut down on evaporative losses and spillage from the bath, although the amount of solvent applied to each vehicle would stay the same. Thus the amount of waste wipes and waste solvent would not decrease.

In deciding upon a method, management determined that three criteria must be met:

1. Solvent emissions must be reduced.
2. The new process must not slow production.
3. Disposal of hazardous waste must be decreased.

When comparing the options that survived the cut after applying these three criteria, management gives only moderate weight to the actual amount of hazardous waste diverted from the landfill. Also, management strongly desires to decrease raw material usage and hopes to minimize operator effort. The degree of workplace safety (an extremely important consideration) is influenced weakly by the amount of solvent stored on site, which in turn is influenced by the amount of solvent applied to each vehicle. The additional operating cost of the new method is also a major consideration. Finally, management wants to weigh the adverse consequences of each option by considering its negative impacts on product quality—a very serious issue.

To decide on a course of action for the company, conduct a K.T. decision analysis.

7.8. You need energy for an upcoming sports competition. You have the following candy bars available: Snickers, Milky Way, Mars Bar, Heath Bar, and Granola Bar. Which do you choose? Prepare a K.T. decision analysis table.

7.9. Prepare a K.T. decision analysis table on selecting an apartment to move into next term (or next year). Consult your local newspaper to learn about the alternatives available.

Potential Problem Analysis

7.10. A minor oil spill has occurred on a small sandy resort beach. The CEO of the company that caused the beach shoreline to become soiled with oil said: "Spare no expense; use the most costly method—steam cleaning—to remove the oil from the sand." Carry out a K.T. potential problem analysis on the direction given by the CEO. (Problem adapted from *Chemtech,* August 1991, p. 481.)

7.11. A procedure in a chemistry laboratory experiment called for students to prepare a 1.0 dm^3 aqueous solution of 30 g of sodium hydroxide. By mistake, one of the students used 30 g of sodium hydride dispersion. This chemical reacted violently with water, evolving heat and hydrogen gas, which then caught fire. The sodium hydride, which was available for a subsequent experiment, was a commercial product. The container bore a warning of the hazard of contact with water, but this warning was not visible from the side showing the name of the compound. Carry out a K.T. potential problem analysis that, if followed, would have prevented this accident. (Problem adapted from *ICE Prevention Bulletin,* December 1991, p. 7.)

7.12. A reactor approximately 6 feet in diameter and 20 feet high in an ammonia plant had to be shut down to repair a malfunctioning nozzle. The nozzle could be repaired only by having a welder climb inside the reactor to carry out the repair. During welding, the oxygen concentration was regularly monitored. Four hours after the welding was completed, a technician entered the reactor to take pictures of the weld. The next day he was found dead in the reactor. Prepare a potential problem analysis that, if followed, could have prevented this accident. (Problem adapted from *ICE Prevention Bulletin,* December 1991, p. 27.)

7.13. Burgermeister has been serving fast-food hamburgers for more than 20 years. To keep pace with the changing times and tastes, Burgermeister has been experimenting with new products in an effort to attract new customers. Product development has recently designed a new Cajun-style chicken sandwich to be called Ragin' Cajun Chicken (see the example on page 166). The developers have spent almost nine months perfecting the recipe for this new product.

One of the developers got the idea for the new product while in New Orleans during last year's Mardi Gras. Product development has suggested that the sandwich be placed on Burgermeister's menu immediately, so as to coincide with this year's Mardi Gras festivities. A majority of the time spent developing the Ragin' Cajun Chicken sandwich was dedicated to producing an acceptable sauce. Every recipe was tasted by the developers, who found early recipes for sauces to be too spicy. Finally, they agreed that the seventy-eighth recipe for the sauce (Formula 78) was the best choice.

After reaching a consensus on the sauce, the development team focused on preparation aspects of the new sandwich. Several tests confirmed that the existing equipment in Burgermeister restaurants could not be used to prepare Ragin' Cajun Chicken. Instead, a new broiler would have to be installed in each of the 11,000 Burgermeister restaurants, at a cost of more than $3000 per unit. The new broiler would keep the chicken moist while cooking it, as well as killing any *Salmonella* (harmful bacteria that are prevalent in chicken).

While testing the cooking techniques for the new broiler, one of the developers became very ill. A trip to the hospital showed that the developer had food poisoning from *Salmonella.* Tests determined that the source of the bacteria was a set of tongs that the developer used to handle both the raw and the cooked chicken.

Next, the development team decided how the sandwich would be prepared. When the Ragin' Cajun Chicken sandwich was prepared using the same buns that are currently used for other Burgermeister sandwiches, the sandwich received a very low taste rating. After much experimentation, researchers determined that a Kaiser roll best complemented the new sandwich. Early cost estimates showed that Kaiser rolls would cost twice as much as the buns used currently for hamburgers, and stay fresh half as long as the hamburger buns.

You are an executive in charge of product development for Burgermeister. Based on the information above, perform a potential problem analysis, considering what could go wrong with the introduction of this new sandwich. (Problem developed in collaboration with Mike Szachta, University of Michigan, 1992.)

7.14. Carry out a potential problem analysis for each of the following situations:

A. A surprise birthday party

B. A camping trip in the mountains

C. The transportation of a giraffe from the Detroit Zoo to the Los Angeles Zoo

D. An upcoming laboratory experiment

E. The transportation of nuclear waste from the reactor to the disposal site

7.15. Orange Manufacturing Corporation has recently learned that important safety changes must be implemented in the operating procedures in its plants in South Africa. These changes must be made as soon as possible. To help things along, the Orange engineering staff has prepared a PowerPoint presentation on how to make the changes. John Thomas, the engineer from the Los Angeles office who identified the problem and developed the solution, has been chosen to fly to Johannesburg to make the presentation on the changes and then to observe that they have been made correctly. Some of the changes are controversial, so John needs to be mentally and physically alert to make the presentation and answer questions.

John has never traveled internationally and is worried about both the trip and the presentation. He is susceptible to leg cramps, gets motion sickness from time to time, and has a little difficulty remembering things when he becomes disoriented. Last month he had an upset stomach and became dehydrated and could not function.

Managers from other South African plants will fly to Johannesburg for John's presentation a week from Monday. John is currently scheduled to arrive the day before the presentation. The travel time between John's home and the Johannesburg office is 24 hours, and there is a 9-hour time difference between California and South Africa. Carry out a potential problem analysis on how John could ensure a successful presentation.

7.16. You are planning to visit a foreign country and you want to leave a good impression of yourself and of America. Carry out a potential problem analysis for visiting one or more of the following countries: Jordan, Norway, Italy, Brazil, other. The Web site WorldCitizenGuide.org may be of use to you in preparing your PPA.

7.17. Use the techniques discussed in Chapter 6 to make up and solve your own K.T. problem/situation for one or more of the following:

A. Situation appraisal

B. Problem analysis

C. Decision analysis

D. Potential problem analysis

FURTHER READING

Keith, Lawrence A. "Report Results Right!," Parts 1 and 2. *Chemtech,* p. 351, June 1991; p. 486, August 1991. Guidelines to help you avoid drawing the wrong conclusions from your data.

Kepner, C. H., and B. B. Tregoe. *The New Rational Manager.* Princeton Research Press, Princeton, NJ, 1981. Contains many worked examples using the K.T. approach. Much more information on the K.T. approach is available from Kepner–Tregoe, Inc., Research Road, P.O. Box 704, Princeton, NJ 08542, 609-921-2806.

8   IMPLEMENTING THE SOLUTION

Many people get stalled in the problem-solving process because they analyze things to death and never get around to acting. In this chapter, we present a number of techniques that will facilitate the **implementation process.** The figure below identifies the phases of the implementation process.

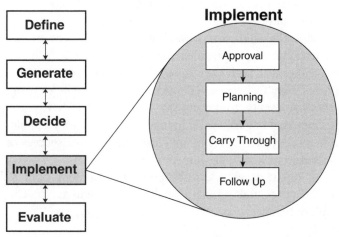

Implementing the Solution

Each of these phases will be discussed in this chapter. In addition, we will explore the topic of experimental projects. These projects may become necessary if you find out during the implementation process that the information necessary to solve the problem doesn't exist and needs to be obtained by an experiment.

APPROVAL

In some situations, the first step in the implementation is to get approval from your organization to proceed with the chosen solution. Many times it may be necessary to sell your ideas so that your organization will provide the necessary resources for you to successfully complete your project. This process may include the preparation of a document or presentation describing (1) what you want to do, (2) why you want to do it, (3) how you are going to do it, and (4) how your project will greatly benefit your organization and/or others. Use the checklist on the next page to help sell your ideas.

- Avoid technical jargon—keep your presentation clear and to the point.
- Give your presentation in a logical and orderly manner.
- Be concise; avoid unnecessary, minute details.
- Anticipate questions and be prepared to respond to them.
- Be enthusiastic about your ideas—or no one else will be.

PLANNING

Now that we have approval for the project, it is time to plan what to do, in what order to do it, and when to do it. The most important aspect of implementing is the **planning phase.** In this phase, we look at the resource allocations of time, personnel, and money; anticipate bottlenecks; identify milestones in the project; and identify and sketch the pathway through to the finished solution. A modified K.T. situation appraisal (see Chapter 7) will help to identify the critical elements of the solution and to prioritize them so that we can prepare a meaningful plan. Gantt charts, deployment charts, budgets, and critical path management[1] can all be used to effectively allocate time and resources. Finally, we proceed to identify what might go wrong and devise ways to prevent these events from occurring; that is, we use K.T. potential problem analysis (PPA; discussed in Chapter 7). In many industries, for example, market surveys are used as a part of K.T. PPA to anticipate the possible success or failure of a product (e.g., chunky chicken ripple chip ice cream) or process.

In the planning stage, we use resource allocation along both K.T. situation appraisal and K.T. potential problem analysis as discussed in Chapter 7 and shown in the figure below.

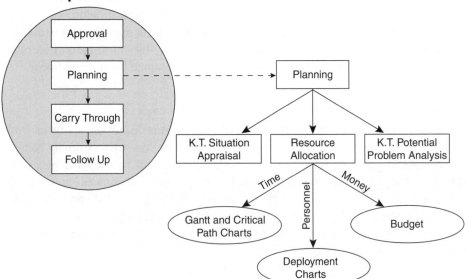

Components of the Planning Process

Resource Allocation

Having been presented with a problem, situation, or opportunity, we need to allocate our time and resources to the various steps wisely so as to bring about a successful solution. We can use a variety of techniques—the Gantt and deployment charts, critical path management, and strategies for budgeting both personnel and money—to arrive at an efficient and effective allocation. Another popular tool for scheduling daily activities is the personal organizer (e.g., the Franklin Day Planner, a series of software-based planners and calendars), which is used by executives and students alike to keep track of important appointments and commitments.

Gantt Charts

One of the most popular ways to allocate specific blocks of time to the various tasks in a project is a **Gantt chart.** A Gantt chart is a bar graph that indicates when a specific task is to begin and how long it will take to complete that task.

"If you don't know where you are going, you'll probably end up somewhere else."
—Yogi Berra

As an example, suppose we have a time constraint of one year to solve the problem and we need to allocate time to each of the five building blocks of the problem-solving process. January, February, and March will be spent working on problem definition; April and May will be devoted to generating solutions. We suggest that time be allocated to evaluate our progress at four points along the way to check that all criteria have been fulfilled: (1) after completion of the definition of the problem, (2) after deciding the course of action, (3) during the implementation, and (4) at the end of the project.

TASK	MONTH											
	J	F	M	A	M	J	J	A	S	O	N	D
Problem Definition	▨	▨	▨									
Generate Solutions				▨	▨							
Decide Course of Action						▨	▨					
Implement								▨	▨	▨	▨	▨
Evaluate				▨			▨		▨			▨

A Gantt Chart

In the Gantt chart, note that at least 25% of the time has been devoted to the problem definition process, which includes the four steps of gathering information discussed in Chapter 3. Many—if not most—of the unhappy consequences of the incorrectly defined problems discussed in Chapter 1 would not have occurred if more time had been spent on defining the problem rather than hurrying to implement a solution. Most experts agree that the project is halfway complete once the real problem is defined, written down, and communicated.

An example of the use of a Gantt chart for the development of a Web site for a small business is shown next.

Developing a Web Site

Jason and Melinda have a partnership to develop Web sites for small companies. A local martial arts school has asked them to develop a Web site to try to increase the school's business. Jason and Melinda meet with the owner to discuss the proposed Web site. During this meeting, they outline the following tasks, which will form the basis for the project:

    Determine the site requirements and needs of the school

    Select the Web site name and register the Web address

    Develop a tentative layout

    Develop content and obtain suitable graphics

    Contract with an Internet service provider to host the Web site on its servers

    Ensure that the site goes live

    Follow up and arrange for periodic updates

    Review the plans with the customer during the development

After the meeting, Melinda develops the following Gantt chart for the martial arts Web site project:

WEB SITE DEVELOPMENT GANTT CHART

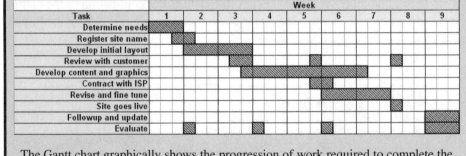

The Gantt chart graphically shows the progression of work required to complete the project.

Evaluate Early

Critical Path Management

Critical path management allows us to identify the critical points in the process. These critical points are readily identified by determining which tasks will cause substantial delays in the implementation of the solution if the schedule is not met.

    Suppose Jason and Melinda decide to use critical path management for the development of the Web site described in the preceding example. In the next figure, the bold lines and boxes indicate the critical path. It identifies items that require a fair amount of time to complete. If the schedule "slips," the Web site's "go live" date will be delayed. In this case, the development of the content and graphics with the customer takes the longest time and the site cannot be finalized until this task is completed; thus it is critical that this task be completed on schedule or the Web site commissioning will be delayed. Non-critical path items, such as contracting with an Internet Service Provider (ISP), can be done as time permits after the critical items are completed.

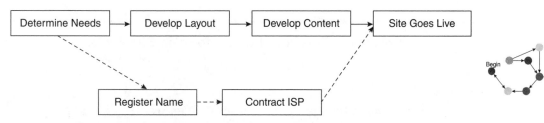

Critical Path Management of a Web Site Development Project

A word of caution is in order here: If non-critical path items are completed too slowly, they can become critical path items. Thus using a critical path diagram is a dynamic process. The diagram should be continually updated as tasks are completed, so that you can view the overall progress of the project as a whole.

Coordination and Deployment

In most circumstances, groups of individuals will work together as a team to solve a problem. Under these conditions, coordination among various team members is imperative if the team is to achieve an efficient solution in the time allotted. The use of a **deployment chart** can help guide the team through the solution by assigning different team members either major or minor responsibilities related to each of the tasks. A deployment chart for the Web site development project is shown here.

Task	Team Member		
	Melinda	John	Web Programmer
Determine needs	▨	▨	▨
Register site name		▨	▨
Develop initial layout		▨	
Review with customer	▨	▨	▨
Develop content and graphics		▨	▨
Contract with ISP	▨		▨
Revise and fine tune	▨	▨	▨
Site goes live	▨	▨	▨
Followup and update	▨	▨	▨
Evaluate	▨	▨	▨

Deployment Chart for the Web Site Development Project

Necessary Resources

We must also estimate the resources necessary to complete the project. These resources usually fall into five categories: available personnel, equipment, travel, supplies, and overhead. Contingency funds are intended to cover unexpected expenses (e.g., permission fees for icons used on the Web site). At the beginning of a project, it is usually important to obtain an estimate of the total cost by preparing a budget similar to the one shown below.

Proposed First-Year Budget for Web Site Project

	Hours/Rate	Cost
Personnel		
Melinda, Project Director	40 hours @ $25/hour	$1000
Jason, Creative Designer	60 hours @ $25/hour	$1500
Web Programmer	60 hours @ $15/hour	$900
Subtotal—Salaries		$3400
Monthly Maintenance/Updates		
Annual Fee	$25/month	$300
Web Site Name Registration		
Annual Fee		$25
Internet Service Provider Web Site Hosting		
Annual Fee	$20/month	$240
Supplies		
CDs for File Backup		$25
TOTAL BUDGET		**$3990**

The budgets for larger projects that are undertaken by larger companies may include fringe benefits—that is, charges for health and retirement programs for the personnel involved in the project. Sometimes "overhead" is charged on a project; it goes toward defraying the costs associated with such items as the salaries of the organization's management, building maintenance, and other general expenses.

Once the budget is submitted and approved, you enter the carry through phase of your problem's solution.

CARRY THROUGH

The **carry through phase** is an essential step in a successful problem-solving process. In this phase, the various people involved in the problem-solving process act upon the plans they have formulated. They may carry out a design, fabricate a product, conduct experiments, make calculations, prepare a report, cook a dinner, go on an activity, and so forth. In some circumstances, the implementation process and the process of deciding the course of action are intertwined. For example, it might be necessary to collect experimental or other data (implement a plan) before the right decision can be made. Great care should be taken with the carry through phase, because all the planning in the world cannot compensate for a poor job of carrying through on the chosen solution. Here is a checklist of things to monitor in the carry through phase.

Carry Through Checklist

- ✔ Make an educated guess about what your solution will look like when you are finished.
- ✔ Make sure there is coordination of tasks and personnel.
- ✔ Constantly monitor your Gantt chart to make sure you stay on schedule.
- ✔ Evaluate each completed task along the way.
- ✔ Continue to learn as much as you can about the solution you have chosen. Read the literature and talk to your colleagues.
- ✔ Continue to challenge and/or validate the assumptions of the chosen solution. Make sure no physical laws are violated.
- ✔ Find the limits of your solution by creating simple models or making assumptions that would clearly both (1) overestimate the answer and (2) underestimate the answer.
- ✔ Construct a quick test or experiment to see whether the solution you have selected will work under the simplest conditions.
- ✔ Plan your computer experiments (i.e., simulations) as carefully as you would plan your experiments in the laboratory.

Flexibility is an essential trait for problem solvers to have if they are to deal with the inevitable changes that occur during projects.

Problem Statements That Change with Time

Sometimes it may feel as if you are shooting at a moving target, as the desired goals change over the course of the project. The problem statement may change for a number of reasons—for example, because of changing market conditions, the introduction of a competing product or services, reduced financing, or other factors. If during the carry through phase some or all of the project cannot be accomplished, the problem statement must be modified. Of course, this type of information is learned only *after* we begin developing the solution. As an example, suppose that during the course of your product development, your competitor launches a more advanced model than you were designing for nearly the same price. Consequently, you are now faced with several alternatives, which include cutting your price to significantly undercut the price of the new product, or improving your design to surpass the design of your competitor's new product.

What Happens When the Goal Keeps Changing?

In the 1870s, a military fort was built in the west near a small village on the northern plains. As the first winter approached, the captain of the garrison sent his men to the forest to obtain firewood. The initial goal was to chop down enough trees to stack eight cords of wood. The captain then asked the corporal to ride over to the village to ask an old settler how cold the winter would be, with the goal of determining whether the soldiers he had cut a sufficient amount of wood to last the winter.

When the corporal arrived at the village and asked the old settler, the old settler put his hand to his forehead, looked toward the fort and said, "Cold winter!" The corporal reported this to the captain, who ordered that eight more cords of wood be cut and stacked.

The captain then asked the corporal to check once again with the old settler as to how cold the winter was going to be. The old settler looked to the sky in the direction of the fort and this time said, "Cold, cold winter!" When the corporal reported to the captain, the captain ordered eight more cords of wood to be cut; he then asked the corporal to check once again with the old settler. The old settler looked toward the fort and said, "Cold, cold, cold winter!"

The corporal said, "Wait a minute. The first time you said 'Cold winter,' the second time, 'Cold, cold, winter,' and now you say, 'Cold, cold, cold winter.' Why do you keep changing your mind and saying the winter is going to be colder and colder?"

"Because," said the old settler, "the soldiers at the fort keep stacking more and more wood for the winter!"

If the goals keep changing, keep two things in mind:

- Where did the goals come from, and why?
- Are the goals still appropriate to the problem as originally defined?

Be flexible and make adjustments as necessary.

FOLLOW UP

In the **follow-up phase,** we monitor our progress not only with respect to ensuring that the time deadlines are met but also with respect to ensuring that our solution does, indeed, solve the problem at hand. In this phase, we periodically check the progress of the carry through phase to make sure it is meeting the following criteria:

Inspect what you expect.

- It follows the solution plan (that is, it meets the solution goals and fulfills the solution criteria).
- It is proceeding on schedule.
- It is staying within the budget.
- It is maintaining an acceptable quality.
- It is still relevant to solving the original problem.

It is important to monitor these points to confirm that the solution is "on track" and satisfies all the necessary goals. Also, check periodically that the problem is still correctly defined during the implementation process. Sometimes a change in conditions can occur during implementation that will invalidate the solution.

EXPERIMENTAL PROJECTS

The use of an **experimental project** needs to be considered whenever you need more information than you have available so as to select the best solution to the problem at hand. In fact, the specific information you need might not even exist (or perhaps you just can't find it in a timely fashion). In these circumstances, you may be required to initiate an experimental program to generate the necessary data or information. How can you do so in an efficient manner? The following figure maps out an efficient path for an experimental program.

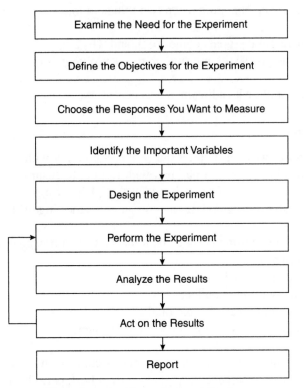

Flowchart for Experimental Projects

Do You Really Need the Experiment?

When you are preparing to initiate an experimental program, be sure to question yourself and others to help guide your progress. The following questions will help you dig deeper into your project:

- Why perform the experiment?
- Can the information you are seeking be found elsewhere (such as literature journals, books, or company reports)?
- Can you do some calculations instead?
- Have sufficient time and money been budgeted for the program?
- Are you restricted to specific materials or equipment?
- Will the safety of the investigators be endangered to such a degree that the program should not be carried out?

These and other appropriate questions must be answered prior to beginning the experimental program so that the need for the experiment is clearly established.

"Five to six weeks in the lab can save you an hour in the library."
—G. Quarderer

Define the Objectives of the Experiment

Prepare a list of all the things you want to accomplish. Then try to prioritize your list, keeping in mind the following issues:

- Which questions regarding your problem would you most like to answer?
- Are you sure you are not losing sight of the overall objectives and other possible alternative solutions (the "can't see the forest for the trees" syndrome)?
- How comprehensive does the program need to be? Are you looking at an exhaustive study or just a cursory examination of a narrow set of conditions? Specific answers to these questions will guide the rest of the project.

Choose the Responses You Want to Measure

An experimental program typically considers two types of variables: independent and dependent. The **independent variables** make things happen. That is, changes in these variables cause the system to respond. The responses are the **dependent variables.** For example, the film speed, flash, and focus are all independent variables related to a camera. Changing any one of these variables will change the system's response—specifically, the quality of the picture (the dependent variable). When you are designing your experimental program, it is essential that you identify the important dependent variables to be measured:

- What are the controlled (independent) variables?
- What are the dependent variables?
- Are instruments or techniques available to make the measurements available?
- Do they need to be calibrated? If so, have they been?
- Will the accuracy and precision of the expected results be sufficient to distinguish between different theories or possible outcomes?

Identify the Important Variables

In any experimental program, there will always be many, many variables you can measure. Nevertheless, you must pare the list down by deciding which independent variables have the greatest influence on the dependent variable.

- What are the *really* important measurements to make?
- What are the ranges or levels of these variables to be examined?
- Instead of changing each independent variable separately, can variables be grouped so as to produce the same end results with fewer measurements? (See Appendix 2, page 280.)

A Night at the Movies

You cannot possibly go to a movie theater without seeing popcorn being sold. James Wilson is an entrepreneur who owns a moderate-size company that markets and packages gourmet popcorn. James believes that his popcorn is superior to the popcorn currently being sold at the movies and hopes that he can sell it to the major chains at a price that is competitive with the price of their current brand. While James maintains his popcorn tastes better (and will even vary with the type of movie—such as a horror versus a musical),* his real selling point is that he gets a far greater percentage of his kernels to pop. He decides to carry out a series of experiments whose results he can then present to the management of the major cinema chains to convince them to buy his gourmet popcorn.

Establish a Need for the Experiment

James believes he has a better product, yet no data are available that compare the popping efficiency of his gourmet popcorn with the brand currently sold at theaters.

Define the Objectives of the Experiment

The objective is to show that James's gourmet popcorn has a greater popping efficiency under a variety of popping conditions.

Choose the Responses to Be Measured

Measure the number (or fraction) of kernels that pop.

Identify the Important Variables

The major variables will be (1) the age of the unpopped popcorn and (2) the media used to pop the corn (oil or air).

We will continue this example after further discussion of experimental design.

* The hypothesis has, indeed, been put forth that the type of movie being viewed has an effect on the taste of the popcorn. Perhaps you could prepare your own experimental plan to test this idea.

Design the Experiment

To obtain the maximum benefit from a series of experiments, we must ensure that they are properly designed. How can we design the experimental program so as to achieve the experimental objectives in the simplest manner with the minimum number of measurements and at the least expense? A *successfully designed experiment* is a series of *organized* trials that enable you to obtain the greatest amount of experimental information with the least amount of effort. You must consider three important questions when designing your experiments.

- What are the types of errors to avoid?
- What is the minimum number of experiments that must be performed?
- When should you consider repeating experiments?

Types of Errors

Two types of errors should be avoided in any experimental design. A **Type I error** occurs when we declare that a variable has an effect on the experimental outcome when, in fact, it really doesn't. A **Type II error** occurs when we fail to identify the actual effect. A Type II error results in lost information: A variable is incorrectly classified as insignificant to the process or ignored and, as a result, no further examination of it takes place. We can avoid Type II errors by researching fundamental principles related to the experiments, gathering sufficient information, and planning thoughtfully.

Performing (and Repeating) the Experiment: How Many Times?

If there is some error associated with measuring the outcome of an experiment, we must consider repeating some of the tests to be sure we have accurate information. But how much data should we consider to be "enough"? The answer to this question depends on how precise (reproducible) the experiments are and on how small a change in the outcome or result of an experiment we wish to detect. Obviously, the less precise the measurements (i.e., the more error present) and the smaller the change we are interested in, the more data we must collect and average to be confident in our result.

To see how this works, let's return to our popcorn example. The popcorn kernels are inherently non-uniform, so we might easily draw erroneous conclusions if we have results from only a limited number of experiments. Conducting several runs under the same conditions and then averaging the data produced from those experiments is the best way to deal with such a situation and ensure reliable results. The number of times that each test should be repeated prior to averaging can easily be calculated using a statistical procedure discussed by Hendrix.[2]

Analyze the Results

How good are our measurements? What modifications, if any, of the existing equipment are necessary to improve the accuracy or precision of the measurements or to better achieve our overall experimental objectives? In the popcorn experiments, we might find that the aging results are inconclusive and learn that we need to control the humidity more tightly in the oven during the accelerated aging process. Thus additional runs would be necessary in this case.

Is software available that can perform least squares analysis (see Appendix 2), set confidence limits, or conduct other statistical analyses on our behalf? Is there any mathematical model or theory available that suggests how the data might be plotted or correlated? What generalizations can be made from the data? Should we perform other experiments to extend the data into different regions? Have we performed an error analysis, listed potential sources of error, and discussed these sources of error in relation to how they might affect the final result (i.e., by what magnitude and in what direction)? Finally, have we satisfied all of our experimental objectives?

Report the Results

Naturally, you must communicate the results of your work with other members of your team. This sharing of information is usually done by means of a technical report. Guidelines for writing such a report can be found in many books. One good source is *Handbook of Technical Writing* by Charles T. Brusaw, Gerald Alred, and Walter E. Oliv (St. Martins Press, 1997), which has particularly useful examples. Typically a report will include the following sections:

If you don't effectively communicate your results, you may as well have not performed the experiment.

1. *Abstract.* This one-page summary of the report is usually written last. It defines the problem, explains how you approached the problem, and highlights the important results that were found.
2. *Introduction.* This section defines the problem, explains why it is an important problem worthy of being studied, gives background information, describes the fundamental issues, and discusses and analyzes how those issues relate to published work in the area.
3. *Materials and Methods.* This section describes the equipment used to carry out the experiments and the instruments used to analyze the data. The purity of the raw materials is specified, as is the brand name of each piece of equipment. The accuracy of each measurement taken is discussed. The step-by-step procedure as to how a typical run was carried out is outlined, and all sources of error are discussed. (If you developed a new model or theory, then a "Theory" section would come after the "Materials and Methods" section. The "Theory" section would develop the governing equations that mathematically describe the phenomena under investigation and justify all assumptions in the development of the theory.)
4. *Results.* This section describes what you found. Make sure all figures and tables in this section have titles and that the units of each variable are displayed. Discuss all sources of error and describe how they might potentially affect your results. Put an error bar on your data where appropriate.
5. *Discussion of Results.* This section explains why the results look the way they do. Discuss whether the results are consistent with theory—either a theory that you developed or a theory proposed by others. You should also describe where theory and experiment are in good agreement and identify those conditions where the theory would not apply.

6. *Conclusion.* This section lists all important information you learned from this work in numerical order. For example:
   a. Dead fish were found in surrounding lakes that were inaccessible to the chemical effluent from the plant.
   b. The effluent from the chemical plant to the river did not cause the fish to die.
   c. A fungus was responsible for the death of the fish.
7. *References.* List all resource material you referred to in this work in the proper bibliographical format.

In addition to the seven sections of a technical report described here, many companies require an **Executive Summary**. It is usually an expanded version of the abstract that includes the conclusion and recommendations.

At least of equal importance to the sections that appear in the report are the *style* and *clarity* with which the report is written. Here is a list of things to look for in an effective report:

Top Ten List for Effective Written Reports

1. Logically organized (introduction, . . . , conclusions)
2. Logical flow of ideas within each section
3. Concisely written
4. Interestingly written, using a wide variety of words
5. Ideas supported by examples, data, and evidence
6. Appropriate use and placement of figures and tables
7. Passive voice
8. Clear purpose
9. No disagreements with Strunk and White[3] (perfect grammar)
10. Report placed in a clear plastic binder (per *Calvin and Hobbes*)

In addition to creating written reports, you will be expected to give oral reports throughout your career. You should refer to some of the references at the end of the chapter to prepare your presentation. The following checklist identifies some key points to consider when you are making a presentation.

Top Ten List for Effective Presentations

1. Be well organized (introduction, body, closure).
2. Have a logical flow of ideas.
3. Present ideas concisely and clearly.
4. Support ideas with examples, data, and evidence.
5. Offer clear explanations.
6. Use good visual aids.

7. Speak clearly and at a reasonable speed.
8. Be well prepared and thoroughly practiced.
9. Dress appropriately.
10. Make sure that your conclusions are supported by the evidence.
11. Match your presentation to the audience.
12. Have a confident appearance.
13. Use good dictation and grammar—avoid slang.
14. Disregard three of the above to make it a top ten list.

SUMMARY

Many people get stalled in the problem-solving process because they get bogged down in the planning process and forget the most critical step—implementation. In this chapter, we presented a number of techniques to facilitate the implementation process.

- **Approval**
  - Sell your ideas for the project.

- **Planning**
  - Sketch the pathway through to the solution.
  - Plan for appropriate resource allocation.
  - Perform a K.T. situation appraisal and potential problem analysis.
  - Prepare Gantt and deployment charts.
  - Identify the critical tasks and prepare a critical path diagram.
  - Prepare a budget for your project.

- **Carry Through**
  - Monitor the progress of the critical tasks closely.
  - Use the Carry Through Checklist.
  - Be alert for possible changes in the original problem statement and chosen solution.

- **Follow Up**
  - Confirm that the solution meets the specified objectives and criteria.

- **Experimental Projects**
  - Formulate your experimental plan carefully to maximize your efforts.
  - Be aware of the various types of errors that can occur.
  - Estimate the minimum number of experiments that you need to carry out.

REFERENCES

1. Peters, M. S., K. D. Timmerhaus, and R. E. West, *Plant Design and Economics for Chemical Engineers*, 5th ed., McGraw-Hill, New York, 2002.
2. Hendrix, Charles D., "What Every Technologist Should Know about Experimental Design," *Chemtech*, p. 167, March 1979.
3. Strunk, W., and E. B. White, *The Elements of Style*, 4th ed., Macmillan, New York, 1999.

EXERCISES

8.1. For Exercises 8.2 through 8.7, choose one of the situations below and perform the required activity. List the five most important things you learned from this chapter. Also list the five most interesting things you learned.

Consider the following situations:

A. Planning a surprise birthday party

B. Planning a wedding

C. Planning a camping trip to Colorado

D. Getting elected mayor of your city

E. Publishing your autobiography

F. Becoming a U.S. Supreme Court justice

8.2. Prepare a Gantt chart for the activity.

8.3. Prepare a deployment chart for the activity.

8.4. Prepare a critical path planning chart for the activity.

8.5. Prepare a budget for the activity.

8.6. Prepare a Gantt chart, a deployment chart, a critical path planning chart, and a budget for a different activity.

8.7. Prepare a write-up (or presentation) to management for the following proposals:

A. You want to attend a professional meeting or take a short course in Europe.

B. You want your company to market a new widget.

8.8. You are going to prepare a three-course dinner for your gourmet dinner group for a party of eight.

Course	Item	Preparation Time	Eating Time
Appetizer	Bacon-wrapped water chestnuts	Cook in oven 10 minutes	10 minutes
Soup	Onion soup	Cook 30 minutes on stove	15 minutes
	Bread sticks	Warm 10 minutes in oven	

Continues

(Continued)

Course	Item	Preparation Time	Eating Time
Entrée	Pot roast	Cook 2 hours in oven	40 minutes
	Mashed potatoes	Cook ready mix 10 minutes	
	Fresh mixed vegetables	Boil 20 minutes	
	Gravy	Cook juice from roast 10 minutes on stove	
Dessert	Apple pie	Cook 35 minutes in oven	15 minutes
	Ice cream	Let stand 5 minutes before scooping	

Prepare a Gantt chart, a stove deployment chart (i.e., oven top), and a critical path diagram for your dinner party.

8.9. Prepare an experimental plan to modify the popcorn example to include popping the corn in at least three different oils (peanut oil, corn oil, olive oil).

8.10. Design experiments to study the following problems given the important variables listed:

A. Coffee making
   - Grind (coarse versus fine)
   - Type of bean (standard versus premium)
   - Percolator versus automatic drip

B. Paper airplane making
   - Wing span
   - Weight distribution
   - Initial velocity
   - Angle of takeoff

C. Plant growth
   - Hours of sunlight
   - Amount/frequency of watering
   - Fertilizer use

D. Paper production
   - Quality of product (strength, brightness)
   - Whiteness (use of bleaching agents)
   - Percentage recycled fibers used
   - Types of fibers used (new and recycled)

E. Fermentation of sugar to alcohol by yeast
   - Temperature
   - pH
   - Nutrients
   - Desired final alcohol content

FURTHER READING

Blanchard, Kenneth, and Robert Lorber. *Putting the One Minute Manager to Work: How to Turn the Three Secrets into Skills.* Berkeley Books, Berkeley, CA, 1984. Increase your productivity using three easy-to-follow techniques.

Hendrix, Charles D. "What Every Technologist Should Know about Experimental Design." *Chemtech*, p. 167, March 1979. Some useful background material on designing experiments to gain the maximum amount of information with the least amount of effort.

Massinall, John L. "The Joys of Excellence." *Chemtech*, 20, p. 393, July 1990. Timely tips for managing a project and keeping work on schedule.

McCluskey, R. J., and S. L. Harris. "The Coffee Pot Experiment: A Better Cup of Coffee via Factorial Design." *Chemical Engineering Education,* p.151, Summer 1989. More interesting background on designing experiments.

Murphy, Thomas D. "Design and Analysis of Industrial Experiments." *Chemical Engineering*, 84, p. 168, June 6, 1977. Excellent overview of factorial design of experiments.

Starfield, Anthony M., Karl A. Smith, and Andrew L. Bleloch. *How to Model It: Problem-Solving for the Computer Age.* McGraw-Hill, New York, 1990. Chapter 6 of this book contains a nice description and additional examples of critical path planning.

9   EVALUATION

Evaluation of our solution to the problem is the last task in our problem-solving heuristic. In this chapter we present guidelines for evaluating a solution to make sure it completely solves the problem specified, is ethical, and is safe for both people and the environment.

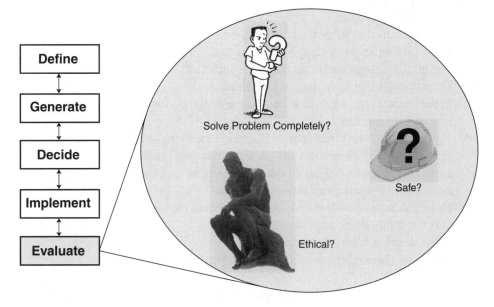

GENERAL GUIDELINES

Evaluation should be an *ongoing* process throughout the life of a project. As each phase of the project is completed, we should examine the goals and accomplishments of that phase to make sure they were satisfied before we proceed to the next phase. We should also evaluate future directions in light of the results of each phase to verify that the direction in which we are proceeding is still the correct one. We must look for any fallacies in logic that might have occurred, especially at key decision points during the project. In addition, we must challenge the various assumptions that were made. Have all unstated assumptions been recognized? For example, was the engineer in our earlier case study justified in assuming that the managers of the plant no longer have to worry about the effluent waste stream no matter how low the river water level becomes because the fish were dying from a fungus?

Evaluation Checklist

To address these types of questions, have someone outside the group that developed the solution review the assumptions and solution logic. During the evaluation process, you must inevitably make qualitative and quantitative judgments about the extent to which the material and methods satisfy the external and internal criteria. Ask evaluation questions such as those given in the following checklist.

Evaluation Checklist

- ✔ Is the solution logical?
- ✔ Does the solution solve the real problem?
- ✔ Is the problem permanently solved, or is this a patchwork solution?
- ✔ Are all the criteria and constraints are satisfied?
- ✔ Does the solution have the desired impact?
- ✔ Is the solution economically, environmentally, politically, and ethically responsible and safe?
- ✔ Have you used the nine types of Socratic Questions—for example, have you challenged the information and assumptions provided?
- ✔ Have all the consequences of the solution been examined—for example, does it cause other, more serious problems?
- ✔ Have you argued both sides—the positive and the negative?
- ✔ Has the solution accomplished all it could?
- ✔ Is the solution is blunder-free?
- ✔ Have you checked the procedure and logic of the arguments?

You need to confirm *all* findings. Check whether any piece of the puzzle (i.e., the solution) doesn't fit and consequently may require the entire solution to be scrapped.

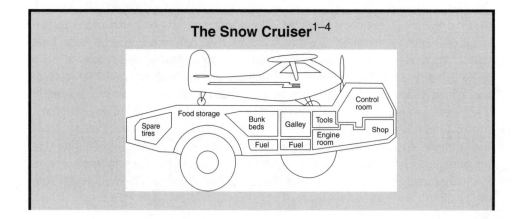

The Snow Cruiser[1–4]

Following Admiral Richard Byrd's second expedition to Antarctica in 1934, excitement over polar exploration was running high in the United States. Thomas Poulter, Byrd's second-in-command, had experienced the difficulties associated with polar expeditions firsthand and had some ideas about how to improve the problems associated with working, living, and transporting goods in subzero temperatures. The embodiment of these ideas became the Snow Cruiser. In 1939, six months prior to the third U.S. expedition to the South Pole, Poulter, with help from more than 70 private companies, set out to design and construct the Snow Cruiser—a vehicle designed to withstand some of the harshest environmental conditions on the face of the Earth. Its design features included

- A range of 5000 miles
- Room for a crew of five and enough supplies for one year
- An airplane carried on its roof to aid in photographic missions
- Outstanding terrain capabilities that included retractable tires for crossing small crevasses

The Snow Cruiser was constructed in Chicago, over a period of about three to four months (August to November). The design and construction period was quite rushed because of the expedition's scheduled summer arrival at the South Pole: The ships were to leave Boston for the Antarctic in November. The specifications of the completed vehicle were very impressive:

- It was 55 feet 8 inches long, 19 feet 10.5 inches wide, and 16 feet high.
- Its gross weight (when fully loaded) was 75,000 pounds.

After construction, the Snow Cruiser was driven cross-country from Chicago to the port in Boston. The trip was quite eventful, and crowds gathered to watch the mammoth vehicle pass. Roads had to be closed to other traffic because of the great width of the Snow Cruiser. In Boston, it was loaded onto a ship, the *North Star,* to begin the expedition to Antarctica.

In January 1940, the *North Star* arrived at the Ross Ice Shelf in Antarctica. With great anticipation, the Snow Cruiser was driven off the ship by Thomas Poulter. Once the vehicle reached the snowy terrain, it became obvious that there was a problem. The Snow Cruiser could hardly move at all! The big vehicle behaved much like a beached whale. The huge tires spun, unable to get traction. As they spun, heat was generated and the Snow Cruiser sank up to 3 feet in the snow. Clearly, something was seriously wrong with the design. Additionally, the vehicle was definitely underpowered. When it was able to gain some traction and move (which wasn't often), the engines overheated after the vehicle had moved only a few hundred yards, leaving it stranded again!

After several months of unsuccessful attempts to improve the vehicle's mobility, the Antarctic winter set in, and the expedition team gave up hopes of using the Snow Cruiser for exploration. They covered it with timbers and snow and used it for shelter. The Snow Cruiser was an enormous flop.

What went wrong? Let's look at the failure of the Snow Cruiser (using 20/20 hindsight) and see how the some of the evaluation checklist questions on page 200 might have prevented this debacle.

Did the developers of the Snow Cruiser challenge the information and assumptions provided? What information was available about the Antarctic environment? How difficult was the terrain? If the vehicle was able to move on dry roads in good weather, what made the developers think it would function on snow and ice? Most polar vehicles up to this time used caterpillar treads rather than tires. Why did the developers think the new tire design would work? Why might other vehicles have used treads? Answering some of these obvious questions might have helped avoid a failed design.

Did the solution solve the real problem? What was the real problem in this case? Clearly, the problem was at least twofold. First, the task was to protect the workers and explorers from the harsh polar environment. The second, equally important aspect of the problem was that the vehicle should have good mobility on the expected terrain so that exploration (the main goal of the expedition) was possible. The design was quite successful from the protection/living accommodations standpoint. The Snow Cruiser was nicer inside than many pre-World War II homes. Unfortunately, the design only partially addressed the mobility problem. Elaborate design features were included to enable the Snow Cruiser to cross the crevasses in the snow that it would certainly encounter, but insufficient consideration was given to ensuring "normal" mobility in polar ice and snow.

Clearly, some incorrect assumptions were made regarding the traction of the tires and the power necessary to move such a mammoth vehicle in the severe conditions found at the South Pole. Challenging all of the assumptions of the design and making sure that the real problem (including all facets of it) is solved are keys to determining a functional solution.

Was the problem permanently solved? If the Snow Cruiser actually functioned as designed, it would have been a permanent solution to polar expedition problems.

Could the solution have had the desired impact? In this case, yes. The Snow Cruiser could have revolutionized the way polar explorations were conducted.

Were all consequences of the solution examined? This question is difficult to answer without knowing what went on at the time, but if the vehicle had operated as designed, many adverse consequences had been anticipated and designed for. Provisions and fuel were available for long periods of time. The Snow Cruiser had a travel range of 5000 miles. Seemingly every contingency had been prepared for—except the fatal mobility flaw.

Are all criteria and constraints satisfied? Was the list of solution criteria surveyed and the solution rated with respect to each criterion? This question might have brought to light some of the design problems, provided the problem was correctly defined in the first place.

If used properly and carefully, the evaluation checklist can point out some otherwise hidden flaws in the solution to a problem and catch costly mistakes before the solution is implemented.

ETHICAL CONSIDERATIONS

Part of the evaluation process includes reviewing all facets of the solution to ensure that an **ethical** solution is in place. Many times the ethical aspects of the situation may not be entirely clear but rather must be uncovered in much the same manner as we would define the real problem or discover what the fault is through a troubleshooting operation. How many times have you heard someone say when discussing a conflict or arbitration, "Gee, I had not thought about it in that light?" When we are thinking in terms of ethics, two questions arise: "What is ethical?" and "How can we make sure we are not ethically blind-sided?" In regard to the first question, many excellent books have been written on ethics and a number of courses offered on this topic. We cannot even begin to recap or summarize them here, but if we were to pick two books, we would recommend *Fundamentals of Ethics*[5] by Edmund G. Seebauer and Robert L. Barry, and *The Power of Ethical Management*[6] by Kenneth Blanchard and Norman Vincent Peale.

Solutions are not always black and white with regard to ethics, but shades of gray.

The Four Classical Virtues

Seebauer and Barry provide a simple model for the origin of moral action, in which *emotions and mind* feed into *will, decisions, and actions.* They also discuss how these components depend on four classical virtues:

- **Prudence:** Thinking about a moral problem clearly and completely
- **Temperance:** Avoiding either being rash or suppressing our emotions
- **Fortitude:** Not moving blindly away from something we do not like
- **Justice:** Having the will to act in truth on the way things actually are and to act with fairness to all concerned

After discussing the four virtues in detail, these authors put forth a key principle: "People should always decide and act according to these virtues as far as possible." Thus Seebauer and Barry describe another way of looking at the ethical decision-making process—namely, as a "four-component model":

- Sensing the presence of moral issues (I had not thought about . . .)
- Reasoning through the moral issues (the four virtues and the five P's)
- Making a decision
- Following through on the decision

We could also use the K.T. decision analysis technique to help us make the decision and the implementation procedure discussed in Chapter 8 to help us carry through on our solution.

Ethics Checklist

In their book *The Power of Ethical Management*,[6] Blanchard and Peale offer a set of guidelines to help us quickly sort through the issues at hand and reach an ethical solution. These guidelines also help us to uncover the moral issues that the decision entails by providing the five P's and a checklist of questions to consider.

Ethics Checklist[6]

> *"There is no pillow as soft as a clear conscience."*
> —*John Wooden, UCLA Bruins*

- Is it legal? Will I be violating either civil law or company policy?
- Is it balanced? Is it fair to all concerned in both the short term and the long term? Does it promote win/win relationships?
- How will it make me feel about myself? Will it make me proud? Would I feel good if my decision were published in the newspaper? Would I feel good if my family knew about it?

If the answer to the first question could be interpreted from any viewpoint or appearance as "No, it is not legal," then there is no need to proceed to the second and third questions. However, if the solution is legal and does not violate company policy, then the second question raises the flag if a decision greatly benefits one person or company, but unfairly takes advantage of others. That is, it may eventually come back to haunt that individual or company (e.g., excessive interest rates on overdue credit cards). Blanchard and Peale's last question is meant to activate our sense of fairness and make sure that our self-esteem is not eroded through an unethical decision. This ethics checklist helps us address one of the knottiest problems in business: *How can we get acceptable bottom-line results and stay competitive, while at the same time making sure we are being ethical?*

The Five P's

Blanchard and Peale identify **five P's** that need to be considered in analyzing the solution to the problem at hand: purpose, pride, patience, persistence, and perspective. The five P's table gives a list of questions for us to answer that will help us further evaluate our solution.

To facilitate the ethical evaluation process, try asking someone to critique your answers to each of the questions for the five P's. This person (called an advisor) could play a passive role—simply listening to your explanation—or an aggressive role—actively questioning your every point. Even when the advisor listens in a passive mode, the mere fact that you must verbalize the application of the five P's to your situation will help improve your evaluation process.

The Five P's[6]

Purpose: What is the objective for which you are striving? Are you comfortable with that as your purpose? Does your purpose hold up when you look at yourself in the mirror? (This P involves the virtue "prudence.")

Pride: Can you take pride in the solution you have developed? Is there any false pride or self-doubt involved? (This P can be related to the virtue "justice.")

Patience: Have you taken the time to think through all the ramifications of your solution? (The virtue "temperance" plays a role in this P.)

Persistence: Are you sticking to your guns and not being dissuaded by other demands? Have you given up too soon on finding a solution that is fair and balanced to all concerned? (This P draws from the virtues "temperance" and "fortitude.")

Perspective: Have you taken the time to focus inside yourself to be sure everything fits with your ideals and beliefs? How does the solution fit into the "big picture"? (This P can be related to the virtues "prudence" and "justice.")

Perspective (the fifth P) is the hub around which the other P's rotate. Part of perspective is developing the inner guidance that is awakened by the other P's and that helps us see things more clearly.

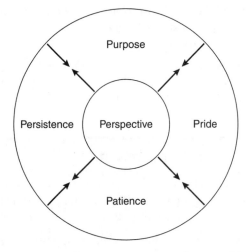

The Interrelationships among the Five P's

Case Study Examples

As discussed earlier, we should carry out an evaluation at each of the key decision points and not wait until the very end of the project to learn that perhaps the solution path that we chose was unethical. Let's consider some examples to see how this process works.

"The greatest battles of life are fought out daily in the silent chambers of the soul."
—David McKay

The Holiday Gift[7]

Henry is in a position to influence the selection of suppliers for the large volume of equipment that his firm purchases each year. At holiday time, he usually receives small tokens from several salespeople, ranging from inexpensive ballpoint pens to a bottle of liquor. This year, however, one salesperson sent an expensive briefcase stamped with Henry's initials. This gift is very much out of the ordinary.

What should Henry do?

1. Keep the case, on the grounds that his judgment will not be affected in any way?

2. Keep the case, because it would simply cause embarrassment all around if the case were returned?

3. Return the case?

4. Other? (Please specify.)

THE FIVE P'S

Purpose: Ask yourself what you would do if you were in Henry's shoes to remain unbiased in selecting the best supplier for a given job.

Pride: Would you feel pride in accepting the case or pride in returning the case?

Patience: Set aside a time to think about whether you should accept the case. Talk to someone whose judgment you trust.

Persistence: Have you pursued all avenues to resolve the issue of either keeping or returning the case?

Perspective: Even if you feel your judgment will not be affected by accepting the case, how will it appear to other colleagues? Are you setting a good example?

The following is the response to a reader survey carried out by *Chemical Engineering* (p. 132, September 1980). The majority of the people (64.9%) thought the case should be returned. However, 27.7% of those respondents who were younger than age 26 thought it would be okay to keep the case.

Option	U.S. Total	U.S. Total	U.S. (by age), %	U.S. (by age), %	U.S. (by age), %	Non-U.S., %	Non-U.S., %
			<26	26–50	>50	British/Canadian	Others
1	20.1	19.7	27.7	17.9	15.4	14.6	39.0
2	3.4	3.3	4.9	2.8	3.1	4.9	4.8
3	64.9	65.8	56.9	68.1	67.6	61.0	43.8
4	9.8	9.5	9.0	9.8	12.1	18.3	11.0

Comments by Respondents to the Reader Survey

- "Keep the case and really not be affected by it, which means that the next holiday you're back on ballpoint pens."

- "As a procurement agent on a limited scale, I have heard of colleagues receiving Porsches. The gifts only get bigger if you accept the first. Eventually, it will affect your judgment."

- "I sometimes feel guilty accepting a gift knowing that the giver won't get anything out of it. But I won't be bribed."

- "My price is very much higher than a briefcase. As a matter of fact it is so high that it would not be profitable to meet it."

- "Henry risks being fired for a crummy $80 briefcase. That's the trouble—it's never two fully paid round-trip tickets to Hawaii, it's always cheap junk."

Rigging the Bidding[7]

Steve is a design engineer for a large chemical company. There are two competitive pieces of equipment that are sold to do a job required by the process he is working on. Equipment from ABC Inc. is widely advertised and sold, but Steve has heard through the grapevine from his competitor's plant that ABC's equipment tends to break down unexpectedly and often. However, there is no way for him to document this information. XYZ Corporation makes equipment that will do the same job, but is much more expensive. Steve knows from his own experience that this equipment is quite reliable. It is company policy to obtain competitive bids, and in such a situation ABC would certainly win. Steve deliberately rigs the specifications by inserting unnecessary qualifications that only the XYZ equipment will meet.

1. Is Steve being ethical in using false specifications to circumvent company policy, even if he believes it is in the company's best interests?

2. Would you do the same if you were in Steve's place?

THE FIVE P'S

Purpose: To choose the best piece of equipment for your company.

Pride: Will you feel pride in having reached the best decision and the way in which you reached it?

Patience: Have you taken the time to check with people in the company to seek their advice about which way to go?

Persistence: Have you checked the grapevine to see if it is a rumor or a fact that the equipment is unreliable?

Perspective: Are you setting a precedent so that you might write future specifications for only one company?

Responses from the reader survey in *Chemical Engineering* (p. 132, September 1980):

Question 1	Total	U.S. Total	U.S. (by age), % <26	26–50	>50	Non-U.S., % British/Canadian	Others
Yes	36.8	36.8	40.8	17.9	32.8	32.9	41.8
No	55.7	55.7	53.5	57.0	54.9	56.7	54.1

Question 2	Total	U.S. Total	U.S. (by age), % <26	26–50	>50	Non-U.S., % British/Canadian	Others
Yes	30.6	30.5	35.9	30.1	24.4	28.0	37.0
No	61.1	61.2	56.9	62.6	61.5	56.8	56.8

Comments by Respondents

- "Can a professional judgment be made based on the grapevine?"

- "Go get that grapevine story verified or busted. Get the facts."

- "Anecdotal reports are a way to document suspicions. One must be careful that one isn't depending on a few disgruntled users; but, surely, it's reason to do more thorough research."

- "To eliminate red tape within a large company and obtain the best equipment, one must often change the rules."

- "Since it'd be me that was called at 2 A.M. when the ABC equipment broke, I'd probably force the choice of XYZ."

- "I have not heard of any design engineer being made to decide based on price and specifications alone. Judgment is a highly sought quality in an engineer. Sometimes, gut feeling counts, too."

SAFETY CONSIDERATIONS

One of the most important parts of the evaluation process is to make sure the proposed solution is safe to both humans and the environment. Carrying out a potential problem analysis (see Chapter 7), a fault-tree analysis, or a hazardous operations analysis (HAZOP) is helpful to make sure you have considered all aspects of the solution that might affect safety.

SUMMARY

Evaluation of the proposed solution to the problem is the last task in the problem-solving heuristic. Evaluation should be an ongoing process throughout the life of a project. Use the evaluation checklist to make sure you have done the following:

- Challenged information and assumptions
- Solved the *real* problem
- Examined all consequences of the solution
- Found a solution that is logical, ethical, safe, and environmentally responsible

Seebauer and Barry provide a simple model for the origin of moral action, in which emotions and mind feed into will, decisions, and actions. Their four-component model involves the following activities:

- Sensing the presence of moral issues
- Reasoning through the moral issues
- Making a decision
- Following through on the decision

These components depend on four classical virtues: prudence, temperance, fortitude, and justice.

You can use the ethics checklist and the five P's to make sure your decision and solution are ethical. The five P's are purpose, pride, patience, persistence, and perspective.

REFERENCES

1. Muller, Peter, "The Antarctic Snow Cruiser," *Invention and Technology,* p. 63, Winter 1993.
2. "The Snow Cruiser: A Mobile Base for Antarctica," *Scientific American,* 162, p. 25, January 1940.
3. "Snow Cruiser to Explore Antarctica," *Popular Mechanics,* 72, p. 494, October 1939.
4. "Dreadnaught Ditched," *Time,* November 6, 1939, p. 40.
5. Seebauer, Edmund G., and Robert L. Barry, *Fundamentals of Ethics for Scientists and Engineers,* Oxford University Press, New York, 2007.
6. Blanchard, Kenneth, and Norman Vincent Peale, *The Power of Ethical Management,* Ballantine Books, Fawcett Crest, New York, copyright ©1988 by Blanchard Family Partnership and Norman Vincent Peale.
7. *Chemical Engineering*, p. 132, September 1980.

EXERCISES

9.1. Nick is chief engineer in a phosphate fertilizer plant that generates more than 1 million tons per year of gypsum, a waste collected in a nearby pile. Over many years, the pile has grown into a mountain containing 40 million tons of waste. There is little room at the present site for any more waste, so a new gypsum pile is planned.

Current environmental regulations call for the elimination of acidic water seepage and groundwater contamination by phosphates and fluorides. Nick's design for the new pile, which has been approved, incorporates the latest technology and complies with U.S. Environmental Protection Agency (EPA) and state regulations. However, he also knows that the old pile—although exempt from the current regulations—presents a major public hazard. When it rains, acidic water seeps through the pile, carrying phosphates into the groundwater.

In a confidential report to management, Nick recommends measures that will prevent the seepage from happening. His company turns down his proposal, stating that, at present, no law or regulation demands such remedy. Use the four virtues, four-component model, evaluation checklist, ethics checklist, and five P's to help you analyze the situation. (Problem adapted from *Chemical Engineering,* p. 40, March 2, 1987.)

9.2. The environmental and safety control group in a circuit-board etching and plating plant has just completed a program to improve the measurement of toxic releases into the atmosphere in response to stricter regulations recently issued by the state health and environmental commission.

Small amounts of a toxic material are detected for the first time by means of a new instrument purchased and installed at the suggestion of Joan, the group leader. The detection method specified by the state does not reveal any trace of chemical.

A search through books and magazines shows that this material is not dangerous in the low concentrations detected, although the state agency says it is, basing its claim on the extrapolation of published data. Use the four virtues, four-component model, evaluation checklist, ethics checklist, and five P's to help you address this situation. (Problem adapted from *Chemical Engineering,* p. 40, March 2, 1987.)

9.3. Each week, operators in a plant regularly dump more than 100 drums of a dry, dusty enzyme (isomerase, used in converting dextrose to fructose) into a large tank, where it is rehydrated for several hours. The dust, although not immediately harmful, is suspected of causing long-term allergies and even lung problems. However, these symptoms show up in fewer than 10% of people who are exposed to the enzyme.

The plant safety code requires that operators wear masks, goggles, and gloves when dumping the enzyme. Because the temperature in the working area is usually about 110 °F, the operators often ignore this requirement.

This is the situation found by Phil, who has very recently taken over supervision of the department. Use the evaluation checklist, ethics checklist, and five P's to help you address this situation. (Problem adapted from *Chemical Engineering,* p. 40, March 2, 1987.)

9.4. You are employed by a small company that is trying to build a plant to produce chemical X. As a result of its low overhead and other factors, your firm should be able to significantly undercut the price charged by your competitor for the same chemical. You have sized all the pieces of equipment except the reactor. You cannot do this because you don't know the kinetic parameters, nor do you have laboratory equipment to determine them. Time is of the essence, so your boss suggests that you take a photograph of your competitor's reactor, which is located outside its plant, and use that information to size your reactor. He suggests you hire a plane to take aerial photographs or a truck similar to those used to repair telephone lines that could see over the fences. Your boss also suggests you could get an estimate of the production rate by monitoring the size and number of trucks shipping the product from your competitor's plant.

How confident are you that your estimates of the sizes will be reasonably accurate? Do you believe it is ethical to estimate the reactor sizes and production rates in this manner? Make a list of reasons and arguments as to why your boss might think it is ethical to make this request. If you don't feel it is ethical, make a list of reasons and arguments as to why the kind of surveillance suggested by your boss should not be done. Suggest alternative ways to obtain the desired information. You may wish to consult the books *Fundamentals of Ethics* by Seebauer and Barry and *The Power of Ethical Management* by Blanchard and Peale to identify and evaluate ethical issues.

If you believe that the situation described here is clearly ethical or unethical, revise the scenario so that it falls into a gray area. For example, would obtaining the needed information in this way be ethical if the reactor were in full view from the street? What if your boss suggested that you tour the plant with a Boy Scout troop and try to take pictures and obtain other information (e.g., read gauges) while on the tour at the competitor's annual "Engineering as a Profession Day" three weeks from now? Use the four virtues, four-component model, evaluation checklist, and ethics checklist to help take the "grayness" out of the situation and make it black or white.

9.5. Jay's boss is an acknowledged expert in the field of data analysis. Jay is the leader of a group that has been charged with developing a new catalyst system. So far the group has narrowed the candidates to two possibilities, catalyst A and catalyst B.

The boss is certain that the best choice is A, but he directs that the tests be run on both catalysts "just for the record." Owing to the fact that inexperienced employees run the tests, the tests take longer than expected, and the results show that B is the preferred material. The engineers question the validity of the tests, but because of the project's timetable, there is no time to repeat the series. The boss directs Jay to work the math backward and come up with phony data to justify the choice of catalyst A—a choice that all the engineers in the group, including Jay, fully agree with. Jay writes the report.

What would you do?

A. Write the report as directed by the boss?

B. Refuse to write the report, because to do so would be unethical?

C. Write the report, but also write a memo to the boss stating that what is being done is unethical—to cover you in case you are found out?

D. Write the report as directed, but refuse to have your name on it as the author?

E. Go over your boss's head and report that you have been asked to falsify records?

F. Do something else? (If so, what?)

Use the four virtues, four-component model, evaluation checklist, ethics checklist, and five P's to help you analyze each of these options. (Problem adapted from *Chemical Engineering*, p.132, September 1980.)

9.6. In exercise 9.5, Jay decided to write the report to suit his boss, and the company has gone ahead with an ambitious commercialization program for catalyst A. Jay has been put in charge of the pilot plant where development work is being done on the project. To allay his doubts, he personally runs some clandestine tests on the two catalysts. To his astonishment and dismay, the tests determine that while catalyst A works better under most conditions (as everyone expected), at the operating conditions specified in the firm's process design, catalyst B is, indeed, considerably superior.

If you were Jay, what would you do?

A. Since no one knows that you've done the tests, keep quiet about the results because the process will run acceptably with catalyst A, although not nearly as well as well as it would run with catalyst B?

B. Tell your former boss (the catalyst expert) about the clandestine tests and let him decide what to do next?

C. Make a clean breast of the whole affair to upper management, knowing that it could get you and a number of colleagues fired or, at least, discredited professionally?

D. Do something else? (If so, what?)

Use the four virtues, four-component model, evaluation checklist, ethics checklist, and five P's to help you analyze each of these options. (Problem adapted from *Chemical Engineering,* p.132, September 1980.)

9.7. Ruth works as a group leader for a company that sells large quantities of a major food product that is processed before sale, by heating. Her product-development group has been analyzing the naturally occurring flavor constituents of the product, and Ruth has discovered that several of the flavor components (actually pyrolysis products, present in minute quantities) are chemicals that have been found to cause cancer in animals when given in large doses. Yet, the product—in worldwide use for literally centuries—has never been implicated as a cause of cancer.

Although in the United States the Delaney Amendment to the Pure Food and Drug Act prohibits companies from adding cancer-causing agents to food, there are no government regulations concerning those that may occur naturally.

What should Ruth do?

A. Quash the report?

B. Submit a confidential report to her superiors and let them decide?

C. Submit an article summarizing the compounds found to a reputable journal, but without mentioning cancer?

D. Notify a consumer-protection organization?

Use the four virtues, four-component model, evaluation checklist, ethics checklist, and five P's to help you analyze each of these options. (Problem adapted from *Chemical Engineering,* p. 132, September 1980.)

9.8. The company that employs Reginald has a practice of using salaried personnel to replace striking workers and paying these people double-time pay for any work in excess of 40 hours per week, plus a $100-per-day strike bonus. (Under ordinary circumstances, overtime pay is never granted to salaried personnel, which includes engineers.) Not having a union themselves, Reginald and his fellow engineers have been hard hit by inflation, and many would welcome the opportunity to earn extra pay.

The plant is presently being struck by union operators over "unsafe" working conditions, which Reginald personally believes may be unsafe but which are not covered specifically under government safety regulations. The company disputes the union's contention about safety. The strike looks as if it could be a lengthy one.

What should Reginald do?

A. Refuse to work, because he thinks the union's allegations may have merit?

B. Refuse to work, because he believes that strike breaking is unethical?

C. Work, because he believes that filling in for striking workers is an obligation of all members of management?

D. Work, because the extra pay is a great way to catch up on some of his bills or earn the down payment on a car?

E. Work, because he believes he may be fired if he doesn't?

F. Do something else? (If so, what?)

Use the four virtues, four-component model, evaluation checklist, ethics checklist, and five P's to help you analyze each of these options. (Problem adapted from *Chemical Engineering,* p. 132, September 1980.)

9.9. Larry's company has been using a flavor additive in one of its products, but there have been problems with the flavor's stability. One of Larry's chemists accidentally discovers that the flavor can be stabilized by adding a mixture of tin and lead in very small quantities. Although both tin and lead are recognized poisons, the chemist points out

the amounts added are not more than the amounts that might be leached out of the sol-
dered seams of the common tin cans used for a multitude of food products. The new
product will be packed in glass, so no further addition of heavy metals will occur.

What should Larry do?

A. Recommend that the additive not be used, because it is unethical to add poisons no
matter what the quantity?

B. Prevent any further problems by suppressing the finding?

C. Recommend the open use of this heavy-metals-stabilized additive?

D. Recommend that the tin and lead additives be used, but that the deliberate addition
of heavy metals be considered a trade secret and kept from leaking to the public
because "it would only cause unnecessary worry"?

Use the four virtues, four-component model, evaluation checklist, ethics checklist,
and five P's to help you analyze each of these options. (Problem adapted from
Chemical Engineering, p. 132, September 1980.)

9.10. Maria is a process engineer for Stardust Chemical Corporation, and she has signed a
secrecy agreement with the firm that prohibits her from divulging information that the
company considers proprietary. Stardust has developed an adaptation of a standard
piece of equipment that is highly efficient for cooling a viscous plastics slurry. (Stardust decides not to patent the idea but to keep it a trade secret.) Eventually, Maria
leaves Stardust and goes to work for a candy-processing company that is not in any
way in competition with her former employer. She soon realizes that a modification
similar to Stardust's trade secret could be applied to a different machine used for cooling fudge, and at once has the change made.

A. Has Maria acted unethically (because she divulged the proprietary modification that
Stardust developed)?

B. Has Maria acted ethically (because she has used only the idea behind the modification, not the specific change developed by Stardust)?

C. Would Maria have acted unethically if the machine used to cool fudge and the one
used by Stardust were identical?

Use the four virtues, four-component model, evaluation checklist, ethics checklist,
and five P's to help you answer these questions. (From *Chemical Engineering*,
p. 132, September 1980.)

9.11. You put together a buoyancy exhibit for a "science day" event. Your exhibit consists
of filling up an aquarium with water and then testing which soda pop cans float. The
idea is that the diet soda pop cans will float because they don't contain sugar,
whereas the nondiet soda pop cans will sink. In preparing your experiment the night
before, you discover that one of your diet soda pop cans floats but the other slowly
sinks to the bottom. You know that if you "spike" the water with salt, thereby
increasing the water's density, all of the diet soda pop cans will float.

What should you do?

A. Spike the water and tell no one?

B. Spike the water and tell only those parents who appear to be looking at your exhibit as a future science fair experiment?

C. Spike the water, but put up a sign next to the exhibit warning people about what you have done?

D. Not spike the water?

E. Do something else? (If so, what?)

Use the four virtues, four-component model, evaluation checklist, ethics checklist, and five P's to help you analyze each of these options. (Problem contributed by Dr. Susan Montgomery, University of Michigan, 1992.)

9.12. You attend your friend's piano recital, knowing that your friend is seriously considering a career as a pianist. Her performance is atrocious. She approaches you after the performance and asks, "Well, what did you think?"

What should you do?

A. Tell her to keep her day job?

B. Tell her it sounded terrific?

C. Try to get out of it by telling her Victor Borge couldn't have done a better job?

D. Tell her it was pretty good, with plans to approach her later to discourage her from making a career of it?

E. Do something else? (If so, what?)

Use the four virtues, four-component model, evaluation checklist, ethics checklist, and five P's to help you analyze each of these options. (Problem contributed by Dr. Susan Montgomery, University of Michigan, 1992.)

9.13. Your company sends you to a foreign country to take part in the bidding for a large construction project. Once you get there, your associates in the country tell you the bribing rates for the officials in charge of taking the bids.

What should you do?

A. Refuse to bribe the officials, knowing you will certainly lose the project?

B. Bribe the officials at double the ongoing rate, to ensure that you get the project?

C. Go along with the bribing scheme, knowing that it is the only way your project will be considered?

D. Do something else? (If so, what?)

Use the four virtues, four-component model, evaluation checklist, ethics checklist, and five P's to help you analyze each of these options. (Problem contributed by Dr. Susan Montgomery, University of Michigan, 1992.)

9.14. Your boss takes you out on the town dining the first weekend of your summer job, not knowing that you are still under the legal drinking age. In the restaurant, everyone at your table orders a drink.

What should you do?

A. Order a beer, wanting to fit in, and hope the server doesn't check your ID?

B. Order a beer, wanting to fit in, and be ready with your false ID in case the server asks for one?

C. Do something else? (If so, what?)

Use the four virtues, four-component model, evaluation checklist, ethics checklist, and five P's to help you analyze each of these options. (Problem contributed by Dr. Susan Montgomery, University of Michigan, 1992.)

9.15. Buffalo Nation is a small Native American tribe whose reservation is located in southwestern Colorado. It has three tribal communities on its reservation. Buffalo Nation has debated the feasibility of producing natural gas from the Buffalo Nation Gas Reservoir for more than 5 years. The tribal council has been split on the issue, however. Younger tribal elders view it as the best way to revive the tribe, as the venture will create significant annual income that will improve the schools, sanitation systems, and roads that have decayed over time, and provide much needed jobs and income. Traditional tribal elders are against any type of development because the reservoir is adjacent to and under the sacred Buffalo Lake. They view development as invasive to their traditional way of life and as a threat to the tribe's cohesiveness. In the past two years, the tribal council has added several elders who are progressive, including one who has a degree in chemical engineering, and replacing those elders who had have become ill or had passed away.

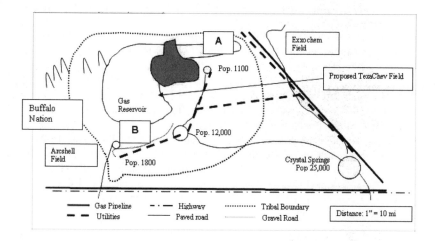

A committee has been formed to reach an intermediate decision about the natural gas proposals. The committee members include the following persons:

– A TexaChev lawyer who has a B.S. in chemical engineering and wants site B to be developed
– The Exxochem field manager, who has a B.S. in chemical engineering and wants site A to be developed
– A tribal lawyer who is a well-respected traditional member from the northern town, is considered to be in line to become the next tribal council leader, and is reluctant to establish a pattern of change for his tribe
– A tribal elder who is a moderate from the central town with education (optional)
– A tribal elder who is a younger member from the southern town and has a B.S. in chemical engineering (optional)

Assume one of the roles of the committee members, and discuss the following issues: evaluation criteria, impact of developing utilities and roads, economic impact, impact of developing a new gas pipeline, environmental impact, cultural impact, impact of potential growth of site, educational impact, and other concerns. *You must discuss each issue from the point of view of your assumed character.* For instance, the industry representatives will favor one of the sites because of the advantages to one particular company. Determine whether a decision to can be made to bring the decision before the full Buffalo Nation tribal council.

(Material provided by University of Colorado faculty and staff Beverly Louie [Women in Engineering Program/Chemical & Biological Engineering Department] and David Aragon [Multicultural Engineering Program], and Thomas Abeyta of Oberlin College, who developed these materials for use in student leadership development activities.)

9.16. Add to the analysis of (a) the Holiday Gift case study and (b) the Rigging the Bidding case study by applying Seebauer and Barry's four-component model and four virtues.

9.17. Write a paragraph describing the difficulties you might encounter in applying the ethics principles discussed in this chapter on the job in industry.

FURTHER READING

Dresner, M. R. "Risk Assessment: How Do We (Irrational Humans) Really Do It?" *Chemtech*, 21, p. 340, 1991. Provides an introduction to the subject.

Matley, Jay, and Richard Greene. "Ethics of Health, Safety, and Environment: 'What's Right?'" *Chemical Engineering*, p. 40, March 1987, and p. 119, September 28, 1987. More scenarios with a health/safety/environmental flavor to further challenge your ethical judgment.

Rosenzweig, Mark, and Charles Butcher. "Should You Use That Knowledge?" *Chemical Engineering Progress*, April 1992 and October 1992. Interesting ethical scenarios that further test your "ethical judgment."

10   TROUBLESHOOTING

Previous chapters in this book discussed each of the five building blocks of our problem-solving heuristic. In this chapter we expand on the problem definition techniques introduced in Chapter 4 to present troubleshooting, another approach commonly used in industry for finding the root cause of a problem. Because troubleshooting is frequently applied to technical situations, the examples offered here will have a more technical flavor than some of our earlier examples.

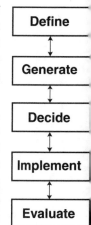

Troubleshooting is used to determine why something new, just constructed, or recently implemented will not work. Troubleshooting is also applicable to an existing plan or process that was working well but then suddenly changed so that it no longer works up to specifications. In each of these situations, we need to carry out a methodical analysis to find and correct the problem. Troubleshooting is an interactive process in which we form a number of hypotheses about where the fault lies and then carry out procedures to test those hypotheses. We can then systematically eliminate or confirm our hypotheses as we obtain the results of the test procedures we proposed. While troubleshooting is far from an exact science, the guidelines and heuristics we have studied so far in this text (e.g., critical thinking, the Duncker diagram, and K.T. problem analysis) will prove extremely useful in the process.

SOME GENERAL GUIDELINES

Successful troubleshooting starts with a solid understanding of engineering fundamentals, the process, and the specific unit questions.[1] It also requires paying attention to detail, developing good listening skills, viewing the problem firsthand, and understanding the symptoms of the problem. These and other troubleshooting guidelines are summarized by Laird et al. and shown next.

Troubleshooting Guidelines[1]

1. Gather information.

2. Apply solid engineering fundamentals.

3. Separate observations from hypotheses or conjectures.

4. Independently verify data using field measurements and observations, when possible.

5. Make rigorous comparisons with satisfactory operations and compare the data obtained under normal operation with the data obtained under faulty operating conditions.

6. Spend time in the unit making direct observations—even if you are not sure what to expect.

7. Consider the entire system related to the problem.

8. Practice good listening skills.

9. Do not reject serendipitous results.

10. Brainstorm all the things that could explain the fault.

11. Use K.T. analysis (either problem analysis or potential problem analysis in modified form) and other troubleshooting strategies to deduce what happened during the faulty run. Present the analysis in the form of a table or chart.

12. Choose the most likely cause or set of conditions that produced the data, and then run the equipment under these conditions to attempt to reproduce the data to verify the hypothesis. Do not fall in love with a hypothesis—seek to reject as well as to accept.

13. Suggest a new troubleshooting scenario. After supervisor approval, collect data and describe how the problem should be approached.

The first step—gathering relevant information—is a key component in any troubleshooting process. Learn how to ask the critical questions. See if you have the necessary information to make a "ballpark" calculation. Walk around the plant, talk to the operators, and compare data from the malfunctioning unit with data from the normal operation. Use the K.T. algorithm for making this comparison:

- What is? What is not? What is the distinction?
- Where is? Where is not? What is the distinction?

The Kepner–Tregoe (K.T.) algorithms and the troubleshooting guidelines from Don Woods's book *Successful Troubleshooting for Process Engineers*[2] should be used whenever possible. An excellent set of "rules of thumb" for troubleshooting can be found in this book, along with guidelines for data gathering and developing critical thinking and interpersonal skills. The critical thinking and troubleshooting focus may then be applied to laboratory experiments and field and plant equipment, as demonstrated by the following troubleshooting worksheet developed by Woods.

Troubleshooting Worksheet[3]

What is the problem? _____

_____

What are the symptoms? _____

1. _____
2. _____
3. _____

Who are the people you will talk to, and why do you want to talk to them? _____

_____

_____

Which data are to be double-checked for accuracy? _____

_____

Fundamentals

What are the guiding principles and equations? _____

_____

Continues

Troubleshooting Worksheet[3] (Continued)

List at least five working hypotheses for the problem:

1. _____

2. _____

3. _____

4. _____

5. _____

Monitoring

If I make this measurement or take this action, what will it tell me?

Measurement/Action _____   Reason/Possible Cause _____

Measurement/Action _____   Reason/Possible Cause _____

Measurement/Action _____   Reason/Possible Cause _____

Measurement/Action _____   Reason/Possible Cause _____

Measurement/Action _____   Reason/Possible Cause _____

Does it fit the observation?

Cause of the Problem	Result of the Cause	Does It Fit the Observation?	Steps Needed to Check Cause	Feasibility
1._____	1._____	1._____	1._____	1._____
2._____	2._____	2._____	2._____	2._____
3._____	3._____	3._____	3._____	3._____

Kepner–Tregoe Problem Analysis

What *is?*	What *is not?*	What is the distinction?
1. _____	1. _____	1. _____
2. _____	2. _____	2. _____

Where *is it?*	Where *is it not?*	
1. _____	1. _____	1. _____
2. _____	2. _____	2. _____

When did it occur (*is*)?	When was everything okay (*is not*)?	
1. _____	1. _____	1. _____
2. _____	2. _____	2. _____

What *is* the extent?	What *is not* the extent?	
1. _____	1. _____	1. _____
2. _____	2. _____	2. _____

Which hypotheses are consistent with all symptoms? _____,_____,_____,_____

Troubleshooters should always keep four or five working hypotheses in mind as they seek to determine what could be causing the fault as they complete this worksheet. Woods stresses the importance of brainstorming as a technique to generate a number of potential explanations.[1] Techniques for brainstorming (e.g., Osborn's vertical thinking, de Bono's lateral thinking) are discussed in Chapter 5.

Another table that is useful for screening potential causes of a problem is the "Does it fit the observation?" table, which was also developed by Woods:

Cause of the Problem	Result of the Cause	Does It Fit the Observation/or Measurement?	Steps Needed to Check Cause	Feasibility

This table can help you organize your thoughts by eliminating hypotheses that are not the true cause of the problem.

We will now apply the procedure outlined on Woods's troubleshooting worksheet to two examples: one nontechnical and one requiring some understanding of the principles of heat transfer, which are commonly discussed in engineering courses.

EARLY MORNING SHIVERS: AN EXAMPLE OF TROUBLESHOOTING

Your spouse shakes you awake at 5 A.M. on a late January morning. The house is cold and it is snowing outside. You usually turn the thermostat back a bit at night, but the temperature in the house is 52 °F (you determine this fact by looking at your desk thermometer). Something is obviously wrong. Your spouse says the house is too cold for your 18-month-old daughter and asks you to do something to get the heat back on. As a temporary measure, your spouse brings your daughter into your bed to keep her warm (temporarily solving one "real" problem). You start to solve the problem by mentally filling out the troubleshooting worksheet.

Troubleshooting Worksheet

What is the problem?

The house is cold and is losing heat.

What are the symptoms?

The temperature inside the house is currently 52 °F and falling.

Who are the people you will talk to, and why do you want to talk to them?

1. Your spouse: Has he or she noticed any unusual problems with the furnace over the past few days?

2. Too early to call anyone else right now.

Which data are to be double-checked for accuracy?

Make sure that the furnace is truly off and that the problem is not caused by an open window or door. (Could someone have broken in during the night?) Upon checking, the house appears to be secure—no windows are open or broken, and all exterior doors are closed.

Fundamentals

What are the guiding principles and equations?

The thermostat (located in the living room) controls the furnace, which in turn heats the house through the combustion of natural gas in the furnace. The flame heats a heat exchanger through which the air passes before it is circulated throughout the house. When the temperature in the house falls below the desired value (the set point), the thermostat calls on the furnace to start. When the house warms up to the desired temperature, the thermostat turns the furnace off. The furnace incorporates several safety devices.

Continues

Troubleshooting Worksheet (Continued)

- A high-temperature sensor that shuts off the natural gas flow if the temperature inside the furnace gets too high.

- A flame sensor that detects whether the pilot light is lit. This very small flame burns continuously and ignites the main gas flow. If the pilot is off, it would be unsafe to open the gas valve, because unburned natural gas would then flow into the furnace and the house, creating an explosion hazard. (Some newer furnaces have a glow plug that heats up to ignite the gas, but the principle is the same: If the glow plug fails to heat up, the safety system prevents the main gas valve from opening.)

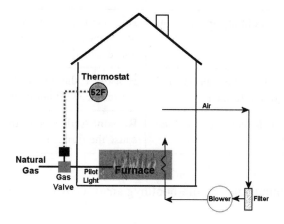

List at least five working hypotheses for the problem:

1. The thermostat is malfunctioning and the furnace does not "think" the house is cold.

2. The electricity in the house is off, or the furnace circuit breaker has tripped.

3. The natural gas supply to the house has been interrupted.

4. The furnace air filter is plugged.

5. The pilot light is out.

6. The sensor for the pilot light is dirty and doesn't sense that the pilot light is on.

Continues

Troubleshooting Worksheet (Continued)

Monitoring If I make this measurement or take this action, what will it tell me?	
Measurement: Check the battery in the thermostat.	**Reason:** A dead battery can cause a malfunction.
Measurement: Check the hot water temperature in the bathroom.	**Reason:** If the water is hot, the natural gas supply to the house is okay, because the water heater also operates on natural gas.
Action: Turn on the light in the bathroom.	**Reason:** This action confirms that there is not an electrical power outage to the house, which would affect the furnace.
Action: Check the circuit breaker box and reset the breaker for the furnace.	**Reason:** If the furnace breaker is tripped, the furnace will not operate.
Action: Remove the furnace filter and see if the furnace will operate.	**Reason:** A plugged or dirty filter can cause the furnace to not operate properly.

We now continue our troubleshootinyg analysis by filling out a K.T. problem analysis table.

K.T. Problem Analysis of the Cold House

	Is	**Is Not**	**Distinction**	**Possible Cause**
What	House is cold	Normal or too-high temperature	Heat added is insufficient to warm the house to the desired temperature	Furnace is off
When	Sometime since bedtime last night	Prior to bedtime	Night is colder, probably causing furnace to run more frequently	Low outside temperature
Where	Entire house is cold	Localized to one room	Something systemic (not a door or window open)	Thermostat problems Natural gas outage Plugged furnace filter
Extent	Only furnace	Water heater or other utilities	Electricity and natural gas are okay	Thermostat problems Plugged furnace filter Other, more complicated mechanical/electrical problems

Does It Fit the Observation?

Cause	**Result**	**Does It Fit the Observation or Measurement?**	**Steps Needed to Check Cause**	**Feasibility**
Thermostat battery is dead	Control system won't ask furnace to start	Yes	Remove and replace battery	Easy, if a spare battery is handy
Furnace filter is blocked or partially blocked	Low air flow to and from furnace results in overheating of furnace, causing it to shut off	Yes	Remove filter and temporarily run without one	Easy
Electricity to furnace is out	Furnace won't operate	Yes	Reset circuit breaker	Easy
Natural gas supply to heat house is shut off	Furnace and hot water heater won't operate	Yes	Check hot water heater	Easy to check—call the gas company
Circuits or connections in furnace are corroded or malfunctioning	Furnace won't operate	Yes	Varies—may need to open furnace up	Need a trained technician

The problem in this example turned out to be a weak thermostat battery. Replacement of the battery corrected the problem.

In this troubleshooting example, we used the troubleshooting procedure to solve a generic problem. The remaining examples in this chapter apply the troubleshooting process to problems of an engineering nature.

TECHNICAL TROUBLESHOOTING EXERCISE

In the next example, we will recall some of the principles of heat transfer and apply them to an actual case history from Marlin and Woods. This example is included for those students who are either enrolled in engineering or are thinking of enrolling in engineering.

Troubleshooting: The Boiler Feedwater Heater

Waste flash steam from the ethyl acetate plant is saturated at slightly above atmospheric pressure. It is sent to the shell of a tube heat exchanger to preheat the boiler feedwater to 70 °C for the nearby boiler house. The boiler feedwater heater is shown in the figure.

Condensate is withdrawn through a thermodynamic steam trap at the bottom of the shell. The water flows once through the $\frac{3}{4}$-inch nominal tubes. There are 1000 tubes. "When the system was put into operation three hours ago, everything worked fine," says the supervisor. "But now the exit boiler feedwater is 42 °C instead of the design value. What do we do? This problem is costing us extra fuel to vaporize the water at the boiler." Fix the problem.

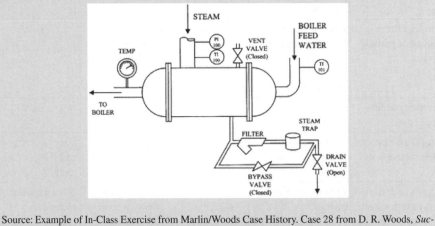

Source: Example of In-Class Exercise from Marlin/Woods Case History. Case 28 from D. R. Woods, *Successful Troubleshooting for Process Engineers*. Wiley-VCH Verlag, Darmstadt, Germany, 2006.

Let's start our analysis of this situation by filling out the troubleshooting worksheet.

Troubleshooting Worksheet

What is the problem?

Heat exchanger malfunction.

What are the symptoms?

The water temperature at the exit of the heat exchanger is 42 °C instead of 70 °C, resulting in boiler feedwater not being heated to the appropriate temperature.

Who are the people you will talk to, and why do you want to talk to them?

The plant engineer says this is the first time workers have used waste steam from the ethyl acetate plant.

Which data are to be double-checked for accuracy?

The temperature of water from the heat exchanger was double-checked and found to be 42 °C.

Fundamentals

What are the guiding principles and equations?

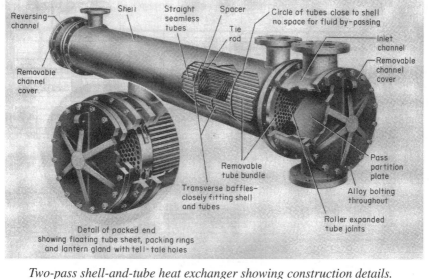

Two-pass shell-and-tube heat exchanger showing construction details.
(Courtesy of Ross Heat Exchanger Division of American Standard. From Max S. Peters,
Elementary Chemical Engineering, 2nd ed. McGraw-Hill, New York, 1984.)[4]

Continues

Troubleshooting Worksheet (Continued)

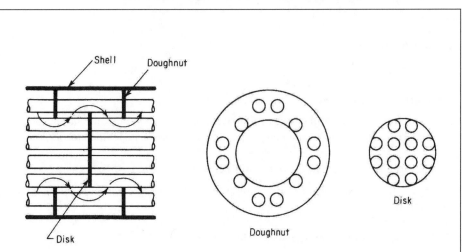

Disk-and-doughnut baffles. (From Max S. Peters, Elementary Chemical Engineering, 2nd ed. McGraw-Hill, New York, 1984.)[4]

The water being heated flows on the inside of the tubes, and the waste steam condenses on the outside of the tubes. The flow of heat, Q, from the condensing steam at temperature T_{steam} to the water at temperature T_{water} at any point in the exchanger is given by the equation

$$Q = U\,(T_{steam} - T_{water})$$

The heat flux at any point is $Q = U(T_{steam} - T_{water})$, where T_{water} is the local temperature. The energy balance is $Q = UA\Delta T_{lm}$. This equation for Q using the log mean temperature driving force may be rearranged to the equation for T_{out}, where A is the heat exchange area and U is the overall heat transfer coefficient, which is a measure of the rate of heat transfer between the shell-side fluid (steam) and the tube-side fluid (water).

The smaller the value of U, the lower the rate of heat transfer. Neglecting the resistance of the pipe wall and assuming that the inside pipe surface area and the outside pipe surface area are the same, the overall heat transfer coefficient U is related to the individual heat transfer coefficients inside (h_i) and outside (h_o) the tubes by the equation

$$1/U = 1/h_o + 1/h_i$$

The smaller the value of h, the smaller the value of U.

Troubleshooting Worksheet (Continued)

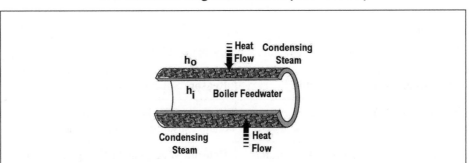

For condensing steam, the outside (i.e., shell-side) heat transfer coefficient is large— on the order of 20,000 W/m^2/°C—compared to the inside (i.e., tube-side) heat transfer coefficient for flowing water (which is approximately 1500 W/m^2/°C). The heat transfer coefficient for stagnant water surrounding the pipes is on the order of 100 W/m^2/°C. If air were present instead of steam, then the shell-side heat transfer coefficient would be approximately 10 W/m^2/°C.

We know that we can find the exit temperature by rearranging the energy balance to obtain

$$T_{out} = T_{steam} - (T_{steam} - T_{in}) \exp(-UA/mC_P)$$

where m and C_P are the mass flow rate and heat capacity of the water, respectively.

Consequently, we see that the outlet temperature from the exchanger to the boiler, T_{out}, would be lowered if the inlet and steam temperatures are lower than expected; the mass flow rate, m, is higher than expected; the overall heat transfer coefficient, U, is lower than expected; and the effective heat exchange area, A, is smaller than expected. The overall heat transfer coefficient will be lower if the individual transfer coefficients inside (h_i) and outside (h_o) were smaller than expected.

List at least five working hypotheses for the problem:

1. The steam trap has become blocked, causing liquid condensate to back up in the heat exchanger and preventing the steam from contacting the pipes in the exchanger.

2. The entering water is subcooled.

3. The steam pressure and the temperature have dropped.

4. The heat exchanger has become fouled.

5. The steam is dirty—that is, it contains noncondensable gases.

Continues

Troubleshooting Worksheet (Continued)

Monitoring

If I make this measurement or take this action, what will it tell me?

Measurement: Inlet temperature.	**Reason:** Subcooled inlet.
Measurement: Water flow rate.	**Reason:** A higher than normal flow rate could cause the fluid not to reach 70 °C.
Action: Check whether the steam trap is closed and not functioning properly. If it is functioning correctly, it should open and close periodically as condensate is formed in the shell.	**Reason:** Water may be filling up the shell side of the exchanger, reducing the condensing steam heat transfer coefficient.
Action: Check whether the filter is plugged.	**Reason:** This problem would produce the same symptoms as a closed steam trap.
Action: Carefully open the vent.	**Reason:** If noncondensable gases have accumulated in the shell, the steam-side heat transfer coefficient would be decreased, reducing U.
Action: Make sure the drain valve is open.	**Reason:** If someone has closed the drain valve, water may be filling up the shell side of the exchanger, reducing the condensing steam heat transfer coefficient.
Action: Check the inlet steam temperature and pressure.	**Reason:** If either of these measures has decreased, the enthalpy of the entering steam will be less than expected, reducing the outlet water temperature.

We now continue troubleshooting analysis by filling out a K.T. problem analysis table.

K.T. Problem Analysis of the Boiler Feed Heater Problem

	Is	Is Not	Distinction	Possible Cause
What	Low exit temperature	Normal or too-high exit temperature	Insufficient heat supply to raise the temperature to 70 °C	Flow rate is too high Inlet water temperature is too low, leading to poor heating
	Correct water and steam temperature measurements	Wrong temperature measurements	Current temperature driving force should be sufficient to heat the water to 70 °C because condensing steam has a high heat transfer coefficient	Something other than incorrect measurements
	Normal water feed rate	High water feed rate	Current temperature driving force should be sufficient to heat the normal water flow to 70 °F	Increase in heat transfer resistance
	Filter and steam trap open	Blocked filter or steam trap	Tubes not surrounded by liquid condensate	Something other than liquid is increasing the resistance
When	Three hours after start-up	Immediately after start-up	Decrease in heat transfer	Buildup of noncondensable gas from waste steam or shell filled with water
Where	Inside heat exchanger	Outside heat exchanger	Entering temperatures are normal	Inefficient heat transfer between shell and tubes
	Entering steam and water temperature normal	Abnormal entering water or steam temperatures	Temperature driving force is not affected	Heat transfer resistance is increased
Extent	Only part of the equipment is affected; some tubes are not affected	All of the equipment is affected; some tubes are not affected	Heat exchange takes place between the shell and tubes	Inefficient heat transfer between the shell and tubes

Does It Fit the Observation?

Cause	Result	Does It Fit the Observation or Measurement?	Steps Needed to Check Cause	Feasibility
Fouling/scale on water side or on steam side	Decrease in heat transfer coefficient	Does not account for a temperature drop over a short period	Instrumentation and measurements to calculate heat transfer coefficient; inspection of tubes	Inspection of the tubes is time-consuming and costly if instruments are not available
Malfunctioning steam trap; clogged condensate valve	Rise in water level and consequent loss of heat transfer area	Water buildup could account for the temperature drop	Observation of water level in condenser shell	Easy—shut down condenser and remove drain
High presence of inert elements in steam; clogged bleed valve	Decrease in heat transfer coefficient	Inert element buildup may account for temperature drop	Shut down, vent inert elements, and restart the system; perform a bleed gas analysis	Availability of skilled technician and equipment?
Inaccurate temperature reading	No actual malfunction in the boiler	Does not account for a temperature drop over a short period	—	—
Steam superheated too high; water flow too high	No malfunction	Does not account for a temperature drop over a short period or a large temperature drop	—	—
Drop in steam pressure owing to a steam-side leak	Change of condensation temperature	No visible/audible signs of a steam leak	—	—

Source: Example of In-Class Exercise from Marlin/Woods Case History. Case 28 from D. R. Woods, *Successful Troubleshooting for Process Engineers*. Wiley-VCH Verlag, Darmstadt, Germany, 2006

The problem in this example turned out to be that "dirty steam" containing noncondensable gases had blanketed the heat exchanger tubes in the shell of the heat exchanger. Consequently, the condensing steam, which has a high heat transfer coefficient, could not effectively reach the tubes carrying the water.

TROUBLESHOOTING LABORATORY EQUIPMENT

When one of the authors of this book (Scott Fogler) teaches the senior unit operations laboratory at the University of Michigan's College of Engineering, the last three weeks of laboratory sessions are devoted to having students apply their newly learned troubleshooting skills. In these sessions, students work in groups of three on one of four different pieces of equipment: a packed bed distillation column, a double-effect evaporator, an Advanced Reactor Safety Screening Tool (ARSST), and a Continuous Stirred Tank Reactor/Plug Flow Reactor (CSTR/PFR) apparatus. Before students try to carry out an experiment on these pieces of equipment, the graduate student instructors (GSIs) generate a specific fault in each one of these pieces of equipment and collect the data. The students are then given two sets of data. One set is taken when the equipment was operated under normal conditions. The second set of data includes the same measurements for the same equipment, but this time obtained under the faulty operation planned by the GSIs.

After the students familiarize themselves with their particular piece of assigned equipment they are asked to perform the troubleshooting algorithm shown on pages 215 and 217. During their troubleshooting exercises, they are allowed to submit three questions in writing to the professor/GSI regarding the data supplied to them. These troubleshooting exercises on real equipment provide students with some very valuable hands-on experience that serves them very well when they become practicing engineers in industry.

SUMMARY

Troubleshooting is used to determine why something new, just constructed, or recently implemented will not work. It is also applicable to an existing plan or process that was working well but then suddenly changed so that it no longer works up to specifications. In each of these situations, we need to carry out a methodical analysis to find and correct the problem. Troubleshooting is an interactive process—as demonstrated by Woods's troubleshooting worksheet—in which we form a number of hypotheses about where the fault lies and then carry out procedures to test our hypotheses. We can then systematically eliminate or confirm our hypotheses as we obtain the results of the test procedures we proposed, thereby identifying the root cause of the problem.

REFERENCES

1. Adapted from Laird, D., B. Albert, C. Steiner, and D. Little, "Take a Hands-on Approach to Refining Troubleshooting," *Chemical Engineering Progress*, p. 68, June 2002.
2. Slightly modified from Worksheet 2-1 from D. R. Woods, *Successful Troubleshooting for Process Engineers*, Wiley-VCH Verlag, Darmstadt, Germany, 2006.
3. After Donald Woods, McMaster University, Hamilton, Ontario, Canada.
4. Peters, Max S., *Elementary Chemical Engineering*, 2nd ed., McGraw-Hill, New York, 1984.
5. Fogler, H. S., *The Elements of Chemical Reaction Engineering*, 4th ed., Prentice Hall, Upper Saddle River, NJ, 2006.
6. Fogler, H.S., S. E. LeBlanc, and S. M. Montgomery, "Interactive Creative Problem Solving," *Computer Applications in Engineering Education*, 4, 1, pp. 35–39, 1996.
7. Fogler, H. S., and N. Varde, "Asynchronous Learning of Chemical Reaction Engineering," *Chemical Engineering Education*, 35, p. 290, 2001.

EXERCISES

10.1. Lake Nyos* in western Cameroon, adjacent to Nigeria, in the elbow region of West Africa, is a water-filled throat of an old volcano. The lake, which is deep and funnel sloped, lies within the Oku Volcanic Field, at the northern boundary of the Cameroon Volcanic Line. The Cameroon Volcanic Line is a zone of crustal weakness and volcanism that extends to the southwest through the Mount Cameroon stratovolcano. The Oku Volcanic Field contains numerous basaltic scoria cones and maars. Lake Nyos itself occupies a maar crater that formed from a hydrovolcanic eruption 400 years ago. Although the volcano is no longer erupting, gas continues to be released very slowly, directly into the deepest water of the lake, by the old plumbing system. This gas is virtually all carbon dioxide, with no traces of deadly hydrogen cyanide or hydrogen sulfide. There are about 30 similar lakes in the region.

Lake Nyos covers an area of about 1.5 square kilometers and is more than 200 meters deep. The region of western Cameroon where it is located averages about 2.5 meters of rain each year. In the rainy season, the excess lake water escapes over a low spillway cut into the northern rim of the maar crater and races down a valley toward Nyos village.

---

*   http://www.geology.sdsu.edu/how_volcanoes_work/Nyos.html

On the morning of August 13, 1986, approximately 1700 people in the villages of Nyos, Kam Cha, and Subum, and virtually all the cattle, birds, and other animals living along the shore of Lake Nyos and in the valley were found dead. The hill people who discovered the disaster found some people still in their beds, some dead on the floor in their houses, and some dead along the water's edge.

The people who lived in the hills above the lake—all of whom survived—recalled hearing a bang around 9:30 P.M. the night before. It was neither a volcanic eruption nor an earthquake, and there were no visible signs of any destruction to the houses or to the trees and other foliage. However, for several days before August 12, there had been a number of unusually cold, rainy days. As a consequence, the cold water ran down the sides of the volcano into the lake, which was at a higher temperature. The water in Lake Nyos is normally a beautiful, deep-blue color. However, the lake now appears to be composed of murky, reddish brown water that apparently formed by the oxidation of iron-rich bottom waters that were carried up to shallower lake levels during the August 1986 event.

There is a rumor that a similar tragedy befell the inhabitants around Lake Nyos more than 100 or 200 years ago.

Use one or more troubleshooting techniques to find the cause of this disaster. After finding the cause, carry out a potential problem analysis to suggest ways to prevent such a disaster from occurring again.

One way to use this troubleshooting exercise in an interactive manner is to write down a list of questions to give to your instructor to answer. Your instructor, who has the solution, will charge a specified number of points for each question you ask; the point value (from 5 to 25 points) charged will depend on the quality of the question and the effort needed to find the answer. You have 100 points to spend, so you will not want to ask all of your questions at once but rather wait until you receive an answer before posing the next question. You want to spend as few points as possible. Each of the following sites may help you ask a pertinent question:

> http://www-personal.umich.edu/~gwk
> http://www-personal.umich.edu/~gwk/research/nyos.html

10.2. Photolithography is a process used to make the computer chips that are found in many electronic devices, including cell phones, MP3 players, digital cameras, and laptop computers. Photolithography uses light to transfer patterns from a "master" (i.e., a mask) to a surface (e.g., a silicon wafer). These patterns ultimately become the electrical components (transistors, resistors, wires, and so forth) of the chip. The pattern of light is generated by shining light through a mask, which selectively blocks the light in a manner similar to an overhead transparency. The light pattern is focused onto a substrate coated with a thin polymeric film called a photoresist. Acid is generated in the regions of the film that are exposed to light. The acid catalyzes a chemical reaction, which in turn allows the exposed regions of the protective film to become soluble. The soluble regions can then be washed away using a "developer" fluid, leaving the unexposed regions intact on the substrate. The exposed areas are further processed by depositing metal, etching, doping, and other means.

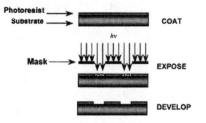

The photoresist typically contains a polymer and a photo-acid generator (PAG). An example of a PAG is shown below. The presence of light causes the molecule to break apart and form an acid (H^+).

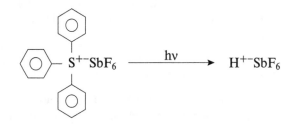

Ideally, the photogenerated acid reacts with a component of the polymeric resist that changes the solubility of the resist. This change in solubility is the critical step, allowing exposed regions of the resist to be dissolved away when placed in a developer. A "deprotection" reaction changes a portion of the polymer coating, allowing it to be dissolved away so that the area is no longer "protected." An example of a deprotection reaction is shown here.

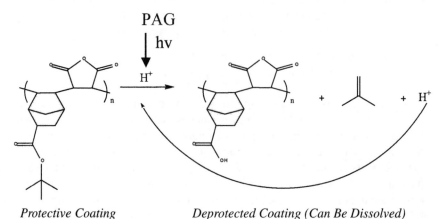

Protective Coating   *Deprotected Coating (Can Be Dissolved)*

The acid acts as a catalyst—it is regenerated during the reaction. A single acid can catalyze many deprotection reactions. This approach to patterning is called "chemically amplified resists," because a single photon is capable of ultimately deprotecting many sites on the polymer by generating a single acid molecule. The ultimate effect is to make the resist (i.e., the protective coating) more sensitive to light, which improves throughput.

Company X has been successfully using the photolithography process described previously for more than a year. Unfortunately, at the end of February the plant's East Wing began producing faulty chips. The faulty production of chips continued through the first few weeks of March. The source of the trouble appears to be that the exposed regions of the chips produced in the East Wing are not all dissolving as expected, causing the resulting chips to malfunction. Operations in the West Wing are unaffected. Although this problem has been occurring only on Friday afternoons for the past few weeks, it is critical that it be solved.

When you gather additional information about the situation, you make the following discoveries. Only one worker handles the chips in each wing of the plant. In the East Wing, the chips are handled by Mary, who has been employed since the beginning of the year. John, the West Wing operator, has been doing this job for several years now. You decide to observe the workers on Friday. The morning seems to go normally, and there are no problems with the process. You decide to have lunch with John and Mary. The company cafeteria changed caterers at the beginning of the year and the food is quite good, with a broad menu capable of satisfying the diverse work force at the plant: dishes ranging from tuna fish casserole to Asian cashew chicken to vegetarian food to beef and potatoes. John remarks how he really enjoys the new steak sandwiches and suggests that you try one. You do and are impressed with the quality. During lunch, conversation focuses on a wide variety of topics, from company politics, to sports (March Madness is in full swing and Mary is a big basketball fan), to Mary's upcoming trip to celebrate Easter with her family in New York. Lunch passes uneventfully, and the afternoon shift begins—and so do the problems with the chips. What do you conclude?

One way to use this troubleshooting exercise in an interactive manner is to write down a list of questions to give to your instructor to answer. Your instructor, who has the solution, will charge a specified number of points for each question you ask, and the point value (from 5 to 25 points) charged will depend on the quality of the question and the effort needed to find the answer. You have 100 points to spend, so you will not want to ask all of your questions at once but rather wait until you receive an answer before posing the next question. You want to spend as few points as possible.

(Problem courtesy of Professor Michael Dickey, Department of Chemical Engineering, North Carolina State University.)

11 PUTTING IT ALL TOGETHER

In the previous chapters of this book, we have presented the building blocks of creative problem solving individually so that we could focus more easily on each block. Of course, when we are faced with a problem in the real world, we bring many of these principles together to bear on the problem at the same time. We have shown the problem-solving heuristic in the form of a job card here. Job cards are usually displayed at the workplace or carried around by individuals to help them recall previously learned concepts that can be applied to their job.

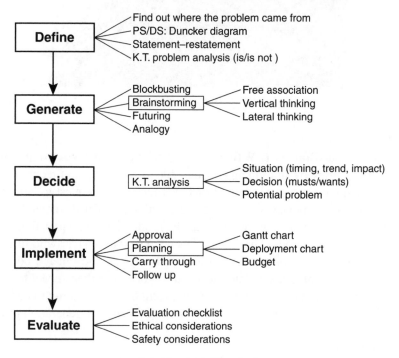

Job Card: A Heuristic

We will now show how the principles we have been studying can be applied to two case studies.

CASE STUDY 1: GENERATING SUSTAINABLE POWER FOR AN AGRICULTURAL PROCESSING PLANT IN INDIA

This case study was contributed by Marina Miletic, Ph.D., Department of Chemical and Biomolecular Engineering, University of Illinois, Urbana–Champaign, Illinois.

The EWB Team in India

Background

Engineers Without Borders (EWB) is an organization that helps communities in developing countries by introducing sustainable engineering and technology. The University of Illinois's student chapter of EWB received a request to help create a sustainable source of power for an off-the-grid village in Bhadakamandara, India. One of the village's sources of income was the production and harvesting of spices and other agricultural goods. These materials were sold to a buyer who further processed them by drying, milling, and grinding the spices and other products. The members of this community wanted to do the processing themselves to generate more income, but did not have the electricity, technology, or training needed to do so. The EWB students accepted the task of starting this power generation project.

Getting Started

This project required everyone on the team to be committed to the goal and to be in the right frame of mind for both solving the problem and implementing the solution. Because this project was voluntary, many participants came and went over time. The few who made the project a priority did much of the planning, went to India, worked until the process was implemented, and then worked to further improve the process even after the project was complete. All students worked equitably toward the goal, and everyone had well-defined roles and objectives throughout the entire project. These students were so focused on the end goal that few personal conflicts arose. The interactions of the group exemplified the team skills discussed in Chapter 2, as evidenced by everyone listening to others' ideas and respecting others' efforts.

There were numerous opportunities for solving many highly important problems, such as the need to purify the unclean water in the area and the need to deliver power to everyone's home in the village. Because of time and resource constraints, however, the problem was limited to providing power for agricultural processing.

Problem Definition

Gathering Information

Data Collection. To further define this problem, data needed to be collected. In particular, the following questions needed to be answered:

1. What kind of power generator will we use?
2. What kind of fuel will it use? (What kind of fuel is naturally occurring and/or available in that area?)
3. Where will the power generator and other equipment be housed?
4. How will we construct the building that will contain the generator and the other processing equipment?
5. How will we obtain the necessary supplies in India?
6. How will we communicate with the local residents? Where do we get an interpreter?

Talk with People Who Are Familiar with the Problem. EWB has undertaken many projects in India and around the world. The University of Illinois chapter of EWB submitted its proposal to work on an international project to EWB-USA headquarters (located in Colorado). The national headquarters office partnered the university team with the Association for Indians' Development (AID-Orissa), with Orissa University of Agriculture and Technology (OUAT), and later with Jagannath Institute of Technology and Management (JITM). All of these organizations had unique information to contribute to help identify the problem.

View the Problem Firsthand. A group of students performed a site assessment to ask local residents about available resources. The team found a vendor for generators in India and identified areas where they could buy related supplies. The team (after talking with villagers) decided on the site for the building where the generator and other equipment would be stored. This information was integrated into the next step of the process.

Problem Definition Techniques

The following critical thinking actions, which were discussed in problem-solving technique 1 in Chapter 4, helped the students define the problem.

Predicting. In predicting, we envision a plan and its consequences. The team had anticipated some of the major challenges involved in this project, both technical and social. This anticipation helped the group with planning a timeline and assigning tasks so that problems were resolved according to schedule.

Analyzing. In analyzing, we separate or break the whole into parts to discover their nature, function, and relationships. By first narrowing down the problem and then breaking the problem down into parts, the EWB team was able to identify the main obstacles for each problem. This helped with identifying what resources were needed (people, time, and money) to complete the project.

Information Seeking. In information seeking, we search for evidence, facts, or knowledge by identifying relevant sources and gathering objective, subjective, historical, and current data from those sources. By speaking with EWB headquarters, AID-Orissa, OUAT, JITM, and local residents, the team was better able to determine which kind of generator and agricultural equipment would be needed and where it would be assembled. They also learned about the potential health and cultural problems they might encounter.

Applying Standards. In applying standards, we make judgments based on established personal, professional, or social rules or criteria. The team agreed that they would go ahead with the project as long as what they did benefited the villagers. Safety was a top priority. These standards were maintained throughout the process and were incorporated in all decisions.

Problem Statement

Ultimately, the students defined their problem as follows: "Generate sustainable power for running agricultural processing equipment."

Generating Solutions

To generate a solution to this problem and answer the questions posed earlier, the team did a lot of brainstorming and research. Many technical blocks had to be removed before implementation of a solution to achieve the goal of powering the process.

Several possibilities for types of generators and fuels were identified. The team quickly identified biofuel- or vegetable oil–run generators as some of the best options given the size and scale of the spice-processing equipment. Ideas regarding the construction materials of the building were generated. Because the building would be constructed on a rice paddy, the students had to think about the materials for the foundation as well as for the building itself. A number of types of building materials were considered (including brick and concrete) based on availability.

Deciding the Course of Action

Students first distinguished which problems needed to be solved immediately and which problems could wait until later. Furthermore, some aspects of the problem had a greater priority than others. The timing of deciding the type of generator and developing a design for it had the highest impact and the highest timing priority. Other aspects of the problem, such as setting up grinding and milling machines, could be dealt with later. The following K.T. situation appraisal chart identifies the students' project priorities.

Situation Appraisal

Project	Timing	Trend	Impact
1. Decide on type of generator and fuel	H	H	H
2. Design generator and fuel system for the specific process	H	H	H
3. Set up grinding and milling machines	L	M	H
4. Purchase auxiliary supplies	L	M	M

Because of the remote location, the students decided to use a proven technology to drive the power generator—specifically, an internal combustion engine. Two viable choices were then identified for internal combustion engine power generators: one that used biodiesel as the fuel and one that used vegetable oil as the fuel. There were several critical criteria that the system had to fulfill, and the solution was identified based on these requirements. Although the formal problem analysis (PA), decision analysis (DA), and potential problem analysis (PPA) processes were not used explicitly, some systematic approaches were used to converge on the best solution. The following K.T. decision analysis is a representation of the process of converging on the chosen solution.

Decision Analysis

	Running on Vegetable Oil	Running on Biodiesel
Musts		
Generator must be available for purchase in India	Go	Go
Generator must use renewable fuel as power source	Go	Go
Generator must use fuel that is available locally	Go	No Go
Generator must use fuel that is safe (no toxic chemicals)	Go	No Go

Wants	Weight	Rating	Score	Rating	Score
System should be easy to maintain	9	6	54	X	X
System should be low cost	7	5	35	X	X
System should last a long time	6	5	30	X	X
System should not involve too many steps	5	6	30	X	X
Total			**149**		

The biodiesel option was eliminated because it required the use of methanol and sodium hydroxide for fuel production. These components were not readily available in the area and were also considered potentially dangerous. Vegetable oil could be used if an oil press were available to press seeds that grew naturally in the area. A disadvantage of using vegetable oil was that it meant modifying the engine to add a fuel preheater and a separate tank.

The Modified Generator for Use with Vegetable Oil

One major concern for the team was the possibility of getting sick during their one- to two-month stay in India. Analyzing potential problems such as snake bites and other illnesses helped the team determine that they needed to have a driver available at all times to take them to the nearest hospital. The following PPA outlines preventive actions and contingency actions for this situation.

Potential Problem Analysis

Potential Problem	Causes	Preventive Action	Contingency Action	Triggers
Becoming sick in India.	Drinking the unclean water.	Bring lots of water filters.	Determine the problem's severity and seek medical attention. Use the driver as needed.	Symptoms such as diarrhea, vomiting, and stomach pain.
	Getting bitten by a snake.	Research what kinds of snakes are in the area and what to do in case of a bite.	Seek medical attention. Take antivenom or remove the venom immediately if possible. Use the driver as needed.	Contact with snake, penetration of skin.

Implementing the Solution

The first step to implementing the solution was the approval process. Approval was necessary from EWB-USA as well as from the various nongovernmental organizations with which the team was working. Most importantly, the villagers had to agree to the solution proposed and the construction process, which would require time and space for its completion. This approval process required substantial communication between all groups. It was only after this approval was granted that implementation could be started.

After identifying the solution and receiving approval, the team set its priorities, identified numerous tasks, and assigned roles to each individual on the team. Responsibilities such as grant writing, communications with local residents, engine design, and process equipment design were broken up between numerous teammates, and deadlines were set. A timeline (Gantt chart) was developed and included in some of the grant proposals the team wrote. Following is an example of a deployment chart, which features the team's responsibilities.

Deployment Chart

Task	Sean Poust	Ben Barnes	Stephanie Bogle	Patrick Walsh
1. Engine design				X
2. Grant writing/travel	X			
3. Project leader			X	
4. Process assembly	Everyone			
4. Solar dryer design		X		

The team faced numerous obstacles while trying to implement the solution. The site that they thought would hold the building with the generator was different than originally planned. The team members had to build the structure on rice paddy land. They purchased bricks for building the structure that would house the generator and other equipment, only to find when these bricks arrived that many were misshapen or broken, though they were told that the bricks would still work in the structure. After trying to assemble the building, the team quickly realized that the structure was unstable. They sought the advice of an expert and insisted that a civil engineer in charge of one of the nongovernmental organizations make a six-hour drive to the site to inspect the structure. The team ended up wrapping the entire building in wire mesh and concrete to ensure its stability. The team recognized when it needed more help and sought it out.

Inside the Building

The Completed Building

After the generator was set up and mounted to the floor of the building, the team encountered another problem: The generator vibrated excessively. This problem required troubleshooting because the level of vibration was unacceptable and could lead to machine failure. The following K.T. problem analysis illustrates the what, where, when, and extent of this problem.

Problem Troubleshooting (PA Analysis): Generator Vibrating Excessively

		Is	Is Not	Distinction	Possible Cause
What	Identify	The generator is vibrating excessively	Any other equipment in the building vibrating	Something specific to the generator	Uncentered motor within generator
Where	Locate	The generator and the pad on which the generator is mounted	Anything else in the building	Only the generator itself or the pad	Poor shock absorption of pad
When	Timing	The problem occurs only when the generator is running and was initially observed when the generator was first turned on	The problem does not occur when the generator is off	Motor motion causes vibration	Mounting pad is not appropriate for motor/generator
Extent	Magnitude	Large unacceptable vibration	Small or no vibration	The generator and the pad are not compatible	Possibly need a different shock-absorbing pad

The team tried mounting the generator on a different pad, one that featured more shock absorption. This change did not seem to help significantly. The generator was mounted very tightly to the pad, and eventually the team heard a loud cracking noise while the generator was running: A fastener bolt that held the generator to the pad had sheared. This breakage caused the generator to be more free-floating and hence reduced the vibrations significantly. Thus the problem was not with the generator but rather with the way it was mounted to the pad. Once the generator was mounted more loosely on the pad, the vibrations subsided considerably. Consequently, *the problem defined as how to generate sustainable power was solved.*

One cultural problem that the team encountered proved difficult to solve, especially because of the language barrier between the students and the local residents. Women were not allowed to be part of the process training, even though it was their idea to start the project in the first place. It was only appropriate for the female members of the EWB team to interact with the village women, so they continued to work on this problem throughout the process. Its solution is still ongoing.

Evaluation

One of the most important aspects of any project is evaluation. The team evaluated their decisions and made corrections at every point along the way. At the end of the project, a final evaluation was completed in which the students determined whether more work needed to be done and which tasks were the highest priorities.

The evaluation of the implementation process can be performed by answering questions from the evaluation checklist.

Does the solution solve the real problem?
The solution does solve the problem originally defined—a lack of sustainable power for running agricultural processing equipment. Although other problems remain, such as the need for better lighting and clean water, this solution does provide the village with a generator that can increase the standard of living for its citizens.

Is the problem permanently solved, or is this a patchwork solution?
Like most solutions, this one will require maintenance and care taking. The most difficult part was setting up the equipment and training local residents to use it. Ensuring that the process will continue to work will require long-term dedication to equipment maintenance, replacement, and operator training.

Have all the consequences of the solution (both negative and positive) been examined?
Despite the benefits, some negative aspects of this solution include finding dedicated people to run the process and sell the product continuously. The

village must maintain a team of people who take responsibility for running the process, making decisions regarding its use, and managing the money generated.

Has the solution accomplished all it could?
The solution might possibly have included providing electricity for the entire village, though this was beyond the scope of the project's timeline and initial resource allotment. The team has been exploring means of providing electricity for these homes as a follow-up project.

Is the solution economically, environmentally, and politically responsible and safe?
Because the process uses vegetable oil—a renewable resource that is available locally through plants—it is environmentally friendly. The process was designed so that the chemicals used would be biodegradable and not hazardous to human health. Furthermore, the extra income it provides can be used to create a better infrastructure for the villagers so that they can improve their water quality, so long as the money is managed properly.

In the end, the team assembled the building, designed the process, trained local residents to use the equipment, and have continued to monitor the progress of the project. Although communication with this remote village is quite challenging, the team tries to maintain contact with the local people who are now running the process to make sure it is still going and attempts to troubleshoot problems remotely. The team has continued to work on other problems faced by the village. In particular, team members have been pursuing the idea of replacing indoor kerosene lanterns, which often cause asphyxiation and other health problems, with small-scale, solar-powered, battery-operated LED lanterns. This project continues to be an exciting challenge for these engineering students, encouraging them to do good and make the greatest impact in the lives of others.
To learn more about EWB, please visit http://www.ewb-usa.org.

CASE STUDY 2: PROBLEMS AT THE BAKERY CAFÉ

Project Assignment

This case study is the result of a term project in the senior-level course at the University of Michigan titled *Problem Solving, Troubleshooting, and Making the Transition to the Workplace*. It was contributed by Carly Ehrenberger, James Herbin, Paul Niezguski, and Sara Schulze, with additional input from Ana Butka, Jessica Moreno, and Jason Rhode-McGauley.

Students were given the following instructions: "Interview employees of Bakery Café on Truman Parkway to determine any problems the employees have. Analyze the problems you uncovered and then generate and evaluate solutions for each problem. Finally, pick the best solution for each problem you identified."

Background

The Bakery Café features fresh food and beverages that are delivered in a comfortable environment for its customers. Customers order at a counter from a diverse menu and wait for a short time while Bakery Café employees prepare their orders. Bakery Café offers its customers amenities including comfortable seating, free wireless Internet, and a catering service. The Bakery Café has more than 30 employees who work a variety of shifts and jobs. Typical jobs include working the register, making sandwiches and salads on the "line," washing dishes, assisting in catering, and acting as a trainer or supervisor. The ages of employees range from 15 to 55 years. They work an average of 30 hours per week, and have worked for Bakery Café for an average of 15 months.

Getting Started: Methodology

Using the "five building blocks" problem-solving process, the following steps were taken:

1. Define the problem.
   - Gathered information about the Bakery Café. Developed, distributed, and collected an employee survey. Interviewed the manager.
   - Used various problem-solving techniques, such as a Duncker diagram and a Kepner–Tregoe potential problem analysis.
2. Generate solutions.
   - Used the idea generation techniques discussed in Chapter 6 to develop a number of solutions to each problem.
3. Decide on the course of action.
   - Chose the best alternative for each problem identified and analyzed.

4. Implement the solution.
   - Recommended future actions for the Ann Arbor store manager to take.
5. Evaluate the solution.
   - Evaluated the feasibility of the solutions recommended.

Problem Definition

Gathering Information

Data Collection
- Researched Bakery Café online to get some background and basic corporate information.

Talk with People Who Are Familiar with the Problem
- *Interviewed manager:* To gain information about the current situation at Bakery Café. We asked critical thinking questions such as "What types of problems do you expect we will find?" to understand the situation at hand and determine the areas of focus.
- *Employee surveys (22 responses):* To help understand the basic concerns or areas obviously in need of improvement at Bakery Café as well as to uncover underlying or unspoken problems.

View the Problem Firsthand
- Visited Bakery Café for dinner and observed employees and customers.

Confirm All Findings and Continue to Gather Information
- *Searched for biases in survey answers:* Survey results were analyzed in light of each employee's age or position to understand potential biases.

Development of a survey was a key means of gathering the necessary information to define the problem. Brainstorming techniques and Socratic Questions were the tools used to help develop the survey. The formulation of the survey was extremely important and required significant thought. Guidelines for survey development were obtained and used from the Web sites http://www.statpac.com/surveys/index.htm and http://www.tele.sunyit.edu/TEL598sur.html, along with other material given in the references at the end of this chapter.[1-7]

Developing the Survey:
Application of Brainstorming Techniques

Uncovering the Unspoken Problems

We began with the problem statement: "What are possible topics that we should ask employees about to reveal their unspoken problems with their jobs?"

Application of three techniques—free association, lateral thinking using random stimulation, and analogy and cross-fertilization—helped to generate survey questions. The following questions were developed.

Free Association

Fellow employees:

- "Are your co-workers generally friendly and willing to help you if needed?"
- "Does Bakery Café deal fairly with all employees?"

Managers:

- "Does the manager value the employee's contribution?"

Shifts:

- "Are you satisfied with the number of hours/shifts you work each week?"
- "Is the way the shifts are scheduled convenient?"
- "Is the way the shifts are scheduled flexible?"

Job tasks:

- "Do you know what is expected of you?"

Stress level:

- "Are you under too much stress at work?"
- "Is there a sufficient number of workers present during each shift?"

Pay:

- "Does your pay match your job performance?"

Benefits/rewards:

- "What do you like most about working for Bakery Café?"
- "Are you recognized when you do a good job?"

Lateral Thinking Using Random Stimulation

Random word: **Knife** → cutting bread → task at work

- "What is your favorite task?"
- "What is your least favorite task?"

Random word: **Voice** → freedom of speech

- "Can you voice your opinions without fear of criticism from your manager?"

Analogy and Cross-Fertilization

What could a Bakery Café manager learn from an elementary school teacher?

Elementary school teachers understand that students need time to learn and are patient with them even when they make mistakes.

- "Does your manager use mistakes as positive learning experiences?"

Elementary school teachers give students grades and report cards to show students their progress and to set goals for the future.

- "Do you receive regular feedback that helps improve your performance?"

The Socratic Questions discussed in Chapter 4 were also employed to help develop survey questions.

Application of Types of Socratic Questions to Developing the Survey

Clarify: Why do you say that?

- "What is your favorite task to do at work?"
- "Why do you like this task?"
- "What do you not like about this task?"
- "What is your least favorite task?"
- "What do you like about this task?"
- "What do you not like about this task?"

Probe Reasons and Evidence: What evidence do you have to support your answer?

- "Why do you feel the customers are not being served efficiently?"
- "Why do you feel there might be a problem with shift scheduling?"

Explore Viewpoints and Perspectives: What is a different way to look at it?

- "Which areas need improvement?"
- "What would you suggest doing to improve them?"

After the survey was administered, the responses were examined to determine the problems. A total of 22 surveys from employees were analyzed. The following main concerns were identified:

- Bottlenecks occur because not enough workers are present during each shift.
- Co-workers do not take responsibility for job tasks.
- Employees do not receive enough training for tasks.

Problem Definition Techniques

A Kepner–Tregoe situation appraisal was performed on these perceived problems to determine their priority order and the next steps to be taken in addressing them.

K.T. Situation Appraisal of Employee Problems at Bakery Café

Problem	Timing	Trend	Impact	Next Process
1. Co-workers do not take responsibility for job tasks.	M	H	H	K.T. potential problem analysis
2. Bottlenecks occur because not enough workers are present during each shift.	M	M	H	K.T. decision analysis
3. Employees do not receive enough training for tasks.	M	M	H	Problem statement triggers (PA)

The rankings of each of the three evaluation criteria are based on the benefit to Bakery Café as an organization, and to this store location in particular.

Problems 1, 2, and 3 are moderately urgent in the *timing* category. All of them directly impact the customers and ultimately the success of the store.

In the *trend* category, problem 1 was assigned a high degree of concern (H): If co-workers are not taking responsibility for their assigned tasks, then unfinished tasks will accumulate and a hostile environment could be created among employees. Problems 2 and 3 have both been given a ranking of moderate concern (M). Not having enough workers on a shift might continually escalate employee and customer frustration as well as leaving tasks unaccomplished. Similarly, a lack of training might increase employee frustration.

In the *impact* category, problems 1, 2, and 3 were all sources of high degrees of concern because they impact both the employees and the customers. The possible impacts of these problems are as follows:

Problem 1: Poor cleanliness and general disorganization
Problem 2: Slow service
Problem 3: Inconsistent service and/or product

If these problems are solved, the result might potentially create a more harmonious work environment for employees. This could, in turn, create better manager–employee relationships as well as more satisfied customers.

Based on the K.T. situation appraisal, the following priority was given to the problems identified:

Problem 1: Co-workers do not take responsibility for job tasks.

Problem 2: Bottlenecks occur because not enough workers are present during each shift.

Problem 3: Employees do not receive enough training for tasks.

This priority should determine the order in which the problems are addressed.

Generating Solutions and Deciding the Course of Action

The next step in the K.T. situation appraisal was to decide on a course of action. For problem 1, potential problem analysis (PPA) was selected because both problems have future implications and their root causes have not been identified.

Problem 1: Co-workers Do Not Take Responsibility for Job Tasks

The PPA helped identify possible causes of the problem and a plan to prevent future pitfalls.

K.T. Potential Problem Analysis for Job Task Responsibility

Potential Problem	Possible Causes	Preventive Action	Contingency Plan
Co-workers do not take responsibility for tasks, leaving the work to be performed by workers on later shifts	Not enough time	Create and use stock-piles of prep material	Add another employee
	Lack of awareness that a task needs to be done	Post checklist of duties near the punch-out clock	Manager completes task
	Blatant neglect on the part of some shifts	Reward employees who complete tasks for other shifts	Confront those shift workers who neglect tasks; schedule the most efficient workers for earlier shifts

Problem 2: Bottlenecks Occur Because Not Enough Workers Are Present During Each Shift

For problem 2, decision analysis was selected as the analytical technique because the cause of the problem had already been identified and a course of action needed to be implemented. Problem 2 was particularly evident during morning and late-evening shifts. The survey revealed that some workers had to wait to use the espresso machine while others were moving as fast as they could while taking orders and serving pastries. Customers would complain as the line of customers became longer. The problem statement was formulated as follows: "Avoid bottlenecks." Alternative solutions identified by brainstorming included hiring more workers, purchasing additional equipment, transferring workers between shifts, or preparing early for shifts. The *musts* and *wants* for the solution are shown in the following table.

K.T. Decision Analysis for Not Enough Workers Present During Each Shift at Bakery Café

		Hire More Workers		Purchase Additional Equipment		Transfer Workers Between Shifts		Prepare for Shift Early	
Musts									
Decrease customer complaints		Go		Go		Go		Go	
Increase preparedness between/during shifts		Go		Go		Go		Go	
Maintain Bakery Café's philosophy of freshness		Go		Go		Go		No Go	
Wants	*Weight*	*Rating*	*Score*	*Rating*	*Score*	*Rating*	*Score*	*Rating*	*Score*
Increase task completion rate	6	5	30	7	42	7	42	X	X
Increase shift satisfaction	9	8	72	5	45	4	36	X	X
Decrease customer wait time	6	5	30	7	42	5	30	X	X
Decrease worker idle time	7	4	28	6	42	6	42	X	X
	Total		**160**		**171**		**150**		

Because the results of the decision analysis were very close, the possible adverse consequences associated with each alternative had to be closely examined.

K.T. Decision Analysis:
Adverse Consequences of Not Enough Workers per Shift

Alternative	Probability	×	Severity	=	Threat
Hire More Employees					
Increase payroll	10	×	3		30
More difficulty in scheduling shifts	6	×	7		42
Total					72
Purchase Additional Equipment					
Maintenance cost	10	×	1		10
Worker training on equipment	7	×	2		14
Total					24
Reallocate Worker Distribution					
Reduced shift productivity	7	×	3		21
Scheduling conflicts	6	×	2		12
Reduced employee satisfaction	5	×	6		30
Total					68

From the analysis of adverse consequences and results of our K.T. decision analysis, it appears that Bakery Café should purchase additional equipment to increase the shift productivity. Specifically, surveys revealed that a bottleneck was created when many customers ordered espressos. Therefore, we suggested that Bakery Café purchase an additional espresso machine identical to the one it currently operates. This purchase would increase productivity without increasing the amount of training required or person-hours logged. Additionally, reallocation of workers to some of the busier shifts (perhaps with some employees working occasional split shifts) would help to alleviate this problem.

Problem 3: Employees Do Not Receive Enough Training for Tasks

Our surveys revealed that employees felt there was a lack of training among their fellow employees. This notion was not limited to employees—managers expressed this perception as well.

Before analyzing this problem and finding ways to solve it, we wanted to verify that the root problem of employee competencies was the employee-training program. Triggers from the problem statement–restatement technique, which was discussed in Chapter 4, were applied to redefine the problem once more. For this technique, a slightly different original problem statement was used: "Some employees believe other employees do not always perform well on the job."

Trigger 1. With this trigger, an emphasis is put on different words or phrases in the original problem statement. The following sentences emphasized different parts of the problem statement to make us think of a new problem statement that will be more tightly defined than the original.

1. Some **employees** believe other employees do not always perform well on the job.
   In statement 1, the word "employees" was emphasized, which led to the question of whether only the employees noticed the poor performance of the other employees or whether customers noticed the problem as well. This trigger also raised the question of whether the manager noticed any poor performances by some of the employees. If this was the case, did the manager ever make sure that all of the employees had the proper information needed to perform well on the job?

2. Some employees believe **other employees** do not always perform well on the job.
   Statement 2 placed emphasis on "other employees." This statement questioned the relationships between the employees, including whether they were all on amicable terms with one another. Delving deeper into the statement recalled a few of the survey comments that complimented the "less-than-par" employees on their personalities and ability to get along, yet criticized their work performance.

3. Some employees believe other employees do not always **perform well** on the job.
   The third statement placed the emphasis on "perform well," which questioned the standards of performance on the job. How were these standards made, and who made them? These questions led back to the employee-training problem: If all of the employees were trained to a specific standard, then would any of them show a significant lack of performance?

4. Some employees believe other employees do not always perform well **on the job**.
   In statement 4, emphasis was placed on the phrase "on the job." This part of the sentence raised the question of what the employees were like outside of the work environment. If the employees were dependable, hard-working people in other aspects of their lives, then they were probably likely to show

the same characteristics while working at Bakery Café. An interview before a new employee was hired could reveal whether the interviewee had the necessary traits for working at Bakery Café.

Placing emphasis on different parts of the sentence gave us some ideas about how to redefine the problem. We continued using the problem statement triggers to see whether the problem could be focused more narrowly.

Trigger 2. Trigger 2 substitutes explicit definitions into the original problem statement. The original problem statement was rewritten as follows:

> "Some people who work at Bakery Café indicated on the survey that other people who work at Bakery Café do not complete all of their assigned job-related tasks while they are working at Bakery Café."

Restating the problem this way led to the question of whether the employees know all of the "assigned job-related tasks"—that is, their work requirements. This led back to the problem in employee training, which, if revised, could make sure all employees know the requirements of working at Bakery Café.

Trigger 3. Trigger 3 was applied to learn whether the training program was the real problem or whether a different problem was at fault. Trigger 3 reworded the original problem statement to say the opposite of what it should. The following opposite statement was found to be quite helpful:

> "What can be done so that all employees feel that all other employees never perform well on the job?"

This opposite statement raised the question of what would cause an employee to always perform poorly. If all employees were trained very poorly, they would probably always perform poorly.

Using these three triggers, the original problem statement was redefined as follows: "Find a way to make sure all employees are well trained and competent."

Duncker Diagram

Once this problem statement was created, we devised the following Duncker diagram:

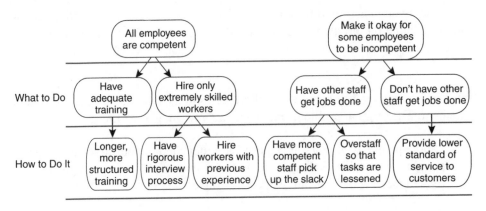

Duncker Diagram for Employee Competence

Generating Solutions by Free Association

We then brainstormed ways to improve employee training using free association. The following alternatives were identified:

- *Practice runs before opening.* The new hire would arrive before the store opens to practice daily tasks such as working the register and making sandwiches. A manager or qualified trainer would supervise these practice runs, and the new hire could become acquainted with various tasks without the added element of customer service.
- *Employee tests.* The new hire would be required to pass tests on all common tasks before completing his or her training. These tests would be monitored by a manager or qualified trainer to ensure that the new hire is capable in all areas before training completion.
- *Specific number of days training.* All new hires would be required to complete a specified number of days in training. Their shifts would also have to include a certain number of day and night shifts to guarantee that the trainee would be capable in all areas. Based on personal experiences and suggestions from current employees, the belief is that training during three opening

shifts and three closing shifts would provide the new hire with the best training experience.

- *Training with a manager.* All training shifts would need to be supervised by a manager. Having a manager present at all times would help with the overall consistency of the training because only one or two people would ever be in charge. The trainee would also be less likely to develop poor habits because the manager is probably the most aware of proper work procedures.
- *Make sure employees are trained on all tasks.* Employees would need to spend time training on all tasks. The person in charge of training could develop a checklist to guarantee that each task is addressed and that the trainee is competent in each area.
- *Employees specifically assigned as trainers.* Having one or more employees specifically assigned as trainers could improve the consistency of the training. The trainers would need to be qualified as knowing the proper procedures for all tasks. They would also need to know the standard training procedure to be followed in all training sessions. This procedure would not only help to make sure that a competent employee is training the new hire, but would also relieve the training pressure on the manager.
- *Computer simulation with built-in testing.* A computer simulation could be built to represent the daily tasks and challenges that an employee might encounter. Quizzes or other interactive activities could be built into the simulation to confirm that the trainees are retaining the information they learn.
- *Employee worksheets with menu and standard procedures for each shift.* New hires would be required to complete worksheets with questions based on the menu and standard procedures for each shift, including opening and closing.
- *Work instructions present and in plain view at each workstation.* Small cards with proper work instructions would be placed in appropriate areas around the restaurant. These work instructions would need to be clear and concise to ensure that the new hire is easily reminded of the tasks to be performed at each station without the instructions becoming a distraction to employees and customers.

Deciding the Course of Action

Next, these alternatives were examined using a decision analysis to determine the best solution to the training problem. Using a situation appraisal to rank problems in order of importance and then analytical techniques such as problem statement triggers, Duncker diagrams, K.T. decision analysis, and K.T. potential problem analysis, we were able to prioritize and propose the most feasible solutions to our initial problems.

Problem Number	Priority	Problem	Feasible Solution
1	1	Co-workers do not take responsibility for job tasks	Task checklists and rewards system
2	2	Bottlenecks occur because not enough workers are present during each shift	Purchase more equipment
3	3	Employees do not receive enough training for tasks	Hire competent people and provide more efficient training

Implementing the Solution

We recommended that the manager of Bakery Café implement these solutions to the identified problems. The situation appraisal showed that the problem of co-workers not taking responsibility for job tasks was the most important and needed immediate action. We proposed setting up task checklists at appropriate stations detailing the task itself as well as any prep or clean-up duties associated with it. To implement this solution, we would need to create and laminate checklists detailing various tasks. If certain tasks consistently are not being done or are being left for later shifts, then a sheet could also be created that employees would have to initial when the tasks are completed. This solution has a very low cost and is easy to implement.

Another idea was to designate one of the workers on each shift as the "checkout" employee. Before other workers end their shifts, they would have to check out with this employee, who would make sure that all clean-up and prep tasks were complete before the next shift began. This person would preferably be one of the more responsible employees during the shift but should also change from day to day so that multiple associates are exposed to this responsibility. This solution would increase the general knowledge of the tasks that need to be done because the "checkout" employee would have to know all of the tasks for several different areas.

We decided that the problem of not enough workers could be solved by purchasing more equipment. It seemed that a bottleneck occurred during busy hours of the day owing to the high demand placed on the espresso machine. This problem seemed to result more from the lack of equipment than from a lack of workers. Purchasing a second espresso machine would help shorten customer waiting times and increase customers' satisfaction. The purchase of a second espresso machine might not be economically feasible, however. The cost of another machine might be offset by increased customer and worker satisfaction, but probably would not increase revenues much. Also, the store might not have space for a second machine or adding a machine might mean sacrificing another device.

An alternative solution would be to create a sign that displays the current drink order number. This sign would give customers a better idea of what to expect in terms of a waiting time and reduce the stress of impatient customers. This expectation would allow them to be more relaxed and free to enjoy the Bakery Café's atmosphere—an area that Bakery Café excels in.

The problem of employees not receiving enough training for tasks is a bit more complex because most training programs are formulated at the corporate level. If we assume that the program itself is not flawed, then either training needs to be implemented more efficiently or it needs to go on for a longer time. Perhaps associates are not being cross-trained thoroughly enough to perform efficiently, or perhaps associates are being trained at too broad a level and are not going deep enough in certain areas. Associates may also be receiving adequate training, but then specialize in certain areas based on which tasks they are assigned. To solve this problem, employees could be given refresher courses in areas where they do not work often.

Evaluation

We would need to follow up with surveys or (preferably) short interviews to see how employees react to the changes made. The changes made should increase worker and customer satisfaction. Evaluation would be a task for the managers at Bakery Café because they see how things run on a day-to-day basis.

SUMMARY

Solving problems can be fun and add spice to an otherwise bland existence. The techniques discussed in this book for defining and solving real-world problems are tried and true, and they can make you a better problem solver. Use the materials in this book to lessen your problem-solving anxiety.

- Take a proactive approach not only to problem solving, but also to your life.
- Have a vision of what you want to accomplish in your organization and in your life, and make sure all of the steps you take head in the right direction.
- Don't be afraid to fail. Most of the time we can learn more from our failures than we do from our successes.
- Observe good problem solvers. Ask them questions and brainstorm with them.
- Don't dismiss the ideas of others out of hand, but instead leverage them—they may trigger the correct solution.
- Get in the habit of planning your time and prioritizing the tasks you must accomplish.
- Practice using the tools and techniques presented in the book. A tool becomes useful only when you are comfortable and familiar with it. Some techniques may sound silly or cumbersome. Don't worry: The same technique will not work for *everyone* and *every* situation. Choose what works best for you.
- Don't force-fit a certain technique that you have used before. If it's not working, choose another technique or move on.
- When you have finished a task, reflect on it. Evaluate it. Is it the best you could have done? If not, can you still improve upon it?

Every time you practice the problem-solving techniques we have presented, you will become an even better problem solver.

REFERENCES

1. Fink, Arlene, *How to Conduct Surveys: A Step by Step Guide,* 3rd ed., Sage Publications, Thousand Oaks, CA, 2005.
2. Oishi, Sabine Mertens, *How to Conduct In-Person Interviews for Surveys,* 2nd ed., Sage Publications, Thousand Oaks, CA, 2002.
3. Creswell, John W., *Research Design: Qualitative and Quantitative Approaches,* Sage Publications, Thousand Oaks, CA, 1994.

4. Frary, Robert B., "Hints for Designing Effective Questionnaires," *Practical Assessment, Research, and Evaluation,* 5, 3, 1996. Retrieved October 19, 2006, from http://PAREon-line.net/getvn.asp?v=5&n=3.

5. Hill, Nick. "Tips for Developing an Effective Questionnaire," 2004, http://www.streetdirectory.com/travel_guide/2244/computers_and_the_internet/tips_for_developing_an_effective_questionnaire.html.

6. "Survey and Questionnaire Design," http://www.statpac.com/surveys/index.htm.

7. "Survey and Questionnaire Construction," http://www.tele.sunyit.edu/TEL598sur.html.

EXERCISES

Choose your group term project from the list below.

Web Projects

11.1. Research global warming, and then prepare and carry out a campaign to make people aware of global warming. Develop a Web site that gives the scientific facts, concerns, and consequences of global warming. If nothing is done to slow global warming, what will be the consequences?

11.2. Research sustainability, and then prepare and carry out a campaign to make people aware of sustainability. Develop a Web site that gives the scientific facts, concerns, and consequences if sustainability is not achieved.

11.3. Research water shortage/conservation, and then prepare and carry out a campaign to make people aware of water shortage/conservation. Develop a Web site as part of your campaign.

Business Projects

11.4. Interview employees of a local restaurant. Determine the problems the employees have, analyze the problems, and generate and evaluate solutions for each problem. Finally, pick the best solution for each problem you identified.

11.5. Interview employees of a local soup kitchen. Determine the problems the employees have, analyze the problems, and generate and evaluate solutions for each problem. Finally, pick the best solution for each problem you identified.

11.6. Interview employees of a local deli. Determine the problems the employees have, analyze the problems, and generate and evaluate solutions for each problem. Finally, pick the best solution for each problem you identified.

11.7. Research a technological need in Rwanda, Africa (e.g., turning solid animal and human waste into fuel). Define the problem, collect information, and outline the solution. Include a Gantt chart and a potential problem analysis as part of your analysis. Prepare a proposal to go to Rwanda consistent with that of Engineers Without Borders (EWB). Use the Web to obtain information about EWB. You can find additional information about investment opportunities in Rwanda on the Web at http://www.thvf.com/.

11.8. Interview 50 students who live in one of the dormitories at your school to determine the problems they have living in the dorm. Classify the problems and develop a number of solutions for each problem. Finally, choose the best solution for each problem.

11.9. Select a business of your own choosing (e.g. your local lumberyard, a bakery, a photo shop, or a hardware store) and get approval from the manager/owner to determine the problems faced by the employees. Analyze the problems, and generate and evaluate solutions for each problem. Finally, pick the best solution for each problem.

Other Projects

11.10. Choose a popular consumer product (e.g., hand soap dispenser, either foam or liquid) currently on the market that you believe could be improved. Interview 25 people, asking them what they don't like about the product (e.g., too much soap dispensed), and then generate and evaluate a number of solutions to each problem.

11.11. Determine the major problems that would affect students, dorms, and businesses should the bird flu pandemic reach your hometown.

11.12. Which businesses would suffer the most if the bird flu reaches the United States?

APPENDIX 1

MCMASTER'S FIVE-POINT STRATEGY[*]

1. **Define:**
   a. Identify the unknown or stated objective.
   b. Isolate the system and identify the knowns and unknowns (inputs, laws, assumptions, criteria, and constraints) stated in the problem.
   c. List the inferred constraints and the inferred criteria.
   d. Identify the stated criteria.
2. **Explore:**
   a. Identify tentative pertinent relationships among inputs, outputs, and unknowns.
   b. Recall past related problems or experiences, pertinent theories, and fundamentals.
   c. Hypothesize, visualize, idealize, and generalize.
   d. Discover what the real problem and the real constraints are.
   e. Consider both short-time and long-time implications.
   f. Identify meaningful criteria.
   g. Choose a basis or a reference set of conditions.
   h. Collect missing information, resources, or data.
   i. Guess the answer or result.
   j. Simplify the problem to obtain an "order of magnitude" result.
   k. If you cannot solve the proposed problem, first solve some related problems or solve part of the problem.
3. **Plan:**
   a. Identify the problem type and select among the various heuristic tactics.
   b. Generate alternative ways to achieve the objective.
   c. Map out the solution procedure (algorithm) to be used.
   d. Assemble the resources needed.
4. **Act:**
   a. Follow the procedure developed under the plan phase; use the resources available.
   b. Evaluate and compare the alternatives.
   c. Eliminate alternatives that do not meet all the objectives or fulfill all the constraints.
   d. Select the best alternative of those remaining.

---

[*] Source: Woods, D. R. *A Strategy for Problem Solving,* 3rd ed. Department of Chemical Engineering, McMaster University, Hamilton, Ontario, 1985; *Chemical Engineering Education,* p. 132, Summer 1979; *AIChE Symposium Series,* 79, 228, 1983.

5. **Reflect:**
   a. Check that the solution is blunder-free.
   b. Check the reasonableness or results.
   c. Check the procedure and logic of your arguments.
   d. Communicate the results.

APPENDIX 2

PLOTTING DATA

In this appendix, we review the techniques for plotting data and measuring slopes on various types of graphs. With the aid of many readily available computer packages, constructing graphs from data is quite straightforward. The background material in this appendix will help you understand the various types of graphs and enable you to determine the important parameters from them. Additionally, we review some statistical techniques available for analyzing experimental data.

LINEAR PLOTS

First, let's look at a quick review of the fundamentals of graph construction and slope measurement on linear plots. Equations of the form

$$y = mx + b \qquad \qquad (A2\text{-}1)$$

will, of course, yield a straight line when plotted on linear axes. Consider an example where we place $100 in the bank in a simple interest-bearing account for five years. A graph of the amount of money in the account at the end of each year is shown below.

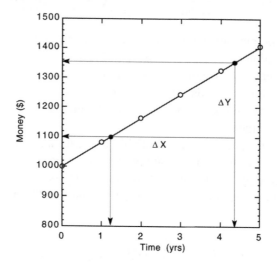

To determine the slope of the line on the graph, we could proceed in two ways.

Method 1: Direct Measurement

We can physically measure Δx and Δy using a ruler, and then, using the linear scale of the graph, determine the slope of the line. For this example, suppose $\Delta x =$ 34 mm and $\Delta y = 20$ mm. The linear scale for the y-axis is $12.50/mm, and the linear scale for the x-axis is (1 yr)/(11 mm). Therefore,

$$\Delta Money = (20 \text{ mm}) (\$12.50/mm) = \$250$$

$$Time = (34) (1yr) / (11 \text{ mm}) = 3.1yrs$$

$$Slope = \frac{\Delta Money}{\Delta Time} = \frac{\$250}{3.1yrs} = \$81/yr$$

The intercept ($1000) can be read directly from the graph at time $t = 0$. While this method works, it is rather crude and its accuracy is limited by the accuracy of the measuring devices used.

Method 2: Direct Calculation from Points on the Line

Pick two points that lie on the line. These points will not necessarily be data points if the data are scattered.

Point 1:   (1.23, 1100)
Point 2:   (4.32, 1350)

$$Slope = \frac{\Delta Money}{\Delta Time} = \frac{1350 - 1100}{4.32 - 1.23} = \$80.9/yr$$

The intercept may be determined from either point using the calculated slope and the equation of the line ($y = mx + b$, $1100 = (80.9)(1.23) + b$, $b = 1000$). As you can see, there is a slight difference in the values of the slopes calculated using the two different methods. This difference can be attributed to the accuracy with which the point values can be read from the graphs and the accuracy of the measurements in method 1.

Many computer packages are available that can determine the equation of the "best" straight line through the data points. These programs employ a statistical technique called regression (or least squares) analysis. A regression analysis of the above data yields the following equation for the "best" line through the data points:

$$Money(\$) = [\$81/yr][Time(yrs)] + 1000$$

$$y \quad = \quad m \quad \quad x \quad + \quad b$$

Notice that the values determined in this manner are very close to those determined earlier.

LOG-LOG PLOTS

When both axes are logarithmic, the graph is called a log-log graph. A log-log graph of the data is used when the dependent variable (u, for instance) is proportional to the independent variable (say, v) raised to some power m:

$$u = Bv^m \qquad\qquad \text{(A2-2)}$$

In many engineering applications, it is necessary to determine the best values of m and B for a set of experimental measurements on u and v. One of the easiest ways to perform this task is to use logarithms on Equation A2-2. If we take the log of both sides of the equation, we get

$$\log u = m\log v + \log B \qquad\qquad \text{(A2-3)}$$

Now, if we let

$$y = \log u$$
$$x = \log v$$
$$b = \log B$$

then Equation (A2-3) becomes

$$y = mx + b \qquad\qquad \text{(A2-4)}$$

Now we can now clearly see that Equation A2-2 has been transformed so that a plot of log $u(y)$ versus log $v(x)$ will be a straight line with a slope of m and an intercept of log B.

Chemical reaction rate data often follow a log-log relationship. Consider the following reaction rate data:

Clearly nonlinear!

Concentration, C_A (gmol/dm^3)	1	2	3	4
Reaction rate (gmol/dm^3/h)	3	12	27	48

If we assume that a log-log plot (Equation A2-2) is appropriate here, we can graph these data to determine m and B. There are two ways that we can proceed: We can manually take logarithms of the data and plot those logs, or we can use log-log coordinates and let the graph do the work. We shall illustrate both methods.

Method 1: Manually Taking Logarithms

Note that $\log = \log_{10}$ in this example.

log(concentration)	0	0.301	0.477	0.602
log(reaction rate)	0.478	1.08	1.43	1.68

We now plot these points on linear paper. It is very important to remember that if you manually take logs, you must plot the points on *linear* paper—*not* on log-log paper (otherwise you'll get a mess!).

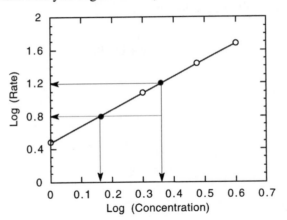

Now we can proceed just as we did for the simple linear plot case to determine the slope and intercept of the line and find the parameters for Equation A2-2. The intercept, b, is clearly 0.478 (from the tabular data). Let's determine the slope using two points on the line.

$$\text{Point 1:} \quad (0.38, 1.2)$$
$$\text{Point 2:} \quad (0.18, 0.8)$$

$$Slope = \frac{1.2 - 0.8}{0.38 - 0.18} = m$$

Because $b = 0.478$,

$$b = \log B = 0.478$$

$$B = 10^b = 10^{0.478} = 3$$

Thus the equation for the line is

$$u = Bv^m = 3v^2$$

Given in terms of concentration and rate, this line is

$$\text{Rate} = 3C_A^2$$

Method 2: Plotting Directly on Log-Log Paper

Plotting directly on log-log paper is relatively simple. You merely plot the points, and the logarithmic scales on the axes take the logs for you. The rate versus concentration data are plotted below on log-log axes.

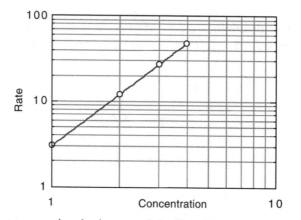

Notice that we again obtain a straight line. These types of plots are more meaningful to the reader, because the points that are plotted correspond to the actual numerical values of the data, rather than to the logarithms of the data. From the plot, the reader can determine immediately that the concentration value associated with the second data point is 2 gmol/dm³. This physical intuition is not available when the logarithms of the data are plotted on a linear scale (e.g., we would know the log of the concentration is 0.303, but we wouldn't know the concentration itself, unless we could perform antilogs in our heads). So now how do we determine the slope and "intercept" from this type of a plot? If Equation A2-3 is a valid equation for the line, then it should hold for every point on the line. Writing this equation for two arbitrary points on the line, we get

$$\log u_1 = \log B + m \log v_1 \qquad \text{Point 1} \qquad (A2\text{-}5)$$

$$\log u_2 = \log B + m \log v_2 \qquad \text{Point 2}$$

If we subtract the equation for point 2 from the equation for point 1, we'll get an expression that will allow us to calculate the slope of the line on the log-log axes:

$$\log u_1 - \log u_2 = m(\log v_1 - \log v_2)$$

$$m = \frac{\log\left(\dfrac{u_1}{u_2}\right)}{\log\left(\dfrac{v_1}{v_2}\right)} \quad \text{or, for this example} \quad m = \frac{\log\left(\dfrac{\text{rate 1}}{\text{rate 2}}\right)}{\log\left(\dfrac{C_{A1}}{C_{A2}}\right)}$$

Once we have determined the value of m, we can find B by substituting the appropriate values for either point back into Equation A2-5. For this example,

$$m = \frac{\log\left(\dfrac{48}{3}\right)}{\log\left(\dfrac{4}{1}\right)} = \frac{1.204}{0.604} = 2$$

$$\log B = \log 48 - 2\log 4 = 0.477$$

$$B = 3$$

Notice that this is the same result that we arrived at previously, as it should be.

We can also determine the slope of a line on log-log axes using the direct measurement technique, as discussed in the section on linear plots. With the availability of computer graphing packages this method is not used very often, but we include it here for completeness. To measure the slope directly using a ruler or similar instrument, we would choose two points on the line, measure Δx and Δy and the cycle length in both directions, and then proceed as follows.

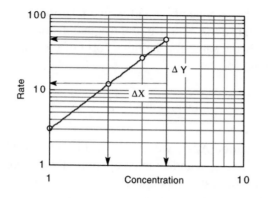

$\Delta y = 2.55$ cm

Cycle length in the y-direction = 3.6 cm/cycle

$\Delta x = 1.55$ cm

Cycle length in the x-direction = 4.35 cm/cycle

$$\left.\begin{array}{l} \Delta y \;=\; \dfrac{2.55 \text{ cm}}{3.6 \text{ cm/ cycle}} \\[3mm] \Delta x \;=\; \dfrac{1.55 \text{ cm}}{4.35 \text{ cm/ cycle}} \end{array}\right] \Rightarrow \dfrac{\Delta y}{\Delta x} = \dfrac{2.55 \times 4.35}{1.55 \times 3.60} = 2.0$$

$$y = bx^2$$

Using the point $(x = 1, y = 3)$, we can now determine the value of b:

$$3 \;=\; b(1)^2, \qquad b = 3$$

$$y \;=\; 3x^2$$

$$\text{rate} \;=\; 3C_A^2$$

Again, this is the same result we obtained earlier.

SEMI-LOG PLOTS

Semi-logarithmic (semi-log) plots should be used with exponential growth or decay equations of the form

$$y = be^{mx} \qquad or \qquad y = b(10)^{mx} \qquad\qquad \text{(A2-6)}$$

To determine the parameters b and m, we take logarithms of both sides of Equation A2-6. We'll use the "e" form of the equation and natural logarithms (ln), although the result is the same for the other form of the equation using common (base 10) logarithms.

$$\ln(y) = \ln b + mx \qquad\qquad (A2\text{-}7)$$

Examining Equation A2-7, we see that a plot of ln$y$ versus x should be a straight line with a slope of m and an intercept of b. If we deposit \$100 into a bank account that gathers interest compounded continuously (a great deal!) and then plot the amount of money in the account at the end of every year for the first 10 years, we obtain the following graph:

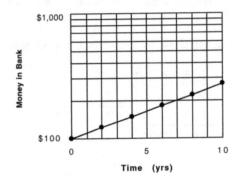

Notice that we have plotted the data (for every other year) directly on semi-log paper. We could have manually taken the logs and plotted the data on linear paper as discussed earlier, but using semi-log axes is easier. We will demonstrate two methods to determine the parameters of Equation A2-6 from the semi-log plot.

Method 1: Algebraic Method

Draw the best straight line through your data points. Choose two points on this line and determine the x and y values of each point.

Point 1: (8 yrs, \$223)   Point 2: (2 yrs, \$122)

Notice that we can write Equation A-7 using the two points and solve for the slope.

$$\ln(y_1) = \ln b + mx_1$$
$$\ln(y_2) = \ln b + mx_2$$

$$\ln\left(\frac{y_2}{y_1}\right) = m(x_2 - x_1)$$

$$m = \frac{\ln\left(\frac{y_2}{y_1}\right)}{(x_2 - x_1)}$$

Substituting the values of the selected points, we get $m = \dfrac{\ln\left(\dfrac{223}{122}\right)}{(8-2)} = 0.1$, and then b is clearly the y value of the line at time $t = 0$; that is, $be^{0.1(0)} = b$. Thus $b = 100$.

$$\text{Amount(\$)} = \$100e^{0.1\text{Time(yrs)}}$$

Method 2: Graphical Technique

A modification of the algebraic method is possible on semi-log paper if we extend the "best" line we can draw so that the dependent variable, y, changes by a factor of 10. For this case, the ratio of y_2/y_1 is 10 and the equation for the slope of the line is

$$m = \frac{\ln(10)}{x_2 - x_1} = \frac{2.303}{x_2 - x_1}$$

The intercept can then be determined as before. This technique is referred to as the *decade method*.

Careful analysis and plotting of the data are important tools in problem solving. In addition to being able to calculate the slopes and intercepts, we should be able to deal with "scatter" in the data. The next section discusses this topic.

Establishing Confidence Limits for Data

Normally, the data we wish to analyze are the results of some type of experiment. There will often be some "scatter"—that is, variability—in these data. If we repeat an experiment a number of times, for example, chances are that our results will show some variation. These variations may be due to experimental error, instrument precision, material variability, or other factors. One approach to dealing with this situation is to perform several experimental runs under identical conditions and average the results. Intuitively, we realize that the more runs we perform, the more closely the average of our experiments will approach the true average for the experimental conditions under consideration. In fact, if we performed an infinite number of repetitions, we would expect to obtain the true average as a result of our hard work. Of course, we cannot afford to perform an infinite number of experiments to determine the true mean of these experiments (μ = true mean), so we would like to have a way to estimate it from a limited number of samples.

Let's define the following quantities:

μ = true mean of the experiments (i.e., population) if a very large (∞) number are performed

n = sample size (the number of experiments that we actually performed)

$\bar{x}$ = mean of the n samples = $\dfrac{\sum x}{n}$

The standard deviation of the samples quantifies the spread of the sample values about the sample mean. The larger the standard deviation, the larger the variability of the individual samples. We can estimate the standard deviation of the entire population (from which we have measured n samples) using Equation A2-8:

$$S(x) = \sqrt{\frac{\sum x^2 - n\bar{x}^2}{n - 1}} \tag{A2-8}$$

To determine the true standard deviation (σ) of the entire population, we would have to know μ, the true mean (which we don't). So, we estimate the standard deviation.

As an example of a distribution, consider the following scenario. Suppose we gather some data regarding the length of time beyond the bachelor's degree that it takes a student at Frostbite Falls University to complete a Ph.D. If we plotted the data, it might look like the following figure.

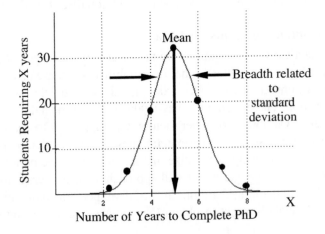

Number of Years to Complete PhD

The mean time to obtain a Ph.D. is five years, and there is clearly a distribution about the mean, which is to be expected. Almost no students take less than two years or more than eight years to obtain a Ph.D. The breadth of this "distribution" is related to the standard deviation.

If we draw several different samples of size n from the entire population and calculate the mean for each, we will most likely get a different mean, $\bar{x}$, for each sample. Additionally, none of these means will probably be equal to the true mean of the entire population, μ. In other words, we will get a distribution of means that is related to the true mean μ. The variability of these means is related to the variability of the entire population (i.e., to the standard deviation).

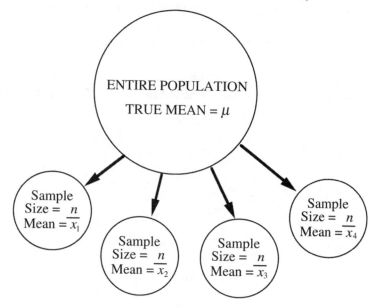

Let $S(\bar{x})$ represent the estimated standard deviation of the means of samples of size n drawn from the entire population, which itself has an estimated standard deviation of $S(x)$ (which we previously calculated). These quantities are related in the following manner:

$$S(\bar{x}) = \frac{S(x)}{\sqrt{n}} \tag{A2-9}$$

We noted that $\bar{x}$ is an estimate of the true mean (μ) of the experiments. But how good an estimate is it? One way to express this relationship is

$$\mu = \bar{x} \pm tS(\bar{x}) \tag{A2-10}$$

This equation states that the true mean lies within $t\,S(\bar{x})$ of the estimated mean, $\bar{x}$. The quantity t is calculated from the so-called t distribution, where t is a function of two parameters: a confidence level and the degrees of freedom. The degrees of freedom in our context is $(n-1)$, where n is the number of experiments performed under a given set of conditions. For a set of experiments, the number of degrees of freedom that we have to model the data is n, the number of runs. For this case, we have used one degree of freedom to calculate the mean. Thus there are only $(n-1)$ degrees of freedom remaining. Another way to look at this concept is to say that we can specify $(n-1)$ data points independently; the nth value is then fixed, because we have already determined the mean value $\bar{x}$ of the data set. The confidence level is defined as the probability that t is smaller than the tabulated value.

Following is an excerpt from a table of the t distribution:

Degrees of Freedom	95% Confidence Level	99% Confidence Level
1	12.706	63.657
2	4.303	9.925
3	3.182	5.841
4	2.776	4.604
5	2.571	4.032
6	2.447	3.707
7	2.365	3.499
8	2.306	3.355
9	2.262	3.250
10	2.228	3.169

In essence, the confidence level tells us how certain we can be that the mean of our data points will lie within the calculated range. For example, with a 95% confidence level, the mean will lie within the range in 95% of the cases, and outside the range in 5% of the cases.

An example will help to clarify this point. Consider an experiment where we pop popcorn using a certain method. We make five runs under identical conditions and obtain the following data:

Run Number	% Unpopped Kernels of Popcorn
1	22
2	18
3	19
4	26
5	25

Population size: $n = 5$

Estimated mean: $\bar{x} = \dfrac{\sum x}{5} = \dfrac{110}{5} = 22$

Estimated standard deviation of the individual points from the estimated mean:

$$S(x) = \sqrt{\frac{\sum x^2 - n\bar{x}^2}{n-1}} = \sqrt{\frac{2470 - (5)(22)^2}{5-1}} = 3.5355$$

Estimated standard deviation of the sample means from the true mean:

$$S(\bar{x}) = \frac{S(x)}{\sqrt{n}} = \frac{3.5355}{\sqrt{5}} = 1.581$$

To estimate the true mean, we'll use Equation A2-10:

$$\mu = \bar{x} \pm tS(\bar{x}) = 22 \pm 1.581t$$

For four degrees of freedom ($n - 1 = 4$), we can be 95% confident that $t \leq 2.776$ (see the table of t values given earlier). Similarly, we can be 99% confident that $t \leq 4.604$. Hence,

$$\mu = 22 \pm 1.581(2.571) = 22 \pm 4.39 \quad \text{(with 95\% confidence)}$$

or

$$\mu = 22 \pm 1.581(4.032) = 22 \pm 7.28 \quad \text{(with 99\% confidence)}$$

Note that the more confidence with which we want to specify the mean, the larger the "error bars" become, or the larger n must be for the same size uncertainty. Data points can be plotted using these values to indicate the uncertainty in the measurement.

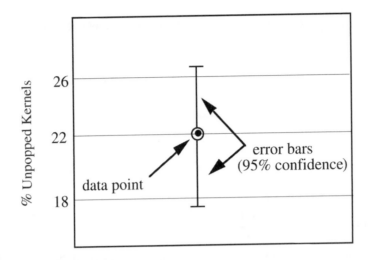

More extensive listings of the *t* distribution can be found in numerous texts on statistics.

PRESENTATION OF DATA

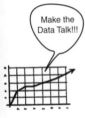

The data that we gather, when properly organized, analyzed, and presented, can serve as the basis for our subsequent decision making. To be of maximum use for problem-solving purposes, the organization and presentation of the information are very important. Drawings, sketches, graphs of data, and other graphical techniques can all be effective communication tools when used properly. Try to display and analyze the data in such a manner so as to extract meaningful information. When your are presented with data, analyze the information to make sure it has not been biased to lead you in the wrong direction.

Display data graphically rather than in tabular form, when appropriate. Tables can be difficult to interpret and sometimes terribly misleading, as demonstrated by Anscombe's Quartet[1,2] (shown on the next page). Graphing, by contrast, is an excellent way to organize and analyze large amounts of data.

From a statistical standpoint (using a regression analysis on the tabular information), all of the data sets are described equally well by the same linear model. However, upon graphing the data, we see some very obvious differences. The graphical presentation (on the next page) clearly reveals the differences in the data sets, which might have gone unnoticed if we had used only the tabular data.

Set A		Set B		Set C		Set D	
X	Y	X	Y	X	Y	X	Y
10.0	8.04	10.0	9.14	10.0	7.46	8.0	6.58
8.0	6.95	8.0	8.14	8.0	6.77	8.0	5.76
13.0	7.58	13.0	8.74	13.0	12.74	8.0	7.71
9.0	8.81	9.0	8.77	9.0	7.11	8.0	8.84
11.0	8.33	11.0	9.26	11.0	7.81	8.0	8.47
14.0	9.96	14.0	8.10	14.0	8.84	8.0	7.04
6.0	7.24	6.0	6.13	6.0	6.08	8.0	5.25
4.0	4.26	4.0	3.10	4.0	5.39	19.0	12.50
12.0	10.84	12.0	9.113	12.0	8.15	8.0	5.56
7.0	4.82	7.0	7.26	7.0	6.42	8.0	7.91
5.0	5.68	5.0	4.74	5.0	5.73	8.0	6.89

Anscombe's Quartet Table

Each of these four data sets A, B, C, and D *all* have the following properties:

$N = 11$ Mean of X's = 9.0   Equation of regression line: $Y = 3 + 0.5 X$

$t = 4.24$ Mean of Y's = 7.5   Standard error of estimate of slope = 0.118

$r^2 = 0.67$ Correlation coefficient = 0.82   Sum of squares $(X - \bar{X})^2 = 110.0$

Regression sum of squares = 27.50   Residual sum of squares of Y = 13.75

Statistically everything looks the same!!

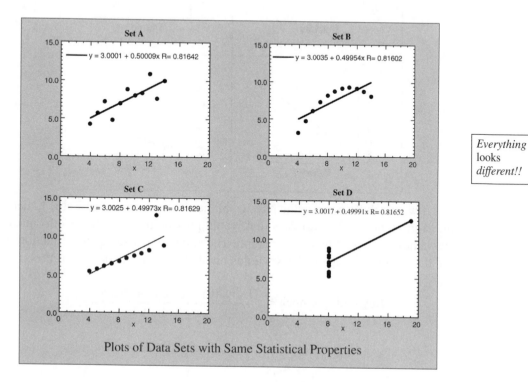

Everything looks different!!

Plots of Data Sets with Same Statistical Properties

GETTING THE MOST OUT OF YOUR DATA: GROUPING THE VARIABLES

Sometimes, a particular quantity that we are interested in measuring depends on a number of different variables. Let's consider the flow of fluid through a pipe at low velocities. Under special low-flow conditions, this flow is termed *laminar*. We perform a number of experiments and determine that the pressure drop through the pipe depends on a number of different parameters: the diameter of the pipe, the density of the liquid, the velocity of the liquid, and the viscosity of the liquid. (The viscosity is a physical property of the liquid. It is related to how "thick" the liquid is. For example, maple syrup is more viscous than water, and molasses is more viscous than maple syrup.)

We can graph the data that we have obtained on separate graphs. That is, we can graph how pressure drop varies with fluid velocity, while we hold all the other variables constant. Then, we could graph pressure drop versus pipe diameter, while holding everything else constant. In this way we would generate a series of four individual graphs.

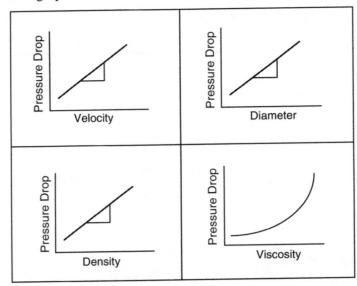

If we carefully analyze the physics of the situation, we may be able to determine a grouping of the variables that would provide us with all the information that we have available in a single graph. The variable that serves this function for fluid flow through a pipe is the Reynolds number, which is defined as follows:

$$\text{Reynolds Number} = \frac{(\text{Density})(\text{Velocity})(\text{Diameter})}{(\text{Viscosity})}$$

Now, if we process the experimental data into the form of pressure drop versus Reynolds number and graph the results, we find that we obtain a single graph that gives us the same information as the four earlier graphs.

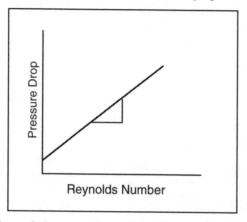

Proper selection of the grouping of the variables will not necessarily be known ahead of time, but if you are aware of this possibility, you may be able to condense your data into a more usable format.

REFERENCES

1. Tufte, E., *Visual Display of Quantitative Information,* Graphics Press, Cheshire, CT, 1983.
2. Anscombe, F. J., "Graphics in Statistical Analysis," *American Statisticians,* 27, pp. 14–21, February 1973.

FURTHER READING

Glantz, Stanton A. *Primer of Biostatistics,* 3rd ed. McGraw-Hill Health Professions Division, New York, 1992.

Volk, William. *Applied Statistics for Engineers,* 2nd ed. McGraw-Hill, New York, 1969.

INDEX

ABOUT THE AUTHORS

H. Scott Fogler is Vennema Professor of Chemical Engineering at the University of Michigan. His research interests include flow and reaction in porous media, fused chemical relations, gellation kinetics, colloidal phenomena, and catalyzed dissolution. Fogler has chaired ASEE's Chemical Engineering Division, served on the Board of Directors of the American Institute of Chemical Engineers, and earned the Chemical Manufacturers Association's National Catalyst Award. He is the author of *Elements of Chemical Reaction Engineering,* now in its fourth edition.

Steven E. LeBlanc is Associate Dean for Academic Affairs and Professor of Chemical Engineering at the University of Toledo. He previously served as the chair of the Chemical and Environmental Engineering Department for 10 years. LeBlanc has served as the chairman of the ASEE Chemical Engineering Education Division and served as a co-chair of the 2007 ASEE Chemical Engineering Summer School for Faculty. He also serves on the Publication Board for *Chemical Engineering Communications.*